# THE COMPLETE GUIDEBOOK TO
# YOSEMITE
# NATIONAL PARK

"On the whole, Yosemite is incomparably the most wonderful feature on our continent."
—A. D. Richardson, 1865

"From the discovery of Yosemite to the present day the wonders of this region of sublimity have been a source of inspiration to visitors, but none have been able to describe it to the satisfaction of those who followed after them."
—Lafayette Bunnell

"You've got a good point, Lafayette, but here goes anyway. . . ."
—SPM

# THE COMPLETE GUIDEBOOK TO
# YOSEMITE
# NATIONAL PARK

## STEVEN P. MEDLEY

REVISED EIGHTH EDITION

YOSEMITE CONSERVANCY
Yosemite National Park

## For Jane and the boys

·································

**YOSEMITE**
CONSERVANCY.

yosemiteconservancy.org

**Yosemite Conservancy's Mission**

Yosemite Conservancy inspires people to support projects and programs that preserve Yosemite and enrich the visitor experience.

Library of Congress Control Number: 2017954165

**Caveat**

Given the rapidity with which things change, the accuracy and completeness of the contents of this book cannot be guaranteed. The publisher and author assume no legal responsibility for the appreciation or depreciation of the value of any premises, commercial or otherwise, by reason of their inclusion in, or exclusion from this book. Further, the names of businesses mentioned here are provided as a service to readers and not as an endorsement or guarantee.

Cover photograph by Pung/Shutterstock.com
Cover design by Nancy Austin Design
Interior design by Nancy Austin Design based on a design
   by J. Spittler/Jamison Design
Maps by Ben Pease, Pease Press Cartography, based on original maps
   by Bill Kuhn and the National Park Service

ISBN 978-1-930238-81-7

Printed in China by Toppan Leefung

1 2 3 4 5 6 – 22 21 20 19 18

# CONTENTS

7 Acknowledgments

## ■ 1. Welcome to Yosemite

9 Introduction

10 Map of Yosemite National Park

12 Yosemite by the Numbers

13 How's the Weather?

14 Lodging in Yosemite

15 Camping in Yosemite National Park

15 How to Reserve Your Campsite

15 Camping in US Forest Service Areas adjacent to Yosemite

17 Hiking and Backpacking in Yosemite

17 Get a Wilderness Permit

18 Wilderness Regulations

18 Route-Planning Information

18 Wilderness Tips

19 Bear-Proof Your Campsite

20 Going Green

21 A Ranger Is a Ranger Is a . . .

22 Yosemite in Winter

24 Where in the Park Can I Find . . . ?

26 What Can I Do with My Children?

27 If You Have Only One Day in Yosemite

29 Yosemite Climbing

32 Where You Can Learn More

33 Connectivity and Technology

## ■ 2. Yosemite History

35 Introduction

36 Yosemite's Native People

38 The Euro-American Occupation

40 The Army Takes Control

41 The Army Years

42 A Yosemite Chronology

44 The National Park Service

45 Historical Sites in Yosemite Valley

46 Map of Historical Sites

48 A Plan for the Twenty-First Century

49 Yosemite in Fiction

50 Key Figures in Yosemite History

53 Selected Yosemite Place Names

## ■ 3. Yosemite's Natural World

57 Introduction

58 Yosemite Geology for Liberal Arts Majors

60 Geologists Disagree: Muir vs. Whitney

61 Yosemite Waterfalls

63 Natural Events

66 Yosemite Plant Life

67 Flowering Plants

68 The Giant Sequoias

69 Mammals

Mule deer

75 Birds

77 Reptiles and Amphibians

78 Fishes

79 The Poisonous, the Itchy, and the Sickening

82 Yosemite's Endangered Species

## ■ 4. Yosemite Valley

85 Introduction

86 Map of Yosemite Valley

88 Can You Find the Visitor Center?

88 Map of Yosemite Village and Shuttle Bus Stops

90 Best Bets in Yosemite Valley

91 Activities in the Valley

94 Three Easy Hikes on the Valley Floor

95 Four Classic Routes to Yosemite Valley's Rim

96 Half Dome: The Hike

97 Hike Smart

99 Valley Camping and Regulations

101 Gas, Food, and Lodging

104 The Nine Best Views from Above

104 Map of Yosemite Valley Views

**A view of Vernal Fall**

## ■ 5. South of Yosemite Valley

**107** Introduction

**108** Map of South of Yosemite Valley

**110** Best Bets South of Yosemite Valley

**111** Wawona

**111** Map of Wawona

**114** Activities at Wawona

**116** Three Wawona Hikes

**116** Map of Wawona Hikes

**117** Activities at the Mariposa Grove

**117** Map of the Mariposa Grove

**119** Activities along Glacier Point Road

**119** Map of Glacier Point Road

**120** Five Great Hikes from Glacier Point Road

**121** Camping South of Yosemite Valley

**122** Gas, Food, and Lodging

## ■ 6. North of Yosemite Valley

**125** Introduction

**126** Map of Hetch Hetchy, Tioga Road, and Tuolumne Meadows

**128** Best Bets North of Yosemite Valley

**129** Hetch Hetchy

**130** Activities in the Hetch Hetchy Area

**131** Map of Hetch Hetchy Area

**132** Activities along Tioga Road

**134** Seven Sensational Hikes from Tioga Road

**134** Map of Tioga Road Hikes

**136** The High Sierra Camps

**136** Map of High Sierra Camps

**137** Tuolumne Meadows

**137** Map of Tuolumne Meadows

**138** Activities at Tuolumne Meadows

**140** Seven Scintillating Tuolumne Hikes

**142** Camping North of Yosemite Valley

**142** Map of Hetch Hetchy Reservoir and Vicinity

**144** Gas, Food, and Lodging

## ■ 7. Getting to Yosemite

**147** Introduction

**148** By Air

**148** By Train

**148** By Bus

**149** By Automobile

**153** Yosemite on the Internet

**154** Photo Credits

**157** Index

**160** About the Author

## ■ Maps

**10** Yosemite National Park

**46** Historical Sites in Yosemite Valley

**86** Yosemite Valley

**88** Yosemite Village and Shuttle Bus Stops

**104** Yosemite Valley Views

**108** South of Yosemite Valley

**111** Wawona

**116** Wawona Hikes

**117** Mariposa Grove

**119** Glacier Point Road

**126** Hetch Hetchy, Tioga Road, and Tuolumne Meadows

**131** Hetch Hetchy Area

**134** Tioga Road Hikes

**136** High Sierra Camps

**137** Tuolumne Meadows

**142** Hetch Hetchy Reservoir

# ACKNOWLEDGMENTS

Many wonderful, helpful people have participated in the production and updating of this book over the years.

Thank you to Pat Wight, Penny Otwell, Holly Warner, Anne Steed, Laurel Rematore, Beth Pratt, Mary Vocelka, Ann Gushue, Jim Snyder, Linda Eade, Len McKenzie, Dean Shenk, Marla LaCass, Laurel Boyers, Craig Bates, N. King Huber, Jan van Wagtendonk, Peter Browning, Jim Alinder, Bill Neill, Mike Osborne, Mono Lake Committee, Keith Walklet, Nancy Lusignan, Kris Fister, Bob Jones, Tori Keith, Jack and Gay Reineck, and Norma Craig. You provided a foundation for future editions and in doing so have assisted many thousands of Yosemite National Park visitors.

For assisting tremendously with the 2012 edition, thanks are due to Bob Hansen, Peter Brewitt, Ben Pease, the staff of Heyday Books, and the National Park Service and its dedicated employees, especially Linda Eade, Mary Kline, Brenna Lissoway, and Laura Patten.

This new edition would not have been possible without the continued assistance of the National Park Service, especially Sabrina Diaz, Jeffrey Trust, Marion Roubal, Sharon Miyako, Robert Loudon, Kara Stella, and Adrienne Freeman. Thank you to all those who contributed updates to the text and the maps: Carolyn Botell, Kathy Chappell, Butch Farabee, Nicole Geiger, Schuyler Greenleaf, Ryan Kelly, Katie Manion, Ben Pease, Adonia Ripple, Laurie Stowe, Molly Woodward, and Lisa Cesaro of Yosemite Hospitality who fielded many, many questions. This book would not be possible without you all.

Summer beauty in Tuolumne Meadows

Summer sunrise at Tunnel View

# 1 | WELCOME TO YOSEMITE

**Yosemite National Park** is one of the best places on earth. Yosemite holds rugged 13,000-foot mountains, two major rivers, living glaciers, and broad alpine meadows. It has the largest (and smallest) trees, one of the tallest waterfalls in North America, and a mountain that looks like it's been cut in half. It is our oldest wilderness park, a mecca for photographers, and a world center of rock climbing. Millions of people visit the park every year, and all of them can find true solitude. If you've come for intense adventures, climbing, skiing, or backpacking, Yosemite is the place for you. If you've come to relax, enjoy the scenery, and take some time out from your life . . . Yosemite is still the place for you. From the joys of the high country and Tuolumne Meadows in the summer to the gushing waterfalls of spring to cross-country skiing in the winter, there is no bad time to visit Yosemite National Park.

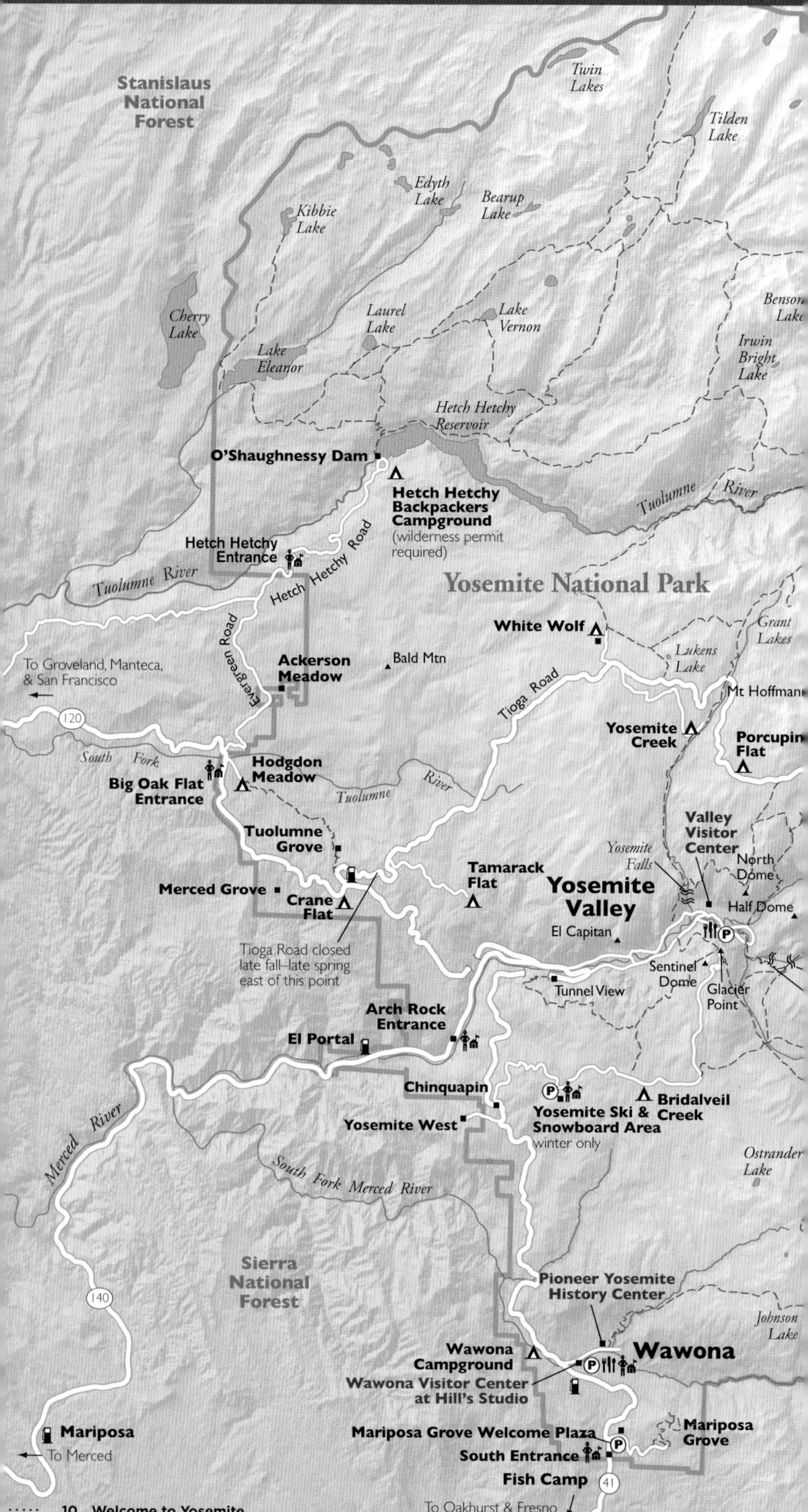

# MAP OF YOSEMITE NATIONAL PARK

Stanislaus
National
Forest

Twin
Lakes

Tilden
Lake

Kibbie
Lake

Edyth
Lake

Bearup
Lake

Cherry
Lake

Laurel
Lake

Lake
Vernon

Benson
Lake

Lake
Eleanor

Irwin
Bright
Lake

Hetch Hetchy
Reservoir

Tuolumne River

O'Shaughnessy Dam

Hetch Hetchy
Backpackers
Campground
(wilderness permit
required)

Yosemite National Park

Hetch Hetchy
Entrance

Hetch Hetchy Road

Tuolumne River

Evergreen Road

White Wolf

Grant
Lakes

Lukens
Lake

Mt Hoffman

To Groveland, Manteca,
& San Francisco

Ackerson
Meadow

Bald Mtn

Tioga Road

Yosemite
Creek

Porcupine
Flat

120

South Fork

Hodgdon
Meadow

Tuolumne River

Big Oak Flat
Entrance

Tuolumne
Grove

Tamarack
Flat

Yosemite
Falls

Valley
Visitor
Center

North
Dome

Merced Grove

Crane
Flat

Yosemite
Valley

Half Dome

Tioga Road closed
late fall–late spring
east of this point

El Capitan

Tunnel View

Sentinel
Dome

Glacier
Point

Arch Rock
Entrance

El Portal

Chinquapin

Yosemite West

Yosemite Ski &
Snowboard Area
winter only

Bridalveil
Creek

Ostrander
Lake

Merced River

South Fork Merced River

Sierra
National
Forest

Pioneer Yosemite
History Center

Johnson
Lake

140

Wawona
Campground

Wawona Visitor Center
at Hill's Studio

Wawona

Mariposa
To Merced

Mariposa Grove Welcome Plaza

South Entrance

Fish Camp

Mariposa
Grove

41

To Oakhurst & Fresno

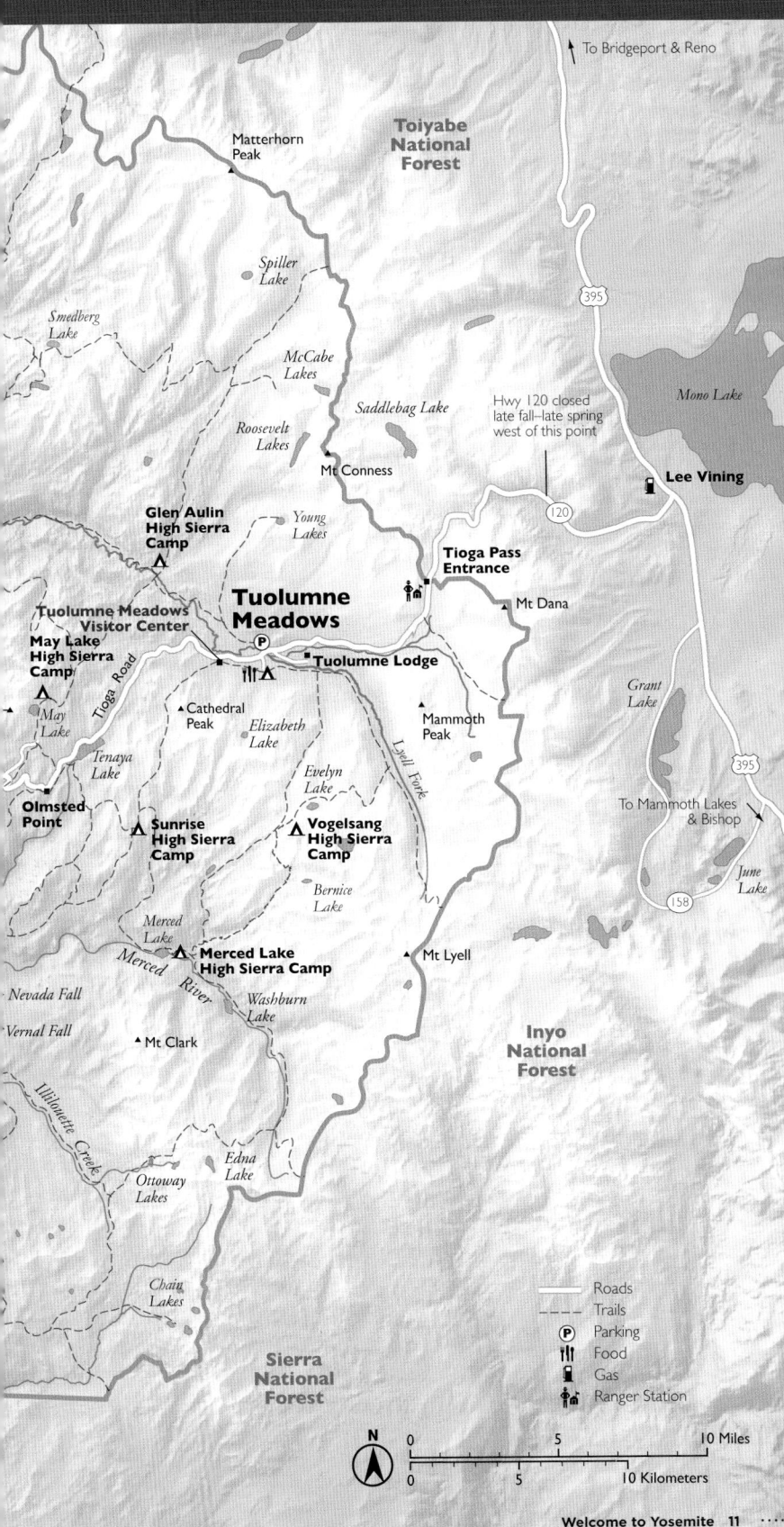

To Bridgeport & Reno

Toiyabe National Forest

Matterhorn Peak

Spiller Lake

Smedberg Lake

McCabe Lakes

Roosevelt Lakes

Saddlebag Lake

Mt Conness

Young Lakes

Mono Lake

Hwy 120 closed late fall–late spring west of this point

Lee Vining

Glen Aulin High Sierra Camp

Tioga Pass Entrance

**Tuolumne Meadows**

Mt Dana

Tuolumne Meadows Visitor Center

May Lake High Sierra Camp

May Lake

■ Tuolumne Lodge

Tioga Road

Cathedral Peak

Elizabeth Lake

Grant Lake

Mammoth Peak

Tenaya Lake

Evelyn Lake

Lyell Fork

Olmsted Point

**Sunrise High Sierra Camp**

**Vogelsang High Sierra Camp**

Bernice Lake

To Mammoth Lakes & Bishop

June Lake

Merced Lake

Merced River

**Merced Lake High Sierra Camp**

Mt Lyell

Nevada Fall

Washburn Lake

Vernal Fall

▲ Mt Clark

Inyo National Forest

Illilouette Creek

Ottoway Lakes

Edna Lake

Chain Lakes

Sierra National Forest

Legend:
— Roads
--- Trails
Ⓟ Parking
Food
Gas
Ranger Station

N

0 — 5 — 10 Miles
0 — 5 — 10 Kilometers

**Welcome to Yosemite 11**

**Established:** October 1, 1890

**Size:** 748,436 acres (302,881 ha), or 1,170 square miles (3,030 sq km); 94 percent of the park is designated wilderness.

**Address:** P.O. Box 577, Yosemite National Park, CA 95389

**Campsites:** 1,520 individual sites parkwide

**Overnight accommodations:** 1,370 units

**Paved roads:** 214 miles (344 km)

**Paved walking & bike paths:** 20 miles (32 km)

**Developed trails:** 800 miles (1,287 km)

**Wildlife species (approximate):**

Amphibians and reptiles: 34
Birds: 260
Fish: 6 native species
Mammals: 90

**Flora species:**

Flowering plants: 1,500
Trees: 35

**Meadows:** Approximately 36,620 acres (14,820 ha)

**Geographic center:** Mount Hoffmann

**Highest paved pass in the Sierra Nevada mountain range:** Tioga Pass, 9,945 feet (3,031 m)

**Major lakes:** 318

**Water bodies:** approximately 2,700 total, with an estimated 245 that contain fish

**Rivers and streams:** 1,200 miles (1,931 km)

**Park speed limit:** 25 to 45 mph (40 to 72 kph); obey posted speed at all times

## Yosemite's Ten Highest Peaks

1. Mount Lyell: 13,140 feet (4,005 m)
2. Mount Dana: 13,057 feet (3,980 m)
3. Kuna Peak: 13,002 feet (3,963 m)
4. Rodgers Peak: 12,978 feet (3,956 m)
5. Mount Maclure: 12,960 feet (3,950 m)
6. Mount Gibbs: 12,764 feet (3,890 m)
7. Mount Conness: 12,590 feet (3,837 m)
8. Mount Florence: 12,561 feet (3,829 m)
9. Simmons Peak: 12,503 feet (3,811 m)
10. Excelsior Mountain: 12,446 feet (3,794 m)

## Park Visitation

1855: 42
1899: 4,500
1922: 100,506
1954: 1,008,031
1995: 3,958,406
2016: 5,028,868

## Entrance Fees

$30  Private Noncommercial Vehicles

$25  Motorcycle Vehicles (each)

$15  Bus Passengers, Bicyclists, and Persons on Foot or Horseback

$60  Annual Yosemite Pass

$80  America the Beautiful—National Parks and Federal Recreational Lands Pass (good at all national parks and federal recreation lands for 1 year from purchase)

$20  America the Beautiful—National Parks and Federal Recreational Lands Pass, Senior Pass (a lifetime pass for US citizens 62 years and older), 1-time issuance fee

Free: America the Beautiful—National Parks and Federal Recreational Lands Pass, Access Pass (for blind or permanently disabled US citizens or permanent residents)

Free: America the Beautiful—National Parks and Federal Recreational Lands Pass, Volunteer Pass (a 1-year pass for volunteers who have acquired 250 service hours)

## Important Yosemite Contacts

Accessibility information
  (see page 93) .................... (209) 379-1035
Camping reservations ...... 1(877) 444-6777
  International callers ....... (518) 885-3639
Deaf services (voice/text) .. (209) 379-5250
  or yose_deaf_services@nps.gov
High Sierra Camps
  reservations .............. (888) 413-8869, #4
Lost and Found:
  NPS yose_lostandfound@nps.gov
  Concessioner ................. (209) 372-1390
Medical clinic ..................... (209) 372-4637
Park information
  recorded .......................... (209) 372-0200
  or nps.gov/yose
Room and activity reservations
  ........................................... (888) 540-5794
  or travelyosemite.com
Visitor Centers:
  Big Oak Flat .................... (209) 379-1899
  Tuolumne Meadows ....... (209) 372-0263
  Valley ............................... (209) 372-0200
  Wawona .......................... (209) 375-9531
Weather and road info ........ (209) 372-0200
Wilderness reservations ..... (209) 372-0740
Yosemite Conservancy
  order line ........................ (209) 379-2648
Yosemite Hospitality .......... (209) 372-1001
Emergencies ..............................................911

**Yosemite's climate** is relatively mild, but prepare for variable weather, especially in the spring and fall. The months of April through October feature warm daytime temperatures and cool nights. In winter, the average maximum temperatures in Yosemite Valley (4,000 feet; 1,220 m) are in the high 40s and 50s. It does get cold in the shade of the granite walls, especially on the south side of the Valley. Of course, weather is significantly affected by elevation, and with a topography ranging from 2,000 to 13,000 feet (610 to 3,960 m) in height, Yosemite can experience dramatic climatic variations on any given day! Precipitation averages 35 to 40 inches (89 to 102 cm) of moisture annually, with the bulk of that falling between December and March. Snowfall in Yosemite Valley averages 29 inches (74 cm) but rarely accumulates to a depth of more than 2 feet. At the 7,000-foot (2,100-m) Yosemite Ski & Snowboard Area (formerly Badger Pass), there is adequate snowpack to support a downhill ski area, and cross-country skiing is popular throughout the higher regions of the park. In spring, increasing runoff swells rivers and creeks, producing a grand display of surging waterfalls. There is negligible precipitation during summer, and many of the park's waterfalls dry up. For weather reports, call (209) 372-0200.

## Yosemite Valley in Winter

High-country conditions are significantly cooler and much snowier during the winter months. Visitors should be prepared for cold temperatures, rain, and snow all year 'round at higher elevations. Winter conditions are not unusual from as early as October until well into May, even in Yosemite Valley. For the latest weather conditions in Yosemite, visit nps.gov/yose.

## Yosemite Valley Weather Data

| | Jan | Feb | Mar | Apr | May | Jun | Jul | Aug | Sep | Oct | Nov | Dec |
|---|---|---|---|---|---|---|---|---|---|---|---|---|
| Rainfall in inches* | 6.5 | 6.7 | 5.2 | 2.8 | 1.7 | 0.7 | 0.4 | 0.1 | 0.7 | 2.1 | 4.6 | 5.5 |
| Rainfall in cm | 16.5 | 17.8 | 13.2 | 7.1 | 4.3 | 1.8 | 1.0 | .25 | 1.8 | 5.3 | 11.7 | 14.0 |
| Max. temp. (°F) | 48 | 52 | 58 | 64 | 71 | 81 | 89 | 89 | 82 | 71 | 56 | 47 |
| (°C) | 9 | 11 | 14 | 18 | 22 | 27 | 32 | 32 | 28 | 22 | 13 | 8 |
| Min. temp. (°F) | 29 | 30 | 34 | 38 | 45 | 51 | 57 | 56 | 51 | 42 | 33 | 28 |
| (°C) | -2 | -1 | 1 | 3 | 7 | 11 | 14 | 13 | 11 | 6 | 1 | -2 |

*37 inches/94 cm annually

| | Jan | Apr | Jul | Oct |
|---|---|---|---|---|
| Hours of sunshine | 3:57 | 7:38 | 9:34 | 6:45 |
| Chances of a sunny day | 39% | 70% | 97% | 81% |
| Afternoon temperatures | 48° | 66° | 90° | 75° |
| Relative humidity | 86% | 69% | 50% | 64% |
| Chances of a dry day | 74% | 80% | 97% | 94% |
| Total precipitation | 6.8"/17.3 cm | 3.3"/8.4 cm | 0.4"/1.0 cm | 1.5"/3.8 cm |
| Snowfall | 25.4"/64.5 cm | 4.5"/11.4 cm | – | 0.2"/.5 cm |

Tent cabins at Half Dome Village in Yosemite Valley

**Most overnight accommodations** in Yosemite are operated by Yosemite Hospitality (a subsidiary of Aramark), a contractor of the National Park Service and the park's chief concessioner. There is a single reservation system for all Yosemite Hospitality lodging units. (If a Yosemite hotel or motel mentioned in this guidebook is not part of the Yosemite Hospitality reservation system, that fact will be noted.) Reservations can be made by phone or online. (Note that reservations for hotel suites must be made by telephone.) The Yosemite Hospitality reservation number is (888) 540-5794 from 7 a.m. to 7 p.m. Mountain Standard Time, 7 days a week. International callers use (602) 278-8888; group sales are (888) 339-3481. Or visit travelyosemite.com to request your reservation online.

## Seven Tips for Getting a Yosemite Reservation

1. Public reservations for Yosemite lodging open exactly 366 days in advance. Call the Yosemite Reservations office at (888) 413-8869 as early as 7 a.m. Arizona time exactly 366 days before your intended arrival.

2. Choose to visit in Yosemite's off-season, particularly the months of November, January, February, and March. You're sure to be accommodated if your stay falls on weekdays.

3. If you want to stay over a weekend, plan your arrival for a Monday, Tuesday, Wednesday, or Thursday. You can reserve up to 7 nights in a row in any given stay. Often, lodging facilities are fully reserved for weekends more than 366 days in advance by people arriving earlier in the week.

4. Be flexible and have several arrival dates in mind. If your first option is not available, one of the others may be.

5. If you're willing to stay in a tent cabin at Half Dome Village (formerly Curry Village), request it. Tent cabins are in the least demand. They can usually be reserved up to 2 weeks before arrival— but are often sold out in the summer. When you arrive, you can always try to upgrade to a room with bath (but there are no guarantees here).

6. Weekends tend to be very busy. On weekdays most calls come in first thing in the morning or in the evening, with a slight uptick at lunch. In general, midday is the quietest and best time to call.

7. Cancellations happen all the time, with increasing frequency as the 7-day cancellation deadline approaches. Call in advance of your desired arrival date. You may get lucky.

**Yosemite National Park** offers visitors almost 1,500 campsites in its multiple campgrounds. If you're planning to camp, be sure to secure an authorized spot, because camping is allowed only in designated campsites. Even if you've got a "self-contained" recreational vehicle, you are not permitted to pull off to the side of the road for the night. Neither should you erect your tent or throw down a sleeping bag wherever you stop; the rangers will send you packing. The impact on the park resources of such haphazard camping is too great. Fortunately, there's a way to ensure that you'll have a Yosemite camping spot when you arrive. The majority of park campsites can be reserved through a campground reservation system called Recreation.gov. Throughout this guidebook, campgrounds with sites that can be reserved through this system are indicated.

## How to Reserve Your Campsite

Campground reservations become available in 1-month blocks up to 5 months in advance. Reservations can be made through Recreation.gov up to 5 months in advance, on the 15th of each month for a 1-month "window" and sell out quickly. For example, on March 15, dates from July 15 through August 14 become available for reservation, and on April 15, dates from August 15 through September 14 are reservable (to ensure that you have the most up-to-date information about this, see nps.gov/yose).

You can reserve campsites through Recreation.gov up to 1 day in advance, in two ways: over the Internet at Recreation.gov, or by telephone at (877) 444-6777. The number for international calls is (518) 885-3639. Phone reservations can be made starting at 7 a.m. Pacific time. Nearly all successful reservations are made online—use the telephone only as a last resort.

The telephone reservation system allows callers to choose from a full month of starting dates for their camping trip. Be sure to pick a number of possible start dates for your trip, and you should be able to secure a reservation.

When making online camping reservations, you can reserve only 2 campsites at a time. For additional information about park campgrounds, refer to the following pages: Valley, page 99; South of Yosemite Valley, page 121; North of Yosemite Valley, page 142. There is a number you can call to find out if there is a rare same-day campsite opening, (209) 372-0266, but don't be too hopeful.

## Camping in US Forest Service Areas adjacent to Yosemite

The US Forest Service operates a variety of campgrounds near Yosemite. Many of them are operated on a first-come, first-served basis; some sites can be reserved in advance. For additional information, call the appropriate USFS district office or InterAgency Visitor Center.

### INYO NATIONAL FOREST
### EASTERN SIERRA, HIGHWAYS 120 & 395

Mono Basin Scenic Area Visitor Center
North of Lee Vining, CA, on Hwy 395
(760) 647-3044

Eastern Sierra InterAgency Visitor Center
Junction of Highway 395 and State Route 136, Lone Pine, CA
(760) 876-6222

### STANISLAUS NATIONAL FOREST
### WESTERN SIERRA, HIGHWAYS 140 & 41

Bass Lake Ranger District
57003 Road 225, North Fork, CA
(559) 877-2218

Oakhurst Ranger District (Seasonal)
40343 Highway 41, Oakhurst, CA
(559) 658-7588

Mariposa InterAgency Visitor Center
5158 Highway 140, Mariposa, CA
(209) 966-7081

### STANISLAUS NATIONAL FOREST
### WESTERN SIERRA, HIGHWAY 120

Groveland Ranger District
24545 Highway 120, Groveland, CA
(209) 962-7825

Happy campers

## Campground/General Location

| | Sites/spaces | Daily fee | Max RV/Trailer size | Water | Toilets | Accessible | Dump station | Showers nearby | Laundry nearby | Groceries | pets allowed | Fishing | Season (approx) | Reservations |
|---|---|---|---|---|---|---|---|---|---|---|---|---|---|---|
| **North Pines** Yosemite Valley | 81 | $26 | 40 ft/35 ft | Tap | Flush | • | • | • | • | • | • | • | April–Oct | Recreation.gov |
| **Upper Pines** Yosemite Valley | 238 | $26 | 35 ft/24 ft | Tap | Flush | • | • | • | • | • | • | • | All year | Recreation.gov all year / Some first come Dec–Mar |
| **Lower Pines** Yosemite Valley | 60 | $26 | 40 ft/35 ft | Tap | Flush | • | • | • | • | • | • | • | Apr–Oct | Recreation.gov |
| **Camp 4** Yosemite Valley | 35 | $6/person | No RVs/trailers | Tap | Flush | • | | • | • | • | | • | All year | First come |
| **Backpackers Walk-in** (see page 100) Yosemite Valley | | | | | | | | | | | | | | |
| **Wawona** Wawona Road, Wawona | 93 | $26 | 35 ft/35 ft | Tap | Flush | • | near | | • | • | • | • | All year | Recreation.gov early Apr–early Sept / First come otherwise |
| **Bridalveil Creek** Glacier Point Road | 110 | $18 | 35 ft/24 ft | Tap | Flush | • | | | | | • | • | Aug–mid Sept | First come |
| **Hodgdon Meadow** off Big Oak Flat Road near entrance | 105 | $26 | 40 ft/30 ft | Tap | Flush | • | | | | | • | | All year | Recreation.gov Apr 15–Oct 15 / First come Oct 15–Apr 15 |
| **Hetch Hetchy Backpacker** (see page 143) Hetch Hetchy Road | | | | | | | | | | | | | | |
| **Crane Flat** Big Oak Flat Rd near Tioga Road | 166 | $26 | 40 ft/30 ft | Tap | Flush | • | | | | | • | | Late June–early Oct | Recreation.gov |
| **Tamarack Flat** Tioga Road | 52 | $12 | not recommended | Creek (boil) | Vault | | | | | | • | | Late June–early Oct | First come |
| **White Wolf** Tioga Road | 74 | $18 | 27 ft/24 ft | Tap | Flush | | | | | | • | • | July–Sept | First come |
| **Yosemite Creek** Tioga Road | 75 | $12 | not recommended | Creek (boil) | Vault | | | | | | • | • | July–Sept | First come |
| **Porcupine Flat** Tioga Road | 52 | $12 | not recommended | Creek (boil) | Vault | | | | | | • | | July–Oct 15 | First come |
| **Tuolumne Meadows** Tioga Road | 304 | $26 | 35 ft/35 ft | Tap | Flush | • | • | | • | • | • | • | July–Sept | 50% Recreation.gov, 50% first come |

**Because there are** some 800 miles of trail in Yosemite ranging through some of the most stunning scenery in the world, backpacking is a popular activity in the park. It allows its practitioners a true wilderness experience, and it is really the only way to reach many areas of Yosemite.

Successful, minimum-impact backpacking requires good physical health, knowledge of backpacking techniques, proper equipment, and a respect for the natural world. Uninformed backcountry users can cause great harm to the wilderness and not even know it. Here are some basic tips for backpackers, as well as wilderness regulations and sources for further information.

## Get a Wilderness Permit

Free wilderness permits are required year-round for all overnight stays in Yosemite's wilderness. To avoid overcrowding and reduce impacts to wilderness areas, Yosemite limits the number of people who may begin overnight hikes from each trailhead each day. At least 40 percent of each trailhead quota is available on a first-come, first-served basis the day of, or 1 day prior to, the beginning of your trip.

These permits can be obtained at any of the following locations in the park: the Yosemite Valley Wilderness Center (just east of the Visitor Center); Tuolumne Meadows Wilderness Center (just off the Tioga Road on the road to Tuolumne Lodge); Wawona Visitor Center (see page 111); Big Oak Flat Information Station (see page 130); and Hetch Hetchy Entrance Station, for those using Hetch Hetchy trails (see page 130).

Wilderness permit reservations can be made 24 weeks to 2 days in advance. The Wilderness Reservation Office is open mid-November through the end of September; reservations are strongly recommended. Reservation requests can be submitted by fax, phone, or mail. For a link to the reservation fax form and additional information regarding the reservation process, please search nps.gov/yose under wilderness permit.

Send mail requests to Yosemite Conservancy Wilderness Reservation Office, P.O. Box 545, Yosemite, CA, 95389, Fax: (209) 372-0739, Phone: (209) 372-0740.

Reservations are not necessary in winter; from November through April, free wilderness permits can be picked up at the Valley Visitor Center or one of the other self-register permit locations.

A nonrefundable processing fee of $5 plus $5 per person is charged for reservations. Fees can be paid by check (payable to "Yosemite Conservancy") or with a major credit card (include the expiration date).

A view of Half Dome from Washburn Point

The following information is needed to process a wilderness permit or reservation: name, address, daytime phone; number of people in group; starting and ending dates of hike; the entry and exit trailhead you use; your primary destination; number of pack stock (if applicable); and alternative dates or trailheads if your first choice isn't available.

Reserved permits can be picked up 1 day prior to departure or the morning of your trip before 10 a.m. If you are picking up your reserved permit on the departure day later than 10 a.m., please call and ask for your reservation to be held for a late arrival, (209) 372-0308. Permits must be picked up during business hours. You must start your trip on the date and trailhead you reserved. Reservations are recommended for hikes leaving from Tuolumne Meadows or with destinations of Little Yosemite Valley, Half Dome, or anywhere along the John Muir Trail, and for trips starting on Friday or Saturday.

## Wilderness Regulations

### GROUP SIZE

Maximum group size in Yosemite Wilderness is 15 people on trails, and 8 people for any off-trail travel.

### CAMPSITE LOCATION

Please use existing campsites at least 100 feet (30 m) from lakeshores and streams to minimize pollution and impact on vegetation. Camp at least 4 trail-miles (6.4 km) from Tuolumne Meadows, Yosemite Valley, Glacier Point, White Wolf, Hetch Hetchy, and Wawona, and at least 1 mile (1.6 km) from any road.

### HUMAN WASTE

Bury human waste 6 inches (15.2 cm) deep in a small hole at least 100 feet (30 m) from any lake, stream, or camp area. Toilet paper should be packed out.

### GARBAGE

Pack out all garbage (no exceptions). Do not bury garbage, scatter organic waste, or leave foil in campfire sites.

### FIRES

Use gas stoves rather than wood fires. Wood fires are not permitted above 9,600 feet (2,926 m) due to firewood scarcity. Use only existing fire rings and dead and down wood in areas below 9,600 feet (2,926 m).

### PETS

Dogs and other pets are not allowed in Yosemite Wilderness.

### SOAP

Putting soap, including biodegradable soap, or any form of pollutant into lakes or streams is prohibited. Discard wash and rinse water at least 100 feet (30 m) from water sources.

## Route-Planning Information

Space considerations preclude listing the thousands of trips that can be made into Yosemite Wilderness. But never fear, there are many resources available to help with your route-planning task. You can obtain maps or trail guides from Yosemite Conservancy, at the wilderness center, at one of the visitor center bookstores, online at yosemiteconservancystore.com, or by calling (209) 379-2648.

## Wilderness Tips

### VISIT THE WILDERNESS CENTER

At the wilderness center, just east of the visitor center on the pedestrian mall in Yosemite Valley, detailed information is available about the park's wilderness. There are educational displays and a trip-planning section, and guidebooks, maps, and backpacking supplies are offered for sale. For additional wilderness information, visit nps.gov/yose.

### KEY PHONE NUMBERS

Wilderness permit reservations: (209) 372-0740.

Current wilderness conditions: (209) 372-0826.

Backpacking in the Sierra Nevada

Wilderness permit late arrivals/cancellations: (209) 372-0308.

For more information about making reservations or obtaining a permit: (209) 372-0740.

For information about wilderness conditions, check nps.gov/yose under wilderness conditions.

### TREAT THE WATER

Unfortunately, microscopic organisms known as *Giardia lamblia* (see page 79) are present in wilderness lakes, rivers, and streams. They can cause illness (sometimes quite severe), so you should not drink from these sources without first treating the water. Your options are to boil it for 3 minutes, to use a chemical disinfectant like iodine or chlorine (less effective than boiling), or to use the *Giardia*-rated water filters available from outdoor equipment stores and at the wilderness center.

### GET ACCLIMATIZED

Many wilderness trips begin at elevations much higher than you may be accustomed to, and then go even higher. It's a good idea to arrive a day early to let your body adapt to the thinner air. Don't overexert, make sure you eat enough, and drink plenty of fluids to avoid altitude sickness.

## Bear-Proof Your Campsite

Yosemite's black bears are clever and very persistent. If you fail to set up your camp and store your food properly, your whole trip may be ruined. Always follow these 6 steps:

1. Use the food storage boxes at your trailhead for storing any food that you will not be taking on your backpack trip. Never leave food or food-related supplies in vehicles left overnight at trailheads. Even toothpaste or deodorant can smell like food to a bear. Along with their keen sense of smell, bears are immensely strong. They will peel down your rear door, rip out the back seat, and crawl into the trunk to get food. They can smell food even if it's hidden from sight, and they know what coolers look like.

2. Store your food in a bear-resistant food storage container. A list of National Park Service–allowed canisters can be found at nps.gov (search under containers).

Bears aside, canisters are proof against birds, marmots, and the many other creatures that will happily eat your food. (Visit any information center, wilderness center, or visitor center for more information.)

3. Do not hang your food—it is illegal and ineffective. Even if you somehow manage to hang it from a limb inaccessible to a small, agile bear, squirrels, raccoons, and birds will definitely be able to get it.

Black bear

4. If a bear approaches your camp, act immediately to scare it away. Yell and make as much noise as possible, and scare the bear. It's more effective if more than one person does this. Throw small rocks no larger than acorns at the bear, but make sure that you do not hurt it—the bear is not trying to harm you. A big rock will hurt a bear just as it would hurt a human.

5. Remain at least 50 yards (46 m) from the bear. Do not advance on a bear that appears to feel threatened or cornered by you. Do not attempt to retrieve food or gear until the bear abandons it.

6. Food taken by bears is your responsibility. Please clean up and report all bear damage to a ranger. Improper food storage can cause not only personal injury and property loss, but also death of conditioned bears. Please do your part to keep Yosemite's bears wild. Visitors can report bear sightings to a ranger or call (209) 372-0322 to help protect this precious Yosemite wild animal.

**Some of the impacts** of climate change are particularly striking in Yosemite. These include impacts to the snow line and wildlife. Both are retreating farther up the mountains as time goes by.

Yosemite's long history as a tourist destination means that it enjoys a richer photographic record than many mountain areas. Old pictures reveal broad glaciers and tourists tobogganing and skiing through a snow-blanketed Yosemite Valley. It still snows in Yosemite Valley sometimes, but a typical winter storm now turns from rain to snow at about 5,500 feet (1,680 m), leaving a dusting in the Valley that quickly melts away. Of course this development disappoints tourists who arrive in January expecting to see the winter, but there are more serious concerns. The snows of the Sierra Nevada melt in the spring, providing most of the water for agriculture in California. Thus the diminution of the snowpack has serious repercussions for the farmers of the Central Valley, and for everyone who eats their food.

The retreating snowpack goes hand in hand with retreating wildlife. In the 1910s and 1920s, UC Berkeley professor Joseph Grinnell and his students made a thorough survey of animal life in California and throughout Yosemite, recording the occurrence and abundance of birds and mammals at many sites composing a long transect from the Central Valley across the park and the Sierra east to Mono Lake. As part of a large-scale, multi-year project, UC Berkeley resurveyed Grinnell's sites in Yosemite and throughout the Sierra

A view east from Washburn Point

nearly a century later. It found all of the same small mammal species in Yosemite that Grinnell had encountered! But about half of them had moved upslope to escape the warming climate. Birds showed similar upslope movements in Yosemite, which has warmed more strongly than other regions of the Sierra, but some species moved downslope in northern regions where rainfall has increased since Grinnell's original surveys. The Grinnell Resurvey Project is conducting similar studies in other national parks and lands throughout the state of California to get a more complete picture of how climate and land-use change will affect where species can survive in the future.

During your time in Yosemite, it may not be within your power to increase the snowpack or provide a home for a pika. There are things you can do, though, to limit your impact. The most obvious is to take free shuttle buses to your destinations. With a little planning, you can get to most places in the park by bus, and for a lot less than you would have spent on gas. If you're staying in Yosemite Valley, you can easily reach most of the Valley floor by bicycle, either your own or a rental bike from Half Dome Village or Yosemite Valley Lodge. If you're camping, consider whether to build that gigantic bonfire—much of the carbon in the atmosphere comes from burning wood. Summer days often find Yosemite Valley filled with smoky haze from campfires.

Many of the park's restaurants, such as those at The Majestic Yosemite Hotel (formerly The Ahwahnee), the Yosemite Valley Lodge (formerly the Yosemite Lodge), and the Big Trees Lodge (formerly the Wawona Hotel), feature dining options that were organically grown, which means minimal oil-based fertilizer. And these foods come from areas near the park, requiring a lot less energy to be transported from the farm to your plate than do similar meals grown far away.

Yosemite is working hard to reach a zero-landfill goal. You can help by avoiding single use packaging and recycling everything possible. Bring a reusable beverage container. Also, most stores and restaurants offer a discount if you use your own cup or bottle.

**Yosemite National Park** is administered by the US National Park Service (NPS), an agency of the Department of the Interior established in 1916. As a bureaucracy based loosely on a military model, the NPS is characterized by a complex ordering of job ranks and by its distinctive field uniforms. The green pants, gray shirt, and universally recognized "Smokey Bear" hat have become the trademark of the park ranger. The key descriptor here is "park," as park rangers differ from forest rangers. Forest rangers work for the US Forest Service, a branch of the US Department of Agriculture, in national forests throughout the country. While the job duties of park and forest rangers are often similar in their respective situations, park rangers work in parks and monuments, and forest rangers work in _____ (you fill in the blank!).

A Yosemite ranger on horseback

Now that you're able to recognize that the person in the flat-brimmed hat before you is a park ranger working in a national park, things start to get a bit more complicated. The National Park Service is divided into any number of departments that range in purpose from visitor protection to interpretation to maintenance to resource management to administration. Confusing things further, employees of the different divisions all wear roughly the same uniform. The traditional park ranger is employed by the Division of Visitor Protection, with duties that include law enforcement, traffic regulation, search and rescue, emergency medical treatment, and many others. In order to work as a traditional park ranger, one must take special training and earn a law enforcement commission.

Park interpreters (interpretive rangers, formerly called naturalists) are responsible for the educational walks, talks, and other such programs at Yosemite. They, too, are rangers, but they generally have not been commissioned and do not perform law enforcement functions. Their uniforms are identical to those of protection rangers, but they don't carry guns and handcuffs.

Identical, too, are the outfits of the various park administrators, such as the superintendent (the park's chief administrative officer), deputy superintendent, chief ranger, and other division chiefs.

Things get a little more confusing with certain maintenance, fire, and resource management workers. They've got the green pants, ditto the gray shirt, but instead of the funny hat, they wear dark green baseball caps with the NPS arrowhead insignia. These employees are not technically rangers, but their roles at Yosemite are all equally significant.

Most people don't realize that the National Park Service has exclusive jurisdiction over Yosemite National Park. That means that state, county, and local agencies do not operate here, and they provide almost no services here: in Yosemite there are no highway patrol officers, no sheriff's officers, no state or municipal firefighters, no state courts, and no incorporated local government. These services fall to the National Park Service, which very ably manages the park.

If you need help of any kind (from emergency assistance to information) while you're in the park, all uniformed NPS personnell are there to be of service. To report an event that may be dangerous or illegal, you can call the rangers at (209) 379-1992.

**Many people have** the impression that when the first day of winter arrives in Yosemite, the whole place closes up tight until spring. They are mistaken, however; the park and its residents do not hibernate, except for some of the bears. Yosemite only "closes" when deep snowfall makes it impossible to plow access roads (which is almost never).

There are notable park changes in winter, but most of them add to the unique qualities of this special season. Much of Yosemite wears a covering of snow, and once-thundering waterfalls quiet themselves in frozen dormancy. Tioga Road and Glacier Point Road close, and visitor activities center on such winter sports as skiing and skating.

Weekdays in winter are perfect for experiencing Yosemite in an uncrowded, serene environment. Yosemite Valley daytime temperatures can be surprisingly mild, and winter walks are some of the best. The biggest reward of all, however, is the sheer beauty and grandeur of a transfigured Yosemite and the surrounding high country.

The major routes to the park remain open throughout the year. The roadway least affected by the weather is Highway 140, which leads from Merced via Mariposa and through the Arch Rock Entrance to the park. Highways 120 (from the west) and 41 are more often subject to closure from heavy snowfall, and use of tire chains is frequently required on them. The roads in Yosemite Valley are plowed throughout the winter.

Winter driving in Yosemite requires special precautions. Because roads are regularly covered with ice and snow, driving speeds should be reduced. You may be required to carry tire chains in your vehicle—whether or not you have 4-wheel drive—depending on conditions. Watch out for snowplows, and never stop in the roadway (find a pullout where traffic can safely pass).

## Skiing and Snowboarding

Both cross-country types and downhillers will discover ski and snowboard opportunities in Yosemite. California's oldest operating ski area, Yosemite Ski & Snowboard Area (formerly Badger Pass), is located at 7,300 feet (2,225 m), about 45 minutes from Yosemite Valley on Glacier Point Road. It's primarily a "family" oriented operation with 9 runs and 4 ski lifts. Yosemite Ski & Snowboard Area is an ideal place to learn to ski, and a ski school is available. Listen to a recorded message on snow conditions at (209) 372-1000. Free shuttle buses are provided during the winter from lodging facilities in Yosemite Valley. Call (209) 372-1240 or visit travelyosemite.com for information about Yosemite Ski & Snowboard Area and the shuttle.

Miles and miles of both groomed and ungroomed trails for cross-country skiers also originate at the ski area. Tracks are laid out on Glacier Point Road, sometimes all the way to Glacier Point, and skating lanes are also provided. Well-signed trails lead into the wilderness and out to the south rim of Yosemite Valley. The cross-country ski school offers classes, individualized instruction, snow tubing, and guided tours. In season, call (209) 372-8444 for cross-country services.

A variety of services are available at the Yosemite Ski & Snowboard Area: snowboard and ski rentals (both downhill and cross-country), ski repair, and food and beverage service. There's also a locker room and restrooms. The National Park Service staffs a ranger station, primarily as a first-aid facility, in the A-frame building. The phone number is (209) 372-0409.

Another popular cross-country ski and snowshoe area is Crane Flat, located at the intersection of Big Oak Flat and Tioga

Snowy morning in Yosemite Valley

Roads, 17 miles from Yosemite Valley. There are no services provided here, but the meadows and forests are full of trails for skiers and snowshoers. There is a winter trails map on the park website covering the Crane Flat area.

## Snowshoeing

You can snowshoe on your own wherever there's adequate snow, or enjoy a ranger-led snowshoe walk with snowshoes provided. Walks are presented several days a week, starting in front of the A-frame at Yosemite Ski & Snowboard Area, and reservations are required. Check the *Yosemite Guide* or call (209) 372-0409.

## Ice Skating

A large outdoor ice rink is operated daily in Yosemite Valley at Half Dome Village (weather permitting) from November through March. It features rental skates, a warming hut with lockers, and a fire pit. For more information visit travelyosemite.com.

## Snow Play

Provisions have been made for individuals and families with a passion for sledding, tobogganing, snow tubing, and snow play generally. Snow tubing is offered at Yosemite Ski & Snowboard Area. There is a designated snow-play area at Crane Flat Campground. Another good snow-play area is found just south of the park on Highway 41 at Goat Meadow, in the Sierra National Forest. There is also sledding on the medial moraine, near the Yosemite Valley stable. Supervise children well, and be careful of sliding into roadways. Many injuries related to snow play occur every year.

## Camping

There are 4 campgrounds in Yosemite that are open for use during winter. In Yosemite Valley, both Upper Pines and Camp 4 (see page 100) have been winterized. The Wawona Campground (see page 121) is the winter camping area south of the Valley, and in the north end of the park, it's Hodgdon Meadow Campground (see page 142). All these campgrounds are first come, first served.

## Backcountry Ski Huts

For the intrepid wilderness skier, 3 different huts are operated in Yosemite's backcountry. Nine miles (14.5 km) from Yosemite Ski

& Snowboard Area to the south of Glacier Point Road is the Ostrander Ski Hut. Set on the banks of a deeply frozen lake and below scenic Horse Ridge, the hut can accommodate up to 25 skiers overnight. There are beds with mattresses, cooking facilities, toilets, a wood stove, and water. Run by Yosemite Conservancy, the Ostrander Ski Hut is so popular that reservations are required. For more information, see yosemiteconservancy.org under Ostrander Ski Hut.

The second hut is located at Glacier Point and is reached by skiing the 10 miles (16 km) out from Yosemite Ski & Snowboard Area to the end of Glacier Point Road. It is operated by Yosemite Hospitality, which also requires reservations. Both guided and self-guided trips are available, with meals and beds included. To learn more about the Glacier Point Hut call (209) 372-8444 or visit travelyosemite.com.

The Tuolumne Meadows Ski Hut is open until the Tioga Road opens in the spring. It sleeps 10 and is available at no charge, first come, first served. The hut is the stone building right at the entrance to the Tuolumne Meadows Campground, approximately 8 miles (13 km) west of Tioga Pass. The NPS operates but does not staff this ski hut. Be prepared to camp out if the hut is full.

## Bracebridge Dinner

Perhaps Yosemite's most long-standing winter tradition is the Bracebridge Dinner. A multicourse Christmas feast is presented at The Majestic Yosemite Hotel in the context of a colorful pageant based loosely on Washington Irving's account in *The Sketch Book of Geoffrey Crayon, Gent.* of a typical Yorkshire Christmas dinner in the manor of Squire Bracebridge. The music, costumes, food, and drama combine for a memorable experience. Tickets for the event (held multiple times) are in great demand, and reservations for the dinner are much sought after. Reservations are accepted 366 days in advance and are processed by lottery when demand exceeds availability. For more information or to reserve tickets to Bracebridge, call (888) 304-8993.

## A public shower?

In Yosemite Valley, there are showers at Half Dome Village (open all year) and at Housekeeping Camp (closed in winter). There are no public showers in the Wawona area. There is a fee for all showers.

## A laundromat?

The only park laundromat (open all year) is at Housekeeping Camp in Yosemite Valley.

## A post office?

The main post office is in Yosemite Village (near the Valley Visitor Center). There is a year-round post office in the Big Trees Lodge Store, and a summer-only post office in Tuolumne Meadows at the grocery store.

## An ATM?

In Yosemite Valley, there is an ATM in Yosemite Village, inside the Village Store; at Yosemite Valley Lodge, inside the main registration area; and at Half Dome Village, inside the gift/grocery store. In Wawona, the ATM is inside the Big Trees Lodge Store, and at Tuolumne Meadows, it's inside the grocery store. There are also ATMs at the Yosemite Ski & Snowboard Area and the store at Crane Flat.

**The Village Store**

## A babysitter?

Limited babysitting is available for registered guests at Yosemite Valley Lodge and The Majestic Yosemite Hotel. Call the front desk or see the concierge for additional information.

## A dog kennel?

The only park kennel is at the Yosemite Valley Stable. Dogs must be gentle, weigh more than 20 pounds (smaller may be okay if you provide a portable kennel), and have proof of shots and a license. Advanced reservations are highly recommended; call (209) 372-8326 for more information.

## A copy machine or a fax machine?

In Yosemite Valley, contact the front desk at Yosemite Valley Lodge, Half Dome Village, or The Majestic Yosemite Hotel. A fee is charged for these services.

## A good time?

If you're not enjoying yourself in Yosemite, with all it has to offer, you need to see your therapist.

## A cup of coffee?

In Yosemite Valley, visit the Food Court at Yosemite Valley Lodge, Degnan's Kitchen in the village, and the Coffee Corner at Half Dome Village.

## A cold beer?

There are 3 real bars in Yosemite, all in Yosemite Valley. The Majestic Yosemite Hotel Bar is probably the classiest spot in the park, with a fine selection of wine, liquor, and mixed drinks in an elegant setting. The Mountain Room, at the Yosemite Valley Lodge, is slightly more casual but does have a pleasant atmosphere and a wide selection of drinks. Half Dome Village also has a bar at the Pavillion Restaurant and Pizza Deck, in the summer season.

There is no actual bar at the Big Trees Lodge, but a full drink selection is available there. You can enjoy a cocktail in their comfortable lounge or with dinner.

For a very casual atmosphere, almost a sports-bar feel, Degnan's Loft, above Degnan's Kitchen, has some wines and usually a pretty good selection of beers, both in the bottle and on tap. In the winter months this switches over to an employees-only hangout. There is also a bar attached to the Yosemite View Lodge restaurant, just outside the park on Highway 140. Yosemite View Lodge also has a small store with a nice selection of beers, as well as other beverages and snacks.

Most of the sit-down restaurants in Yosemite serve drinks and have a few beers on tap. If all you're looking for, though, is a fine beer at the end of the day and you don't want to go to the effort and expense of a bar or restaurant, your best bet is to

Relaxing by Tenaya Lake

buy a few bottles or a six-pack from the Village Store or the Tuolumne Store and take it back to your campsite or wherever you're staying.

## Groceries and Supplies

Most people don't come to Yosemite to go shopping. But when your needs turn from natural beauty to a hearty meal or cold drink, you need not fear. The park is well supplied with grocery stores as well as other modern conveniences. Of course the stores sell camping food and souvenirs, but if you look you can find anything that you might want (within reason) in the park. Be aware that you'll pay a little more than you would at home. Head to the following places to satisfy your needs.

The Yosemite Village Store and the Tuolumne Store (open only in summer) are much like traditional grocery stores. The Village Store is by far the best grocery option in the park. Yosemite locals do a fair amount of their grocery shopping here. It features a surprisingly strong wine rack and beer selection, and a good amount of organic food. The Tuolumne Store is smaller, but it has enough for you to base your summer trip out of Tuolumne Meadows on and not have to go to the Valley to buy anything.

The Half Dome Village Store, Yosemite Valley Lodge Store, and Big Trees Lodge Store carry limited supplies but are all good options.

There are several locations where you can find snack food: the Crane Flat Gas Station, Glacier Point Snack Stand and Gift Shop, White Wolf Store, Big Trees Lodge Golf Course Pro Shop, Yosemite Conservancy Depot at the Mariposa Grove, and the Yosemite View Lodge Store. All are open only in the summer season except the Yosemite View Lodge, which is open all year.

The El Portal Market, just outside the park on Highway 140, in the small community of El Portal, offers a good selection of groceries and supplies, including fresh produce, frozen foods, picnic fixings, beverages, and baked goods.

Dining out in Yosemite

**Though just being in** Yosemite should be enough to keep young people occupied and engaged, there are lots of activities and programs that will enhance their visit to the park. During your stay, be sure to check the *Yosemite Guide* for scheduled events that are specially designed for kids.

## Take a Hike

With just about every park locale offering flat to moderate walking, a family hike is a great way to burn youthful energy and to reach undeveloped, uncrowded spots with remarkable views and natural beauty. Take a picnic and make a day of it! See pages 94, 95, 96, 97, 116, 118, 120, 130, 134, 135, 140 and 141 for hiking ideas.

## Enjoy a Bike Ride

The best park bicycle riding is in Yosemite Valley, which features miles of bike trails. Bring your own, or rent bicycles at Yosemite Valley Lodge or Half Dome Village. See page 91 for details. Don't forget your helmets—you can rent them along with your bikes.

## Visit Happy Isles

The Happy Isles Art and Nature Center in Yosemite Valley, open in summer only, is devoted to kids and the junior ranger program, with wildlife exhibits, nightlife display, and other presentations. There are books for sale, and Explorer Packs on a variety of topics can be checked out. They include activities designed to help children learn more about the natural world they live in.

## Help Them Become Junior Rangers

There are two self-guided junior ranger programs for kids in Yosemite. Children 3 through 6 can become little cubs and earn a button by completing the activities set out in *The Little Cub Handbook,* available at visitor centers throughout the park. The *Junior Ranger Handbook* is for those aged 7 to 13, and completion of the program allows them to become junior rangers and receive a certificate and patch. Any questions? Check with a ranger for more information.

## Explore the Indian Village and Yosemite Museum

Within the Yosemite Museum in Yosemite Valley, a room has been dedicated to the culture of the local American Indian people. Besides a number of educational displays, there is often someone demonstrating basket making or some other cultural aspect of the Miwok and Paiute people. Behind the museum is a garden area that includes exhibits about the local American Indians.

## Take in a Campfire Program

What better way to finish off a day than attending a traditional campfire program? During the summer, there are usually programs offered by rangers in campgrounds throughout the park. Check the *Yosemite Guide* for schedules.

You can also have a campfire at your own campsite. Make sure that you are aware of campfire regulations. You can buy wood, hot dogs, and s'mores material at the Yosemite Village Store.

## Visit the Skating Rink

From November through March when weather allows, an outdoor ice rink operates at Half Dome Village beneath the shadow of Glacier Point. You can rent ice skates, and there's a warming hut as well as lockers, a fire pit, and a snack bar. For more information go to travelyosemite.com or call (209) 372-8319.

## Engage in Snow Play

During winter, grab your sleds, toboggans, and inner tubes and head to the snow-play areas at the Crane Flat Campground or just outside the South Entrance at Goat Meadow on Highway 41. Relatively gentle and clear slopes afford hours of slipping and sliding.

## Go Skiing or Snowboarding

The ski area at Yosemite Ski & Snowboard Area is perfect for families, with 9 runs, multiple lifts, and lessons offered by a first-rate ski school. Rental equipment is available for snowboarding and downhill and cross-country skiing. See page 22.

## Snowshoe with a Ranger

Snowshoe walks are offered at Yosemite Ski & Snowboard Area by National Park Service rangers for adults and children 10 years and older. Rental snowshoes are available. Check the *Yosemite Guide* for schedules.

**If by some horrible twist** of your itinerary you find yourself with but a single day in Yosemite National Park, you will be sorely cheated. The park is so large and so studded with fascinating features that usually 3 or 4 days are required to really "do the place justice." But take heart, for there are some remarkable highlights that can be enjoyed in a day, many of them centered in Yosemite Valley.

While Yosemite Valley's 7 square miles (18 square km) comprise but a tiny fraction of the park's total area, they are jam-packed with spectacular scenic beauty. First of all, get out of your car at any of the day-use parking areas in the Valley and board a free Yosemite Valley shuttle bus. Buses stop at practically every point of interest in the eastern end of Yosemite Valley, and they are the only means (besides bicycle or on foot) to enter the areas there that are closed to automobile traffic. Listed below are several activities that can be enjoyed in a day from stops along the shuttle bus route. See page 89 for more information on free shuttle buses. You might also consider taking a Yosemite Valley Floor Tour: operated by the park's concessioner (but with a ranger doing the talking) and leaving from Yosemite Valley Lodge, the flatbed trailer tour covers many popular sites. Call (209) 372-1240 for times and availability.

## Valley Visitor Center

Here is a logical starting point for your visit. See page 88. Park information, an orientation film, exhibits, and books are all available here. If time allows, take in the Yosemite Museum, and walk through the Indian Village behind it. (15 minutes to 2 hours)

## Lower Yosemite Fall

Walk from the bus stop to the base of Lower Yosemite Fall—about .25 miles (400 m). See page 94. Be prepared to get wet in spring when runoff is at its peak; in any season you'll be impressed by the imposing height of one of the world's most famous falls. (30 minutes to 1 hour)

## Happy Isles

This is the trailhead for hikes to Vernal and Nevada falls, Half Dome, and other high-country destinations (except in winter). Walk to the Vernal Fall bridge (.7 miles; 1.1 km) for a breathtaking view of this beautiful cataract, or continue on to the top of the fall (if you've got the energy). This route is known as the Mist Trail for reasons that will be obvious. During the summer, the Happy Isles Art and Nature Center offers art classes, exhibits, and books. This location also serves as the center for the junior ranger program. There are snacks at the kiosk behind the Happy Isles Shuttle Stop (1 to 3 hours)

## Mirror Lake

From the shuttle bus stop, Mirror Lake is a .5-mile (.8-km) walk up a slight grade. See page 94. While the lake only offers the mirrorlike surface for which it was named in spring and early summer (it's filling up with silt), one of the best views of Half Dome is to be had from its banks. The hike around the lake is easy and rewarding. (1 to 2 hours)

## Bridalveil Fall

Follow road signs to Wawona Road (toward Wawona and Fresno). Immediately after turning onto Wawona Road, turn left into the Bridalveil Fall parking lot. The short trail leads to the base of the fall, where a sheet of water floats downward 620 feet (189 m) to the Valley floor. (15 to 45 minutes)

Bridalveil Fall

## Tunnel View

Turn left back onto Wawona Road and drive approximately 3 miles (4.8 km) to the Tunnel View turnout, which is just below the entrance to the Wawona Tunnel. Before you will be the classic panoramic view of Yosemite Valley that greeted the first Euro-American visitors here. (10 to 30 minutes)

## Glacier Point

Thirty-two miles (51.5 km) from Yosemite Valley, Glacier Point is unquestionably a "must see" for visitors. Within 200 yards (183 m) of the parking lot is the top of the sheer southern wall of Yosemite Valley. Not only does the Valley lie 3,200 feet (975 m) below you, but also the entire park is revealed, with astounding vistas in every direction. Most of Yosemite's major peaks are identified, and exhibits explain the geologic processes that created this amazing landscape. There is possibly no better view of Yosemite Valley and the surrounding high country. The road to Glacier Point is closed in winter. See page 119 for more information. (1 hour for the drive from Yosemite Valley plus wait time when the free shuttle is running and 30 minutes to 1 hour at Glacier Point)

## Mariposa Grove of Giant Sequoias

If you have already seen Yosemite Valley and Glacier Point and you've still got time (hard to believe!), the Mariposa Grove is located near the park's south entrance from Highway 41 (see page 117). This magnificent stand of sequoias is Yosemite's largest and includes trees thousands of years old. A free shuttle transports visitors into the grove (during summer months, check the *Yosemite Guide* for schedule), or you may enter on foot. (The hike into the upper part of the grove area is fairly rigorous.) Famous trees, like the Grizzly Giant and the fallen Tunnel Tree, should not be missed. (2 to 3 hours)

## Tuolumne Meadows and Tioga Road

Open in summer and early fall only, Tioga Road bisects the park and leads through Tuolumne Meadows, a beautiful subalpine meadow surrounded by soaring granite crags and polished domes (see page 137). If your trip out of the park takes you to the east, you will be able to enjoy the scenery lining Tioga Road and the exhibits describing it (see page 132). Be sure to stop at Olmsted Point for its remarkable view of Tenaya Canyon and the back side of Half Dome, and of Tenaya Lake, the deep-blue, icy-cold waters of which form Yosemite's largest natural lake. (2 to 2.5 hours for the trip from Yosemite Valley to Tioga Pass)

## Just Passing Through?

If it happens that you are simply driving through Yosemite (a regrettable situation), be sure to stop by a visitor or information center, located at or near every park entrance, for recommendations from park staff on what to see.

The View from Glacier Point

**Because of its granite** landscape, Yosemite is a mecca for rock climbers from all over the United States and the world. Climbs range from short routes of 50 feet (15 m) or less (a pitch) to multiday ascents of Yosemite's biggest walls (like El Capitan), which are made up of many pitches. Yosemite Valley has been the location of so many climbing developments and innovations that it has become the yardstick against which all other climbing areas are measured. In every season of the year, climbers can be seen clinging to rock faces or hanging by their hands and feet from upward-leading cracks.

Passionate rock climbers populate a world foreign to most "normal" people and have developed a subculture with customs, clothing, language, and tools of its own. In Yosemite, that world revolves around Camp 4. Across Northside Drive from Yosemite Valley Lodge, Camp 4 is the climbers' permanent temporary home. Its role in the evolution of rock climbing has been recognized by the United States government, and Camp 4 is on the National Register of Historic Places. Many of the hardcore climbers move to Tuolumne Meadows during the summer.

Climber tackling Yosemite granite

Not that long ago, climbers utilized many artificial techniques to accomplish their climbs. These included drilling holes in the rock and inserting permanent metal bolts, chiseling holds in the rocks, and hammering in steel pitons that damaged the rock and could not always be removed. Such techniques made certain routes climbable that might not otherwise be.

Today, a less destructive and harmful climbing ethic has developed. Bolts are placed much less often, chiseling is frowned upon, and high-tech devices like "chocks," "friends," and "cams" that are inserted into cracks and easily removed provide protection for climbers. It's known as "clean climbing," and it's a matter of high priority for climbers who wish to protect and preserve a natural climbing environment.

This cleaner, less invasive style is also called "trad" (for "traditional") climbing. Yosemite's vertical crack systems have allowed climbers to pioneer the style without taking unacceptable risks. The climbing community has been and continues to be split over the issue of how much bolting, if any, is acceptable.

Overall, trad climbing is more of an American style—European geology makes it harder to place removable safety gear. Hand in hand (or hand in granite) with this cleaner style came the rise of free climbing. Climbing free means propelling yourself up a route without pulling on the rope, or using artificial aid for anything other than arresting a fall. Most Yosemite climbing is done free, but using artificial means remains the standard on long, demanding routes up the Valley's big walls. For example, the Nose on El Capitan, perhaps the most iconic route in American climbing, is done many times a year using aid, but it has only been "freed" by a few of the best climbers in the world. The first free ascent of the Nose, in 1993 by the magnificent Lynn Hill, is considered one of the greatest achievements in climbing history.

For climbers not sufficiently challenged by free climbing, there is free soloing, in which climbers ascend a route in much

Climbing in Yosemite's high country

the same way that children ascend a jungle gym—with no protective gear of any kind. Many of Yosemite's landmarks have been free soloed in less than a day. This book does not recommend free soloing. While most roped climbing can be fairly safe if done properly, one small mistake will likely kill you if you climb unroped.

While Yosemite is filled with climbable granite, El Capitan is the one feature that dominates all others, to climbers and laypeople alike. For decades, no one thought it would ever be climbed. But in 1958, after 47 unbelievably strenuous days on the wall, Warren Harding along with several others clambered up the Nose, ensuring that our 29th president can only ever be the second-greatest man named Warren Harding. Nowadays a typical team spends 4 days climbing the route. The current speed record, set in October 2017 by Brad Gobright and Jim Reynolds, is 2 hours, 19 minutes, and 44 seconds. Alex Honnold free soloed El Capitan's Freerider route in June 2017 in 3 hours and 56 minutes. If you visit Yosemite in spring or fall, you may be able to pick out climbers, tiny against the rock, gliding (or lurching) their

way up El Capitan. Bring binoculars to El Capitan Meadow and look for the flash of sunlight on metal gear. If you go by at night, check for the headlamps as teams camp out on ledges thousands of feet above the ground.

One interesting aspect of the climbing subculture is its system of naming and rating climbing routes. The first climber to successfully undertake a new path up a section of rock (a "first ascent") is entitled to name that route. That climber, and those who come after, attempt to rate the difficulty of climbing that route. The Yosemite Decimal System is used for this purpose and is an elaborate scale with ratings from 5.0 to 5.15 with grades from "a" to "d" at the higher levels signifying different degrees of difficulty.

The technology of climbing has advanced considerably over the past several decades. Special ropes made from synthetic fibers are used, and they stretch to absorb the weight of a falling climber. Their strength under pressure has also increased. Shoes covered with sticky rubber that adheres to practically any surface are now commonly used. And devices such as cams made from high-strength alloys have expanded climbing opportunities as well.

But good equipment or not, climbers must still have the skill and strength to climb the rocks. The mastery that has been achieved by many "rock jocks" is astounding, and routes that many once considered unclimbable are now accomplished almost daily. New routes are being explored and climbed, and other climbing firsts, like paraplegic Mark Wellman's 1989 ascent of El Capitan, continue to occur.

Rock climbing is not recommended for the casual park visitor. If you would like to learn more about the sport, consider taking a lesson from the Yosemite Mountaineering School & Guide Service, contact them at (209) 372-8344, email yms@aramark.com, or visit travelyosemite.com under Things to Do in Tuolumne Meadows. In summer only, call (209) 372-8435. Without proper equipment and without proper technique, you could severely injure yourself or die. If you are planning on climbing in Yosemite, be sure to check the park website under Things to Do for current climbing restrictions, safety advice, and more.

Scaling a rock face

. . . . . . . . . . . . . . . . . . . . . . . . . . . . . . . . . . . . . . . . . . . . . . . . . . .

**Q: My friend and I are going to do some climbing this fall in Yosemite. Is it true that October is a great time to climb?**

**A: Autumn is a popular climbing season because the weather tends to be moderate. However, weather extremes do occur in the fall; heat is possible but so is heavy rain and even the first snows. Yosemite climbers have died in October from hypothermia. It is important that you are prepared for any weather extremes.**

Climber appreciating Yosemite granite

**Many people, upon arriving** in Yosemite, are bowled over by the vast array of experiences the park offers. Do you want to spend your day in skis, climbing shoes, or slippers? Do you want to see waterfalls, glaciers, or John Muir? Was that bird a junco, a raven, or a golden eagle? Where to stay? What to eat? How much to spend? You don't need to climb atop Yosemite's mountains and ask a guru in a cave. Along with its many choices, Yosemite offers many places to learn about the park and shape your experience into what you want it to be. The best place to start (of course) is the book in your hand, but if you want to delve deeper or learn more, here is a list of places to look.

## Half Dome Village (Yosemite Valley)

Half Dome Village Gift & Grocery (books, guides, maps)

The Yosemite Mountain Shop (historic displays, advice)

Occasional presentations at Half Dome Village

Sierra Club presentations at the Yosemite Conservation Heritage Center

Happy Isles Art and Nature Center (books, exhibits)

## Yosemite Village (Yosemite Valley)

The Village Store (books, maps, DVDs)

The Valley Wilderness Center (exhibits, maps, advice)

The Ansel Adams Gallery (books, all things photographic)

The Valley Visitor Center (advice, forecasts, many exhibits)

Yosemite Conservancy Bookstore (books on all things remotely related to Yosemite)

The Yosemite Museum and its rotating special exhibits (books, exhibits, and presentations focusing on all things about American Indians in Yosemite)

The Yosemite Theater, featuring *Spirit of Yosemite* (an excellent short film about Yosemite history and culture) and *Yosemite: A Gathering of Spirit* (a short film by Ken Burns celebrating the 150th anniversary of the Yosemite Grant).

Presentations at the Yosemite Valley Lodge

## Wawona/Mariposa Grove

Yosemite Conservancy Depot (books, advice)

Big Trees Lodge Store (books, advice)

Pioneer Yosemite History Center (historic exhibits)

The Wawona Visitor Center (advice, forecasts, maps)

## Glacier Point

Glacier Point Snack Stand and Gift Shop (books, advice)

Ranger presentations at Glacier Point

## Big Oak Flat

The Big Oak Flat Information Station (books, maps, forecasts, advice)

The Crane Flat Gas Station (books)

## Tioga Road

Ranger presentations at the Tuolumne Meadows campground

Presentations at Parsons Memorial Lodge

The Tuolumne Meadows Visitor Center (books, forecasts, advice)

Find information and advice here

Wilderness Center (maps, forecasts, advice)

Many gift shops, coffee shops, gas stations, and restaurants in communities surrounding the park have information of all kinds, from maps to guest speakers.

And there are many, many interpretive signs all over the whole darn place.

**Both cell and Internet** service coverage and access continue to increase and improve in the Sierra Nevada. To check on current status in Yosemite, go to nps.gov/yose under Plan Your Visit.

## Cell Phone Coverage

The cell coverage described here is primarily for Verizon, via the local carrier service. AT&T service also covers some areas of Yosemite Valley, but AT&T has limited or no service in Wawona, El Portal, or Yosemite West. T-Mobile works in the Yosemite Village area. Your best bet for coverage remains Yosemite Valley. You will hit occasional dead spots, but in general coverage is pretty solid, especially in the heavily trafficked east end of the Valley. The signal may fade if you're too close to one of the Valley's walls. Above the walls, on Glacier Point and Sentinel Dome, you should be able to get service. Please be aware of other hikers if you talk on your cell phone on the trail.

**Q: I'm headed into Yosemite Wilderness. I can use my cell phone in an emergency, right?**

**A: Wilderness is characterized by the absence of cell coverage (weak signals are possible in a few pockets). Your best defense in a wilderness area is to be prepared for self-sufficiency; after all, this is part of your outdoor experience. Thorough planning and preparation are your best companions.**

With some carriers there is some reception in other areas. The signal in El Portal, in the Merced Canyon, is a little uneven, but Foresta, 2,000 feet higher, is pretty well covered. Yosemite West has very limited reception, but there's enough that it's worth a try if you need to make or take a call. Fish Camp, south of Yosemite, has patchy reception that improves as you go higher up. There is a little reception in Wawona, in the area surrounding the Big Trees Lodge. Along Tioga Road, Crane Flat has decent reception, but then you have to wait until you reach Tuolumne Meadows before coverage picks up again.

Coverage tends to improve as you go farther up or farther west, out of the canyons. A small rise can make a big difference.

Do not rely on your cell phone while hiking. There is very little coverage in the backcountry. As NPS ranger Brad Benter says, a cell phone is not a first aid kit. Don't put yourself into a risky situation and assume that you can phone for help and get out of trouble. If you decide to go somewhere dangerous, in the high country or in Yosemite's canyons, make sure that your party has the necessary skill and supplies to deal with emergencies.

Using your phone while driving in Yosemite is a terrible idea. There are simply no stretches of highway that are straight and have consistent reception. Contending with RVs, tour buses, weather, and wildlife is enough of a challenge on Yosemite's narrow, winding roads without trying to put in your earpiece (as required by California law) and hold a patchy conversation. Your call can wait.

## The Internet

Public Internet access is limited in Yosemite National Park. Most lodging in the Valley provide free Internet for their guests. There is also WiFi available to hotel guests at Degnan's Kitchen and Loft in the Yosemite Village area. Half Dome Village Guest Lounge offers visitors access to WiFi for a fee that is payable at the front desk.

The public libraries of Wawona, Yosemite Valley, and El Portal offer public Internet access. Each spot has variable hours that are dependent on the season and the day. Schedules can be found on the Mariposa County library website, mariposalibrary.org. In the Valley, the Mariposa Library offers free WiFi at their site at the Girl's Club on Village Drive, across from the Administration Building. There are also numerous restaurants and coffee shops in the towns surrounding Yosemite National Park on Highways 41, 140, and 120 with wireless Internet access.

**Q: Can I fly my drone in Yosemite?**

**A: Drones are prohibited in the park. They disturb wildlife and interfere with the ability of aircraft to respond to visitor emergencies. Plus, they impact the experiences of other visitors who may not share your passion. Please leave your drone at home.**

The Holmes Brothers and a Stanley Steamer in Yosemite, c. 1901

# 2 YOSEMITE HISTORY

**The recorded history** of Yosemite National Park is as fascinating and important as it is short relative to other parts of the US and the world. While American Indians were long-term residents, Euro-Americans did not enter Yosemite Valley until 1851 and did not occupy it in any meaningful way until the 1860s. Yet Yosemite's history over the past century and a half is particularly significant, because the actions of both people and governments here have pioneered conservation efforts on behalf of natural areas all around the globe. There is little question that at Yosemite the concept of national parks was born, and the park still serves as a model and symbol for the entire world.

**People resided in** the Yosemite region for about 8,000 years before Spain occupied California. Anthropologists suggest that the earliest inhabitants came from the east side of the Sierra Nevada looking for water and food in particularly dry years. Later, as populations increased and competition for homelands grew, groups from the Central Valley (predominantly Miwok-speaking) moved into the foothills and greater Yosemite. These groups merged and established permanent villages near the Merced River throughout Yosemite Valley.

There is no written history of people in Yosemite until very recent times. Anthropologists believe that the several cultures here evolved gradually; a lifestyle of seed and plant gathering, hunting, and trade remained little changed for many generations. Yosemite's American Indians generally departed the elevations above 4,000 feet (1,219 m) during the winter and spring, and then moved back upslope to Yosemite Valley and elsewhere for the summer and fall. Once snow melted off the high country there was a good deal of trading and intertribal connection across the Sierra to the east side. The first Europeans that native Californians came into contact with were Spanish missionaries, soldiers, and settlers in the eighteenth century. As more and more Europeans settled in the central and southern parts of the state, white encroachment on traditional Indian territory increased. Some people believe that at the beginning of the 1800s the Indian people of Yosemite were struck with a "fatal black sickness," a plague of some type. Reportedly, the few survivors abandoned the Valley and relocated to the eastern Sierra and were assimilated by other groups there. For a number of years (the exact number unknown), Yosemite Valley may have been uninhabited.

One of the Yosemite people who grew up with the Mono Paiutes was Tenaya (see page 50). As a youth, Tenaya heard stories of the beauty and bounty of Yosemite Valley. He finally visited the former home of his people quite late in his life. Being favorably impressed, he and 200 others (some Yosemite descendants, some not) resettled the Valley. Tenaya was named chief of the group.

These people lived in the Valley they called "Ah-wah-nee" until the Gold Rush and the fateful Euro-American occupation of the Sierra foothills began in 1849. Ahwahnee (as it is spelled now) probably means "place of a gaping mouth," although Lafayette Bunnell of the Mariposa Battalion reported that through hand signals the native people had indicated its meaning was "deep, grassy valley."

As friction between gold seekers and American Indians in the foothills increased, negative sentiments blossomed. Groups native to the Central Valley moved higher into the foothills, and conflict resulted between rival Indian groups as well as between whites and native people. As Tenaya and his fellows defiantly protected their mountain stronghold, the Mariposa Battalion was formed to locate and capture the residents and relocate them to reservations. The members of the Mariposa Battalion were the first white people in the Yosemite Valley. Soon "Ahwahnee" became "Yosemite." The local Indians called themselves the Ahwahneechees. The white soldiers called them the "Yosemites." Some say this came from the Miwok word "uzumati," or grizzly bear. The origin that is now considered correct is that it is a corruption of the word "Yo-che-ma-te," which means "some among them are killers." Whatever the word's meaning, it is true that the local Indians were known as fierce fighters and that they lived in an area where grizzly bears were fairly common.

Following Tenaya's death in 1853, what was left of the band of Ahwahneechees dispersed. Some went east to the Mono Lake area, while others joined neighboring

An American Indian family in Yosemite, c. 1900

peoples along the Tuolumne River. Never again did the remaining Ahwahneechees gather together as a people.

Within 20 years, the number of American Indians living in the Yosemite area dwindled to below 50. With white settlement of Yosemite Valley and ever-increasing tourism, the native culture was irrevocably corrupted. Hotelkeepers and other concessioners employed some of the Ahwahneechees for odd jobs and manual labor, but the truth is that they were only tolerated at best.

## A Gentle Lifestyle

During their hundreds of years of life in Yosemite Valley, the native people of Yosemite were remarkably gentle in their use of the land. There were at least 40 different village spots on the floor of the Valley. Most of them were summer encampments only. Because of heavy snow and extremely cold temperatures, the bulk of the Valley residents moved to the El Portal area and the foothills below to pass the severe winter months.

The typical house was a conical lean-to covered with 3 layers of cedar bark slabs, affording reasonable shelter from the elements. There were also earth-covered dance houses and sweathouses, and small elevated granaries for storing acorns and other edibles.

The staple of the American Indian diet in Yosemite and much of the rest of California was acorn, which was painstakingly prepared and eaten as mush. Mushrooms as well as ferns, clover, bulbs, and other plant foods were also eaten. Fish and game included deer, squirrels, rabbits, trout, and the Sacramento sucker. Some insects, like certain fly pupae, caterpillars, and grasshoppers were considered delicacies.

American Indians in Yosemite wove fairly coarse twined baskets and finer coiled baskets with elaborate patterns, as well as cradles. They also made bows and arrows, obsidian tools and implements, bone awls and scrapers, and ceremonial costumes.

Today American Indians play an important part in the cultural preservation and interpretation of Yosemite Miwok/Paiute sites in the park. Be sure to visit the Yosemite Museum, where expert interpreters demonstrate traditional native skills.

## Basket Culture

Yosemite's American Indians were part of a trading network that extended from the desert east of the mountains to the Pacific coast. In return for shells, obsidian, and other goods, they offered their finely woven baskets. Many people today don't recognize the value of these baskets, but for native Californians, baskets were the only way to contain or transport many things, from food to trade goods to babies.

Through the arrival of Euro-Americans and the destruction of native culture, basketry survived. Part of this was a matter of utility—native people use baskets for cooking, carrying, and gathering to this day. Some baskets are so watertight and sturdy that they can be used to boil water with the use of heated rocks, a necessity for cooking acorns. For the visitors flocking to Yosemite, though, baskets came to represent local American Indian culture, and fine baskets are now worth thousands of dollars. Tourists presented an opportunity for the Miwok/Paiute women living in the Valley to demonstrate their skills to the rest of the world, and to supplement their incomes. Basketry takes work, though—large baskets like those found in the Yosemite Museum can take 3 to 4 years to create.

The skills of collecting and preparing materials and then forming these materials into baskets have been passed down from generation to generation since the earliest times. In Yosemite, these skills still live today, through the family of Julia Parker. Julia learned how to weave from her mother-in-law, famed Miwok weaver Lucy Telles. The Parker family ancestry is Coast Miwok and Kashaya Pomo, and Julia lived in Yosemite from the age of 17. She demonstrated basketry to Yosemite visitors for more than 50 years, and taught traditional weaving to thousands of people, including her daughter, granddaughter, and great-granddaughter. Visitors can still experience a demonstration of native skills and culture, including basket weaving, at the Yosemite Museum, thanks to Julia and her family. Handmade baskets are available for purchase at the museum shop, and basketry classes are offered through Yosemite Conservancy, as Julia's descendants carry on the practice and sharing of native skills and culture.

**It's long been accepted** that Yosemite Valley was probably sighted by Euro-Americans for the first time in 1833. A party of explorers headed by Joseph R. Walker was crossing the Sierra Nevada that fall, and in their efforts to determine the best route, several of the group may have come upon the north rim of the Valley. The cliffs were described as "more than a mile high," and after several efforts the mountaineers determined that they were "utterly impossible

Yosemite Falls by artist Thomas Ayres

for a man to descend, to say nothing of our horses." Recent research indicates that the Walker Party may, in fact, have passed to the north of the Valley. The identities of the first Euro-Americans to see Yosemite Valley may remain a mystery forever.

It was not until nearly 20 years later that non-natives first entered Yosemite Valley.

In response to actions by the Yosemite Indians and their neighbors in defense of their homeland, a group of men was organized as the Mariposa Battalion to kill Indians as they deemed necessary and to transport survivors to reservations in the Central Valley. A punitive expedition was mounted in March of 1851, and their quest led the battalion into Yosemite Valley, where they beheld what no other group of pioneers had seen before.

It wasn't long before the word began to spread about Yosemite's wonders. Letters from members of the Mariposa Battalion to San Francisco newspapers aroused the interest of James Mason Hutchings, who organized the first tourist party to Yosemite Valley in 1855. He brought the artist Thomas Ayres to sketch the region's geologic features and used the sketches to disseminate Yosemite's fame even more widely.

An ever-increasing stream of visitors arrived primarily on foot and horseback, but as the years passed, wagon roads were developed to permit yet greater visitation.

Hutchings became the chief entrepreneur and publicist for Yosemite, homesteading land and operating a hotel. Other hotels and residences were built, livestock was grazed in the meadows, crops were planted, orchards were established, and Yosemite Valley was treated as a resource to be exploited.

## The State Grant

Fortunately, not everyone viewed the Valley as a capitalist's dream come true. Some amazingly farsighted persons took it upon themselves to work for the protection of Yosemite Valley for the public good. These early-day conservationists, I. W. Raymond and Frederick Law Olmsted (the landscape architect who, with Calvert Vaux, designed New York's Central Park) prominent among them, appealed to Congress. Senator John Conness introduced a bill to grant Yosemite Valley and the Mariposa Grove of Big Trees to the State of California for preservation and protection. The bill was passed, and in the midst of the Civil War, President Abraham Lincoln signed the legislation on June 30, 1864.

It was a landmark event. Never before had a government set aside a piece of land for its inherent natural and scenic qualities to be preserved for public use, resort, and recreation "inalienable for all time." Yosemite became, in effect, the first state park in the world. It unquestionably served as a model for the development of other parks and led to the birth of the national park system as we know it in the US today.

Galen Clark in Yosemite

## Public Management

Responsibility for management of the Yosemite Grant (as it came to be called) fell to a board of commissioners appointed by California's governor and to the "guardian" that the board hired. Yosemite's first guardian was Galen Clark (see page 50).

The 1860s and 1870s saw improved access to the Valley thanks to the completion of several wagon roads, and the guardian had to contend with an astounding increase in the number of visitors.

Many new hostelries were built, including the extravagant Cosmopolitan Bathhouse and Saloon, Black's Hotel, Leidig's Hotel, La Casa Nevada Hotel, the Stoneman House, and others. Competition was fierce among the various operators, and unsuspecting visitors found themselves heavily lobbied by concessioners keep seeking their business.

Despite the much-publicized scenery, things in Yosemite were far from peaceful and quiet. Given the intense public interest in Yosemite as well as the disappointment of the original settlers, who saw their opportunities to make a killing disappear, Yosemite politics were never boring. Several lawsuits were brought by individuals who were dispossessed by the Yosemite Grant (Hutchings foremost among them), and criticism was regularly leveled at the board of commissioners.

## Greater Yosemite

While Yosemite Valley and the Mariposa Grove had been recognized and protected, the thousands of acres of wilderness surrounding these relatively small park strongholds had not. Led by John Muir (see page 51) and by easterner Robert Underwood Johnson (editor of the then-influential magazine *The Century*), a group of preservationists began to focus attention on the need to protect the greater Yosemite area, including the beautiful high-country regions, such as Tuolumne Meadows.

As resource degradation in the form of mining, logging, and stock grazing increased, so did the efforts of Yosemite champions. Muir and Johnson did their best to influence Congress and to inform the American people about the threats to Yosemite. They derived important support from the Southern Pacific Railroad and its president, Edward Harriman, who were strongly interested in boosting tourism in the Sierra Nevada.

On October 1, 1890, the US government acknowledged the preciousness of these wildlands by enacting the law that established Yosemite National Park as the nation's third national park. Interestingly, the new park did not include Yosemite Valley or the Mariposa Grove, but encompassed an enormous area around them. The park was actually 30 percent larger than it is today.

Early tourists, c. 1880

**The brand-new** national park needed management, and in 1890, the National Park Service had not yet been established. It was determined that the US Army would assume the administration of Yosemite, and members of the cavalry became a common sight in the park. Because a deep blanket of snow covered much of the area during the winter months, the army limited its occupation of Yosemite to summers only. Usually soldiers from the San Francisco Presidio would ride or march to and from their headquarters in Wawona each summer.

The duties of the cavalrymen were multiple and varied. They chased sheepherders from high-country meadows, explored previously uncharted regions of the park, blazed trails, surveyed boundaries, prepared maps, and prevented poachers from illegally taking park game. The work done by army personnel was prodigious, and their mark on Yosemite's history was a major one.

During the Spanish-American War, when many US troops were engaged, civilian rangers were hired by the army to assist at the park. They were the first of their kind.

The existence of two different administrations, one for Yosemite Valley and the Mariposa Grove of Big Trees, the other for the greater Yosemite National Park, inevitably led to duplication, overlap, and conflict. Many individuals and organizations (including John Muir and the Sierra Club) began to push for a unification of all of Yosemite under the management of one entity.

## A Single Yosemite

The mood of the public was apparently shared by lawmakers and government officials. In 1906 the federal government formally accepted the "recession" of Yosemite Valley and the Mariposa Grove from the State of California, an action that obviated the Yosemite Grant once and for all. The price of the agreement was the reduction in overall size of the park to conform it to natural boundaries and to exclude private mining and timber holdings. But at last there was one Yosemite National Park with a single administration.

The US Army continued its management of the park, moving its headquarters to Yosemite Valley (to a site near the present-day Yosemite Valley Lodge). In 1914 a civilian administration was established, with the Department of the Interior authorizing and employing park rangers.

Troop F, 6th US cavalry on the Fallen Monarch in the Mariposa Grove, 1899

Buffalo Soldiers, the 24th Mounted Infantry

**The years between** 1890 and 1914 were characterized by a transportation revolution. Regular stage lines began operation, and private wagons commonly made the trip to Yosemite. The remarkable increase in visitation continued, and then the completion of the Yosemite Valley Railroad from Merced to El Portal in 1907 effectively heralded the end of the stage era in Yosemite. But more earthshaking changes in transportation were still to come.

It was in 1900 that the automobile first entered Yosemite Valley. The Secretary of the Interior rescinded the ban on automobiles in the park in 1913, and when they came, they came with a vengeance. Two years later, all horse-drawn stages connecting train passengers to Yosemite Valley were replaced by motor stages. By 1920, two-thirds of all visitors were coming to Yosemite via private automobile.

The period also witnessed growth and proliferation of concessioner facilities. Camp Curry was established, Best's Studio was founded, and Camp Ahwahnee was built at the base of Sentinel Rock. Competition remained hot and heavy, and considerable conflict resulted between concessioners.

A regrettable chapter in Yosemite's history was written during the army years. The famous and bitter battle over the damming of the Hetch Hetchy Valley was settled in 1913 with the enactment of the Raker Act and the resulting inundation of the area. See page 129 for more about the Hetch Hetchy controversy.

## Buffalo Soldiers

When tourists arrived in Yosemite between 1891 and 1914, they would be greeted by soldiers wearing the blue uniforms and gold braid familiar to everyone who's seen a Western movie. A surprise to some of the tourists then and many researchers now is that several of the units that guarded Yosemite were made up of black men—the famous Buffalo Soldiers. During that era, black cavalry and infantry (under the command of white officers, as dictated by army policy) built roads, blazed trails, fought fires, and guarded mountains. Unfortunately, the stories of these men have been lost, overlooked even by Yosemite historians, who have focused on the stories of Galen Clark, John Muir, and the Firefall. But soldiers, black and white, played a pivotal role in the story of the national parks.

In an era when the dominant approach to land in America was to make as much money out of it as possible, the army kept out herders and poachers, enforcing the law and preserving the park (as the modern Park Service's mission statement has it) for the "enjoyment, education, and inspiration of this and future generations." The experience of patrolling Yosemite's meadows and canyons, and the authority that came with their positions, provided the Buffalo Soldiers with opportunities that were denied them in most of America. Like many people, these long-ago Americans came to Yosemite and found a freedom like none they'd ever known.

**1833**—Yosemite Valley was possibly first seen by Euro-Americans. Crossing the Sierra, the Joseph Walker party encountered a valley with "precipices more than a mile high" that were "impossible for a man to descend."

**1851**—The Mariposa Battalion, under the command of Major James Savage, became the first group of pioneers to enter Yosemite Valley. They were pursuing "intransigent" Indians.

**1852**—The Mariposa Grove of Big Trees was discovered by a party of prospectors.

**1855**—The first tourist party visited Yosemite Valley, with James Mason Hutchings as guide. Thomas Ayres, an artist with the group, made the first known sketches of Yosemite Valley.

**1856**—The first permanent structure, the Lower Hotel, was built in Yosemite Valley at the base of Sentinel Rock. The first trail into Yosemite Valley was completed by Milton and Houston Mann.

**1859**—The first photograph in Yosemite Valley was made by C. L. Weed. His subject was the Upper Hotel.

**1864**—Yosemite Valley and the Mariposa Grove of Big Trees were set aside by the federal government as the world's first state park. Florence Hutchings was the first white child to be born in Yosemite Valley.

**1866**—Galen Clark was named the first Yosemite guardian.

**1868**—John Muir made his first trip to Yosemite.

**1871**—The first ascent of Mount Lyell, Yosemite's highest peak, was accomplished by J. B. Tileston on August 29.

**1874**—The first road into Yosemite Valley, the Coulterville Road, was completed. The Big Oak Flat Road was finished a month later.

**1875**—George Anderson made the first ascent of Half Dome before the installation of ropes or cables. The first public school was opened in Yosemite Valley.

**1878**—The first public campgrounds in Yosemite Valley were opened by A. Harris near the site of the present-day Majestic Yosemite Hotel (formerly known as The Ahwahnee).

**1890**—Yosemite National Park was established. The park did not include Yosemite Valley or the Mariposa Grove of Big Trees, but it encompassed a large region around them.

**1891**—Telephones were installed in Yosemite Valley for the first time.

**1898**—The first civilian park ranger, Archie Leonard, was employed at Yosemite.

**1900**—Oliver Lippincott and Edward C. Russell drove the first automobile (a Locomobile) to enter Yosemite.

**1903**—President Theodore Roosevelt went camping with John Muir in Yosemite for 3 days.

**1907**—The first railway line to Yosemite, the Yosemite Valley Railroad, began operation.

**1913**—Automobiles were officially admitted to Yosemite.

**1916**—The National Park Service was established. Washington B. Lewis was named the first NPS superintendent at Yosemite.

**1917**—The first High Sierra Camp, Tuolumne Meadows Lodge, was installed.

**1919**—The first airplane in Yosemite Valley, piloted by Lt. J. S. Krull, landed on May 27.

**1926**—The Yosemite Museum opened to the public.

**1934**—Water from the Hetch Hetchy Reservoir first flowed into San Francisco.

**1935**—Badger Pass Ski Area was developed.

**1940**—Ostrander Ski Hut was opened for winter use.

**1946**—The first ascent of the Lost Arrow Spire was accomplished by 4 climbers on September 2.

**1949**—The first use of a helicopter for rescue purposes in Yosemite was made at Benson Lake to fly an injured boy to safety.

Theodore Roosevelt and John Muir at Glacier Point, 1903

**1954**—Annual park visitation exceeded 1 million for the first time: 1,008,031 visitors were recorded.

**1958**—The first climb up the face of El Capitan was completed.

**1961**—Pioneer Yosemite History Center opened to the public.

**1966**—The current Yosemite Valley Visitor Center was built.

**1967**—For the first time, over 2 million visitors to Yosemite were recorded.

**1969**—The Firefall from Glacier Point was discontinued. The famed Wawona Tunnel Tree toppled over from the weight of its winter snow load.

**1970**—The free shuttle bus system was initiated in Yosemite Valley.

**1974**—Hang gliding was officially allowed from Glacier Point, and 170 flights were made.

**1980**—The Yosemite General Management Plan, the park's first systematically developed, long-range planning document, was approved.

**1981**—Captive-born peregrine falcon chicks were successfully reared in a nest on El Capitan.

**1984**—Yosemite was added to the World Heritage List. The California Wilderness Bill designated 94 percent of the park as wilderness.

**1987**—Annual park visitation exceeded 3 million for the first time: 3,266,342 visitors were recorded.

**1990**—Yosemite celebrated its 100th birthday as a national park.

**1994**—Annual park visitation exceeded 4 million visitors for the first time.

**1995**—The Yosemite Wilderness Center opened its doors, and the wilderness permit reservation system was initiated.

**1996**—A massive rockfall in Yosemite Valley downed several hundred trees, damaged the Happy Isles Nature Center, and killed one visitor.

**1997**—Due to major flooding in the Valley, some 450 campsites, 350 motel and cabin units, and 200 concessioner housing units were lost. The Valley was closed to visitors for 3 months.

**1999**—Camp Curry celebrated its 100th anniversary.

**2006**—Yosemite became a sister park to two national parks in China: Huangshan and Jiuzhaigou.

**2007**—Yosemite became a sister park to Torres del Paine in Chile.

**2008**—A major rockfall hit several cabins in Half Dome Village (formerly Curry Village), prompting the closure and removal of over 70 structures.

**2010**—Yosemite National Park instituted a day-hiker permit system for Half Dome.

**2012**—Tioga Road closed on January 17, the latest closing on record.

**2013**—The Rim Fire, the third largest wildfire in California history, swept the western portion of Yosemite National Park. Of the more than 255,000 total acres (103,195 ha) burned, approximately 77,254 acres (31,264 ha) were in the park.

**2014**—Yosemite established a sister park relationship with Berchtesgaden National Park in Germany

**2015**—Yosemite signed sister park agreements with Mongolia's Lake Hovsgol and Tengis-Shishged National Parks, and Horidol-Saridag and Ulaan Taiga Strictly Protected Areas.

**2016**—The western boundary of Yosemite National Park expanded to include Ackerson Meadow, 400 acres of wetland and meadow habitat, the largest addition of land to the park since 1949.

**Ackerson Meadow**

**2016**—Yosemite achieved goal of having sister parks on all 6 continents, upon the signing of agreements with Chitwan, Langtang, and Sagarmartha National Parks in Nepal, Ngorongoro Conservation Area in Tanzania, Cumbres de Monterrey National Park in Mexico, Blue Mountains National Park in Australia, and Wadi Rum Protected Area in Jordan.

**2016**—Annual park visitation exceeded 5 million people for the first time: 5,028,868 visitors were recorded.

**2017**—Mariposa Grove of Giant Sequoias reopened after extensive restoration.

**A major change** came about in the national park system with the creation of the National Park Service in 1916. It had been recognized that administration of the parks required more than the part-time attention of the army and that there was a war to be fought in Europe. The NPS was the Interior Department's chosen alternative.

It was Frederick Law Olmsted Jr. (whose father had been influential in the establishment of the 1864 Yosemite Grant) who proposed that the new agency should "conserve the scenery and the natural and historic objects and the wildlife therein, and . . . provide for the enjoyment of the same in such manner and by such means as will leave them unimpaired for the enjoyment of future generations." This phrase became the cornerstone of the act that created the NPS and guides the agency still.

The years following 1916 were significant not only for Yosemite but also for all US national parks because the basic policies of the agency were being developed and implemented. The process of interpreting the NPS mandate to preserve the parks while allowing for their use was ongoing. Yosemite consistently was the park where new ideas were first tested and applied.

Yosemite's new National Park Service superintendent was Washington B. "Dusty" Lewis, who was responsible for many innovations and changes at the park. During his 12-year tenure the concessions were consolidated under one principal operating company (The Yosemite Park & Curry Company), roads including the Tioga Road were improved and tolls eliminated, new accommodations were built in Yosemite Valley (now the Yosemite Valley Lodge and The Majestic Yosemite Hotel) and at Glacier Point, a new administrative center

was built, and utilities, roads, and buildings were modernized.

## Interpretation

It was also shortly after the birth of the park service that Yosemite personnel inaugurated the educational program so familiar to park visitors today. The original program was the inspiration of Dr. C. M. Goethe, and Harold Bryant and Loye Miller were hired as Yosemite's first "nature guides" in 1920. At the outset the interpretive program was pretty much limited to nature walks, but it has evolved to include visitor center displays, campfire programs, informal talks, multimedia presentations, and informational literature.

A logical extension of the interpretive program was the Yosemite Museum, plans for which were hatched about 1921. Several years later a permanent museum was completed in the park, thanks to a gift from the Laura Spelman Rockefeller Memorial. At the same time a Field School of Natural History was established in Yosemite to provide for the training of future interpreters and nature guides.

These formative years of the NPS reflected the realization that protection of the parks depended on a strong program of education designed to increase public awareness of the special values embodied by Yosemite and other outstanding natural areas. The Yosemite model has been emulated throughout the world and is still as vital as it was at the start.

## The Modern Years

The past 100 years in Yosemite have seen consistent management and burgeoning visitation. With scientific research and experience, resource policies have changed. Fire is no longer viewed as evil, wild animals are managed to be wild, and artificial attractions like the Firefall from Glacier Point have been eliminated.

The greatest challenge facing Yosemite today is its popularity. With visitation regularly reaching between 4 and 5 million people each year, the park sometimes suffers from overcrowding, congestion, and air pollution. Resources are degraded and the visitors' experience is diminished. Hopefully, solutions to these issues will be found (see page 48) and Yosemite will endure as the preeminent national park in the world.

An interpreter makes time for music during a tour

**The following locations** have special historical significance or were the sites of early development in Yosemite Valley. They are listed in order of locale, beginning at the west end of the Valley, continuing to the east along Southside Drive, focusing on the east end of Yosemite Valley, and then heading back to the west along Northside Drive. In your explorations, remember that all cultural resources should be left unimpaired, and that digging and the use of metal detectors are not allowed.

## Bridalveil Meadow

### ABOUT .5 MILES (.8 KM) BEFORE THE WAWONA/HIGHWAY 41 TURNOFF

This spot is where the Mariposa Battalion camped in March 1851. The party was in search of American Indians and was the first group of whites ever to enter Yosemite Valley. Around a campfire here, the group proposed and applied the name "Yo-sem-ite" to this marvel of nature's handiwork. It was also here that President Theodore Roosevelt and John Muir camped in 1903 and discussed the need to preserve our nation's wilderness areas.

## Bridalveil Fall

### JUST PAST THE TURNOFF FOR WAWONA

This is roughly the place where the 1875 wagon road from Wawona entered Yosemite Valley. Toward the Merced River through the trees, a large sewer plant operated for many years. The sewer plant was removed in 1987, and more than 3 acres were freed of development. Yosemite Valley sewage is now carried by pipeline to a new processing facility in El Portal.

## El Capitan View

### LOOK FOR THE LONG STRAIGHTAWAY WITH EL CAPITAN TOWERING TO THE LEFT

Just upriver from here is the site of the bear-feeding platform used in the 1920s and 1930s. Garbage was dumped on the lighted platform, drawing bears and gawking tourists each night. Enlightened managers have long since dispensed with the spectacle.

## Sentinel Rock View

### IMMEDIATELY PAST THE SENTINEL BEACH PICNIC TURNOFF ON SOUTHSIDE DRIVE

Here was a portion of Lower Yosemite Village, which included the Yosemite Chapel (later moved to its present location east of here); Leidig's Hotel, which operated from 1869 to 1888; and Camp Ahwahnee (1908–1915). This is also the trailhead for James McCauley's Four-Mile Trail to Glacier Point, where for several years a tollhouse was maintained to collect fees from hikers and horseback riders. Some locust trees are the only visible remnants of this earlier occupation.

Swinging Bridge over the Merced River

## Swinging Bridge Turnout

### THE TURNOUT IS ABOUT .25 MILES (.4 KM) PAST THE SENTINEL ROCK VIEW ON THE LEFT

The remainder of Lower Yosemite Village was located here. Black's Hotel stood from 1869 through 1888. Photographer George Fiske's residence and studio were near the river to the west. Galen Clark had a residence here. The Coffman & Kenney Stables operated for several years. A boardwalk nearly .5 miles (.8 km) in length was constructed through the meadow to the east to connect the Upper and Lower Village areas.

## Chapel Parking Area

### ABOUT .5 MILES (.8 KM) BEYOND SWINGING BRIDGE ON THE RIGHT

This area was covered by extensive development from the 1860s until the 1950s. Here were the Upper Hotel (known at various times as Hutchings House, the Sentinel Hotel, and the Yosemite Falls Hotel); photographic studios (Boysen's, Foley's, and Pillsbury's); Best's Studio; Degnan's Store and Restaurant; the world-famous Cosmopolitan Bathhouse and Saloon; the Village Store; and many other structures. In 1925 the "new" Yosemite Village site (the present location) was selected, and an administration building, museum, post office, and several artist studios were built. Slowly the Upper (old) Village was dismantled and razed. The Village Store was the last major building to go, in 1959. The observant historian can still find plenty of evidence of Yosemite's yesteryears with a little exploring here.

Yosemite Chapel in Yosemite Valley

## Stoneman Meadow

### NEAR HALF DOME VILLAGE

This meadow has been the center of much activity over the years. Within it stood a large wooden hotel called the Stoneman House, built by the state of California in 1886, that burned in 1896. James Lamon, a settler in the park's earliest days, built a cabin near here and planted two apple orchards in 1859. One now serves as the Half Dome Village parking lot, and the other is behind the Valley Stable (shuttle bus stop 18). Stoneman Meadow will also be remembered as the site of a riot in 1970 which pitted young people against NPS personnel in a clash over curfews, noise levels, and lifestyles.

## The Majestic Yosemite Hotel

### SHUTTLE BUS STOP 3

Before the present hotel was built, an active stable business was operated at this spot. Known as Kenneyville, the stable was extensive and there were horses, shops, barns, and houses mingled here. When automobile travel became popular, the need for such a large stable was eliminated. In 1926, to make way for The Ahwahnee (now The Majestic), the stable was moved to its present location and the old buildings torn down. Many people are unaware that during World War II between 1943 and 1945 the hotel was closed to the public and converted to use as a Naval Convalescent Hospital. During that time almost 7,000 patients were rehabilitated.

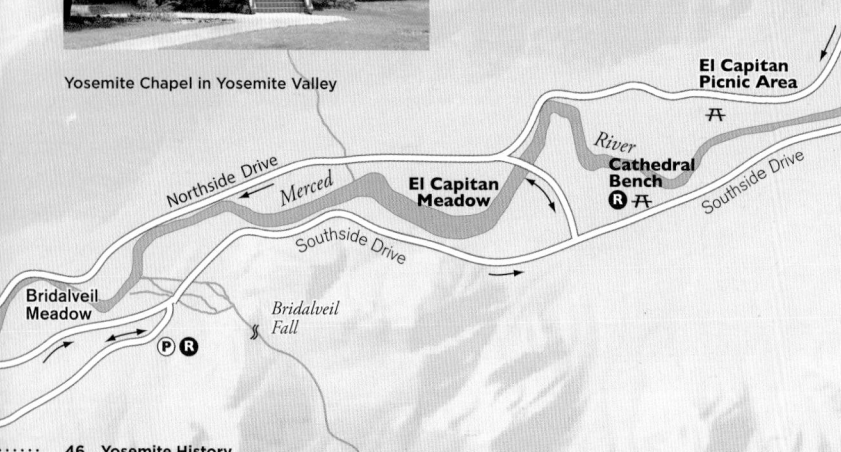

## Yosemite Cemetery

**JUST WEST OF AND ACROSS THE STREET FROM THE YOSEMITE MUSEUM, IN YOSEMITE VILLAGE**

This is the cemetery where local residents were buried between the 1870s and the 1950s. There's a wide variety of personalities interred here, from Indian Lucy, Sally Ann Castagnetto, and other American Indians to such pioneer settlers and innkeepers as Galen Clark and James Mason Hutchings. A guide to the cemetery is for sale in the Visitor Center.

## Yosemite Falls

**JUST WEST OF YOSEMITE VILLAGE, NEAR SHUTTLE BUS STOP 6**

In the forested area between the restrooms and Lower Yosemite Fall, James Mason Hutchings built a sawmill for preparation of lumber to upgrade his hotel. John Muir was employed to run the sawmill for a time and constructed a cabin for himself nearby. It featured running water: one strand of Yosemite Creek flowed right through it. Camp Yosemite, also known as Camp Lost Arrow, stood near the base of the fall and to its east from 1901 to 1915.

## Yosemite Valley Lodge

**SHUTTLE BUS STOPS 7 AND 8**

The lodge area was first developed as army headquarters for the park in 1906. The facility included 2 large barracks buildings, 2 bathhouses and lavatories, 156 tent frames, and a parade ground. When the army administration ended in 1914, so did the need for the headquarters, and they were converted to accommodate visitors in 1915.

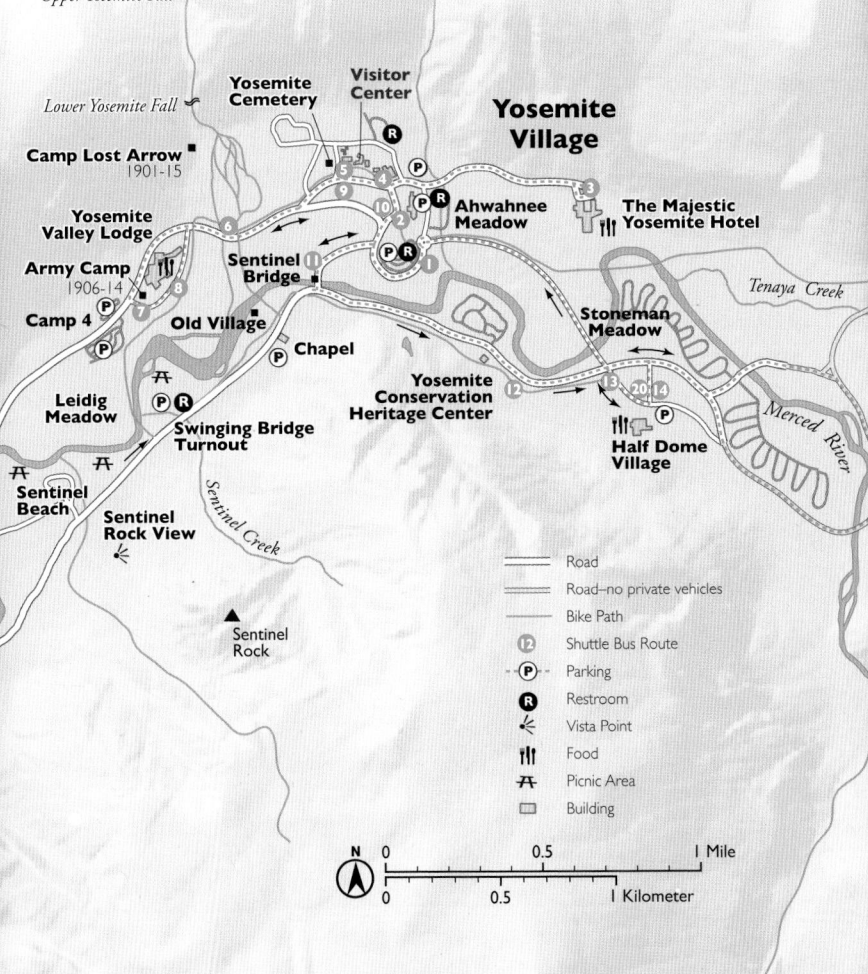

**The Yosemite 2020 Strategic Vision**, produced in 2012, was an effort to consolidate the many plans, aspirations, and needs of the park. The National Park Service has accomplished a goodly number of items on its long to-do list, such as:

## Supporting Youth in Yosemite

More than thirty youth programs operate in the park. Supported by park partners, these programs are increasingly diverse and are reaching more urban youth and youth with special needs each year.

## Stewarding of Natural Resources

When Yosemite Valley and the Mariposa Grove were set aside as a public reserve, noted landscape architect Frederick Law Olmstead was charged with preparing a report and setting out the policy that should guide the management of the grant. Olmsted's plan was a visionary document. Among his key points was that "The first requirement is to preserve the natural scenery and restrict within the narrowest limits the necessary accommodation of visitors." This is a challenge to be sure, and one that certainly has not always been respected. But there are recent signs that Olmsted's vision is being resurrected, such as the recently completed restoration of the Mariposa Grove of Giant Sequoias, widespread meadow and riverbank restoration, and successful restoration of threatened and endangered species including the Sierra Nevada bighorn sheep, the California red-legged frog, and the Sierra Nevada yellow-legged frog.

## Sustainability

Each year, the park ends up with 2,200 tons (2,000 metric tons) of garbage, enough to fill 3,919 dumpsters. In 2016, Yosemite joined in a pilot program with Subaru of America (a leader in zero waste) and the National Parks Conservation Association, and since then Yosemite's Zero Landfill Initiative has expanded these efforts. The ongoing goal is to increase diversion to 80 percent. What can you do during your visit do to help with Yosemite's trash problem? Follow the effort at #dontfeedthelandfills.

## Enhancing the Visitor Experience

Yosemite continues to work with public transportation agencies to address traffic congestion and wait times at entrance stations for more than 4 million annual visitors. See page 148 for some of those expanded opportunities and consider leaving your car at home.

## Reaching Past Borders

Yosemite's established Sister Park relationships on all six continents promote and enhance international conservation efforts.

Despite these achievements, Yosemite still faces ongoing challenges posed by a changing climate; increasing drought and wildfires; being part of an ever-changing federal department; the need to attract and retain staff; coordinating with more than 50 park partners; and an exponential increase in visitation in recent years. . . . You get the idea that Yosemite managers face daily decisions that impact the park and the region, and influence others 'round the world. Mull this over during your visit to the park, while sipping a cold beverage from a reusable container as you wait for a free shuttle ride.

An early example of resource protection: The Grizzly Giant

**Since people started** writing about it in the 1850s, Yosemite has figured as a grand locale for fiction. From mass-appeal romances to beatnik epics, the array is impressive. Following are some of the better or more unusual literary works set in Yosemite.

## The Forge of God

This science fiction novel by Greg Bear (New York: Tom Doherty Associates, 1987) is set in "futuristic" 1997, when profound changes to the solar system threaten Earth with destruction. People migrate to Yosemite to await their imminent demise. The book climaxes with a cataclysm that yields a great description of the collapse of the Royal Arches, the blockage of Yosemite Falls, and the destruction of Half Dome.

## Star Trek V: The Final Frontier

This book by J. M. Dillard (New York: Pocket Books, 1989) is a media spin-off in reverse. It grew out of the movie by the same title, part of which was filmed in the park. At one point, Captain Kirk attempts a free climb of El Capitan and falls to his apparent doom, only to have Spock (wearing levitation boots) catch him by the ankles in midair.

## The Dharma Bums

The beat generation goes hiking! Here is Jack Kerouac's classic account of a 1955 climb of Yosemite's Matterhorn Peak (New York: Viking Press, 1958) by Kerouac, Gary Snyder, and John Montgomery, written as fiction. The description of two crazed beatniks bounding down the side of the Matterhorn, yodeling and laughing, is particularly joyful.

## The Affair of the Jade Monkey

Detective Huntoon Rogers tracks a suspicious character to Yosemite in this mystery by Clifford Knight (1943; reprint 1993, Yosemite Association). A body is found, and then a hiker is murdered and a small jade monkey appears in another's pack. Can Huntoon solve the case and thwart an enemy plot against the nation?

## Angels of Light

Jeffrey B. Long's Yosemite climbing novel with a twist (New York: William Morrow, 1987) is based loosely on the true story of the drug plane that crashed at Lower Merced Pass Lake in the park's backcountry. Before the rangers caught on, hundreds of pounds of marijuana were packed out by Yosemite climbers. The author characterizes it as the end of innocence for the park's climbing subculture.

## Images on Silver

Believe it or not, a Harlequin Romance set in Yosemite. In this novel by Rayanne Moore (Toronto: Harlequin Books, 1984), highly acclaimed wildlife photographer Christy Reilly meets Ranger Travis Jeffords. Travis keeps asking Christy why she has worked alone for so long. Christy's secret is something no man can understand.

## Fires of Innocence

A steamy novel by Jane Bonander (New York: St. Martin's, 1994) set in the 1860s. In a snowbound cabin, Alex Golovin, a government attorney bent on buying up land for the national park, and Scotty MacDowell, daughter of a Valley homesteader, come to know each other. Thrilling her with "searing kisses and teasing caresses," he will not let the "sensuous spitfire" stand in the way of his work.

## Gloryland

As told from the perspective of a Buffalo Soldier, this historical novel (Berkeley, CA: Counterpoint, 2010) features troubled Elijah Yancy who finds solace in Yosemite. Written by Shelton Johnson, a Yosemite ranger, this lyrical book is based on a character he created and portrays in the Yosemite Theater.

## A Body to Dye For

This one's about a hairdresser/detective who finds the dead body of a Yosemite park ranger in the bed of one of his regular customers. With a colorful cast of characters, author Grant Michaels (New York: St. Martin's Press, 1990) details the detective's efforts to solve the case by following leads back to Yosemite.

## High Country

Famed national park mystery writer Nevada Barr finally inserts her protagonist Anna Pigeon into Yosemite (New York: Putnam & Sons, 2004). She's working undercover as a waitress at The Ahwahnee, where her coworkers' odd behavior leads her into a backcountry showdown with some evil druggies: Yosemite as the dark side.

## Chief Tenaya

Chief Tenaya, leader of the native people in Yosemite when Euro-Americans first arrived in the Valley in 1851, has been called not only a brave warrior but an unusual personality who commanded the respect of his people.

Accounts have it that a tribal shaman warned Tenaya that "horsemen of the lowlands" (probably a reference to the Spaniards) represented the gravest threat to his people and should be guarded against. When in 1849 gold miners began entering the foothills and interacting with the native residents, Tenaya apparently felt threatened. He reportedly informed the invading whites that his people would be peaceable, but only if they could continue to occupy Yosemite Valley and not be disturbed.

This arrangement was unacceptable to the new foothill residents. The Mariposa Battalion was dispatched to subdue Yosemite's native people and in May 1851 the greatest portion of the band was rounded up and marched to a reservation in the Central Valley. Problems arose, the federal government never ratified a treaty, and by the end of the year, Tenaya and his people had either escaped or been permitted to return to Yosemite Valley.

The following year, American Indians in the Valley allegedly attacked a party of miners, and further efforts to remove them resulted. Tenaya's group fled to the high country of Yosemite and to the east side again. In 1853 they returned once more to Yosemite Valley, but their fate was practically sealed.

Despite his best efforts, Tenaya was unable to protect his people and their homeland from the incursions of the whites. He was killed by stoning late in 1853. There are two versions of his death; the more commonly accepted one is that the Ahwahneechees stole horses from their eastern Sierran neighbors, who attacked in retribution.

Tenaya's name is common in the park today, having been attached to a canyon, a lake, and other features.

## Galen Clark

Known as the "Guardian of Yosemite," Galen Clark was as intimately involved in Yosemite's early history as any other person. He moved to the park in 1856 at the age of 42, suffering from a debilitating lung disease that doctors had said would quickly end his life. The Yosemite fresh air and inspiring scenery must have been therapeutic; Clark lived to be 95.

He first settled in Wawona, developing his place as a stopping point on the stage route to Yosemite (Clark's Station). He visited the Mariposa Grove of Big Trees in 1857 with Milton Mann, then explored the trees and publicized them. He recognized the value and uniqueness of the sequoias and Yosemite Valley, and he worked to bring about the enactment of the 1864 law that set aside the Yosemite Valley and Mariposa Grove of Big Trees as the world's first state park.

In 1866 Clark became the first "Yosemite Guardian," employed by the State of California to oversee the grant. He continued in this job until the political winds changed in 1880 and a new guardian was employed. He worked odd jobs for 9 years and then was hired once again to be the guardian. His second term lasted 7 years, and he closed out his life by guiding, writing books about the park, and helping wherever he could.

As guardian, Clark made many needed improvements, worked to relocate homesteaders, and persevered in his efforts to protect Yosemite. John Muir called him "the best mountaineer I ever met . . . one of the most sincere tree-lovers I ever knew." Following his death, Clark was buried in the Yosemite Cemetery in a grave shaded by sequoias he had planted and headed by a granite marker upon which he had chiseled his name.

## James Mason Hutchings

James Hutchings will be remembered most for being Yosemite's first and best publicist. A native of England, in 1855 he organized and led the first "tourist" party to visit the Valley, bringing with him the artist Thomas Ayres, who sketched Yosemite's wonders. Hutchings published the sketches and paired them with his descriptions of the place, drawing national attention to a previously unknown scenic treasure.

Like Galen Clark, when his health failed Hutchings chose to come to Yosemite, and in 1862 he purchased a hotel that became known as Hutchings House. The hotel was

very primitive; only sheets of muslin hung to separate the rooms. Hutchings built a sawmill along Yosemite Creek to prepare the lumber for more effective partitions and for a time employed John Muir to run the mill.

When the Yosemite Grant was set aside in 1864, Hutchings became embroiled in lengthy and bitter litigation with the government as a property owner dispossessed. His political fortunes changed, however, in 1880, when he was named to succeed Galen Clark as Yosemite guardian. He worked in that capacity for 4 years.

Hutchings' many writings outlived him. His *Hutchings' Illustrated California Magazine* is full of historical gems, and he published a series of guidebooks to the Yosemite Valley and the Big Trees. His most famous work is *In the Heart of the Sierras*, which is representative of the best travel writing of that era.

Killed in a wagon accident on the Old Big Oak Flat Road in Yosemite Valley in 1902, Hutchings is buried in the Yosemite Cemetery.

## John Muir

For his efforts on behalf of the park, John Muir has come to be recognized as the most significant individual in the history of Yosemite. This reputation is certainly deserved; Muir's contributions to the place through the years were considerable, particularly his efforts to create Yosemite National Park in 1890. He will also long be associated with the park thanks to his eloquent, loving writings.

John Muir first visited Yosemite in 1868 and returned the following summer to work as a shepherd in the high country. Late in 1869, he could no longer resist the lure of Yosemite Valley and found work doing odd jobs there for James Mason Hutchings. He built a small cabin on Yosemite Creek and began a long-term residence in his beloved Yosemite.

Muir roamed and studied the park, learning its aspects as intimately as he could. He became renowned as a guide and entertained Asa Gray, William Keith, Ralph Waldo Emerson, and other luminaries of the day. His marathon hikes with few or no provisions have become legendary. He recorded his experiences and documented the natural world around him in a series of journals.

In 1871 Muir published a newspaper article about Yosemite; it was the first of a series of articles and books he would write during his life. Topics of his writing included the glaciers, the forests, winter storms, and everything else about Yosemite that came to fascinate him.

In the 1880, Muir married and left Yosemite, beginning a new life in Martinez, California. In 1889 he returned to the park with Robert Underwood Johnson. It was during this visit that the two hatched a campaign to establish Yosemite National Park. Using articles, personal visits, and other lobbying efforts, the two saw the 1890 act to create the national park through to its successful passage.

Muir was later to write *My First Summer in the Sierra* and *The Yosemite*, both of which—among many others—would become Yosemite classics. His tireless work in opposition to the damming of the park's Hetch Hetchy Valley (a fight that he lost) drained him physically and contributed to his death in 1914.

## David and Jennie Curry

The Currys were pioneer innkeepers in the park. In 1899 they moved to California from Indiana and established a small camp in the eastern end of Yosemite Valley. Starting with 7 tents for guests and a dining tent that seated 20, the Currys initiated an enterprise that experienced immediate growth.

By the end of their first season, the camp had increased to 25 tents, and almost 300 guests had been accommodated. The operation soon became known as Camp Curry, and thanks to their warm hospitality and outgoing personalities the Currys prospered.

David Curry specialized in entertaining his guests with both disarming informality and brash showmanship. Every night at the campfire, people were encouraged to add wood to the fire and, while it burned, to tell stories or lead the group in songs. Curry also revitalized the Firefall, the spectacle that involved pushing burning embers from the brink of Glacier Point to create a stream of fire down the cliff face.

"Mother" Curry, as she was affectionately called, was considerably less flamboyant, but she continued the Camp Curry tradition when David died in 1917. She was assisted by family members and saw her camp grow to include lodging for 1,300 guests.

In 1925 the Curry Camping Company and the Yosemite National Park Company merged to form the Yosemite Park & Curry Company, which operated until 1993.

## Ansel Adams

The man who best communicated the beauty of Yosemite through photography during the twentieth century was Ansel Adams, and his influence continues to be felt. His images have been a source of inspiration, delight, and enjoyment to millions of people, and they have defined the Yosemite landscape for many. Further, he was a dogged conservationist who worked hard to protect the environment he photographed with such skill.

Interestingly, Ansel Adams was a gifted artist in two fields. He almost became a professional pianist, but the camera won out, particularly as Adams became more and more attached to Yosemite. After moving to the Valley in 1920 to run the Sierra Club Lodge, he made the acquaintance of the proprietor of Best's Studio, painter Harry Best, who allowed Ansel the use of a piano. It brought Adams in contact with Best's daughter Virginia, whom he later married.

For several years Adams worked as a commercial photographer doing publicity pictures for the Curry Company and other such jobs. As the years passed, his promotional work gave way increasingly to his more artistic expression. His prints were offered for sale in gift shops and at Best's Studio, and before long he was gaining national recognition for his fine landscape work.

Many of his photographs were used to illustrate the beauty of natural areas that environmental groups hoped to have protected by Congress, and he undertook special assignments from the National Park Service to photograph the national parks. His landscapes became well known for their detail, tonal ranges, unique composition, and fine printing. A multitude of awards were bestowed upon Adams for his photographic excellence.

He remained active as a photographer and conservationist until his death in 1984, teaching, lecturing, lobbying, and making new images all the while. Best's Studio is now operated as the Ansel Adams Gallery, and a peak on Yosemite's eastern boundary was named for him in 1985.

## Ahwahnee

The local American Indian name for both a large village near Yosemite Falls and for the greater Yosemite Valley. The people were known as the Ahwahneechees. Lafayette Bunnell reported that the name meant "deep, grassy valley," although this is unsubstantiated. Linguists believe that "place of a gaping mouth" is the correct translation.

## Big Oak Flat

A small town near Yosemite's northwestern boundary from which the Highway 120 route took its original name. The massive oak (reportedly 10 feet in diameter) that inspired the name is long since dead, the victim of miners' axes in the 1860s.

## Chilnualna

This name, common in the Wawona area, is of unknown origin and meaning. An unsupported theory suggests its meaning is "leaping water."

## Clark

Yosemite Valley's first guardian, appointed in 1864, and one of the first nonnatives to find the Mariposa Grove of Big Trees was Galen Clark. His name now graces a mountain, a mountain range, and a viewpoint on the way to Nevada Fall.

## Conness

A senator from California in the 1860s, John Conness introduced the bill in Congress that set aside Yosemite Valley and the Mariposa Grove of Big Trees as a state preserve. Mount Conness is an imposing peak on the park boundary north of Tioga Pass.

## Crane Flat

Most probably named for a group of sandhill cranes encountered there by Lafayette Bunnell (John Muir also noted cranes at the location), although some assert the origin was a man named Crean who at one time resided at the spot.

## Curry

David and Jennie "Mother" Curry established a small tent camp for the public in Yosemite Valley in 1899. It grew to become Camp Curry and later Curry Village and now Half Dome Village. The merger of their operation with the Yosemite National Park Company resulted in the Yosemite Park & Curry Company, a longtime concessioner.

## Dana

Josiah Whitney's California Geological Survey named a prominent peak east of Tuolumne Meadows for James Dwight Dana in 1863. Dana was a Yale professor and considered the foremost American geologist of his time.

## El Capitan

This massive granite cliff was named by the Mariposa Battalion in 1851. "El Capitan" is the Spanish replacement of the local American Indian name, "Too-tok-ah-noo-lah." Other names assigned the rock at one time or another were Crane Mountain and Giant's Tower (go Giants!).

## El Portal

This is Spanish for "gateway" or "entrance" and was used to name the terminus of the Yosemite Valley Railroad on the park's western doorstep. Now a small town on Highway 140, the site houses some of the park's administration offices. Because of its searing summer heat, some have dubbed the place "Hell Portal."

## Glen Aulin

James McCormick, at the behest of R. B. Marshall of the USGS, named this idyllic spot on the Tuolumne River with the Gaelic phrase for "beautiful valley" or glen in the early 1900s. A High Sierra camp was built there in 1927.

## Half Dome

Credit the Mariposa Battalion with describing this split mountain as a half-dome. American Indian legend has it named "Tissiack," for a woman who some say can be seen in the rock face. Of all the landmarks in Yosemite, Half Dome has worn the most names over the years, among them Rock of Ages, North Dome, South Dome, Sentinel Dome, Cleft Rock, Goddess of Liberty, Mount Abraham Lincoln, and Spirit of the Valley. Somehow a T-shirt imprinted with the phrase "I climbed the Goddess of Liberty" wouldn't quite work.

## Happy Isles

One of Yosemite Valley's early guardians named the 3 small islets on the Merced River for the emotion he enjoyed while exploring them ("no one can visit them without for the while forgetting the grinding strife of his world and being happy").

### Hetch Hetchy

Hetch Hetchy bears an American Indian name that has been interpreted in several ways. The most popular is that it means a kind of grass or plant with edible seeds that abounded in the Valley. Some believe Hetchy means "tree" and Hetch Hetchy refers to two yellow pine trees that grew at the entrance to the place. At one time a remarkably beautiful companion valley to Yosemite Valley, the Hetch Hetchy Valley was dammed by the city of San Francisco in the 1920s.

### Illilouette

This French-sounding name is actually an English transliteration (poor indeed!) of the American Indian word "Too-lool-a-we-ack." James Mason Hutchings opined that it means "the place beyond which was the great rendezvous of the Yosemite Indians for hunting deer."

### Lembert

John Baptiste Lembert was an early settler in the Tuolumne Meadows region. He built a cabin at Soda Springs in Tuolumne, and his name is attached to the granite dome nearby.

### Lyell

Yosemite's highest peak (13,114 feet) was named for Sir Charles Lyell, an eminent English geologist, by the California Geological Survey in 1863.

### Mariposa

The Spanish word for "butterfly" was first applied to a land grant, later to the community, and then to the county. Because Mariposa County encompassed the south end of Yosemite when Galen Clark discovered them in 1857, the sequoias there were named the Mariposa Grove of Big Trees.

### Merced

The Moraga party named this river, which originates in Yosemite's high country, when they crossed it in the San Joaquin Valley. This was in 1806, 5 days after the feast day of Our Lady of Mercy, which is why the river was formally known as El Rio de Nuestra Señora de la Merced (River of Our Lady of Mercy). All other names utilizing "Merced" in Yosemite are derived from the river's name.

### Mono

At what is now known as Mono Lake, the resident American Indians harvested, ate, and traded millions of alkali fly pupae—a favorite foodstuff of the native people of the region. The Shoshonean tribe grew to be known as the Mona or Mono, a name derived from the Yokuts word "monoi" or "monai," meaning "flies." Many landmarks east of Yosemite bear this name.

### Nevada

The Mariposa Battalion assigned this name to the waterfall on the Merced River in 1851. The word signifies "snow" in Spanish, and members of the battalion felt this was appropriate because the fall was in the Sierra Nevada and because the white, foaming water was reminiscent of a vast avalanche.

### Olmsted

A turnout from Tioga Road near Tenaya Lake with a remarkable view was named for Frederick Law Olmsted Sr. and Jr. The senior Olmsted was involved in the creation of the 1864 Yosemite Grant and served as chairman of the first board of Yosemite Valley commissioners. His son worked as an NPS planner in Yosemite and had a position on the Yosemite Advisory Board.

Half Dome as seen from Olmsted Point

### Sierra Nevada

This is the Spanish phrase for "snowy mountain range." Father Pedro Font applied it to California's greatest range of mountains when he glimpsed it from near Antioch in 1776. Because "sierra" implies plural mountains, it is both grammatically and politically incorrect to use the term "Sierras." If you do you will be castigated by self-righteous Yosemite word snobs.

Tenaya Lake

## Stoneman

A large hotel built by the State of California in 1885 once stood in the meadow just north of Half Dome Village. Known as the Stoneman House for then-Governor George Stoneman, it burned in 1896. The meadow and nearby bridge still bear the name.

## Tenaya

The chief of the resident tribe when the Mariposa Battalion entered Yosemite Valley in 1851 was named Tenaya. A later military incursion captured some American Indians living near the banks of a lake not far from Tuolumne Meadows. They named the lake after the chief.

## Tioga

This in an Iroquois word meaning "where it forks," "swift current," or "gate." Miners at work on the Sierra crest near Yosemite established the Tioga Mining District in 1878, apparently importing the name from Pennsylvania or New York.

## Tuolumne

A tribe residing in the Sierra foothills near Knights Ferry was known as "Taulamne," reportedly pronounced Tu-ah-lum'-ne. This name was applied to the river originating in Yosemite that flowed through their territory.

## Vogelsang

Colonel Benson, an army officer and acting superintendent of Yosemite National Park from 1905 to 1908, named a peak south of Tuolumne Meadows for either Alexander Vogelsang or his brother Charles, both of whom were affiliated with California Fish and Game. The German word "vogelsang" refers to birdsong, which is apt for the site of the Vogelsang High Sierra Camp.

## Wawona

Popular opinion has it that "wawona" is an American Indian word for "big tree": the sequoias were considered sacred and called "woh-woh'-nah." The word is formed in imitation of the hooting of an owl, which bird is said to have been sacred to the native people, the guardian spirit and deity of the sequoias.

## White Wolf

A meadow on the old route of the Tioga Road was named by John Meyer, who, while pursuing American Indians, came to a temporary camp of the band's chief. His name was White Wolf.

## Yosemite

This name was assigned to the world's most beautiful valley by the Mariposa Battalion in 1851. The exact meaning of the name is disputed. Lafayette Bunnell, a member of the battalion, later wrote that it signified "grizzly bear" (derived from the Miwok word for the bears, "uzumati"). Others consider it a corruption of the Miwok word "Yo-che-ma-te," which means "some among them are killers" and is said to have referred to the Ahwahneechee people of Yosemite.

Coyote

# 3 | YOSEMITE'S NATURAL WORLD

**Yosemite is filled with** living things of every description existing in a remarkable setting created by the various forces of nature. From its famous black bears and big trees to nocturnal owls, seldom-seen reptiles, pesky mosquitoes, and mysterious fungi, the park is abundant with flora and fauna that are rich and varied. Because wildlife is protected in Yosemite, the park has served as an "island" sanctuary of sorts, where natural processes have continued and biological diversity is still great. Other factors contributing to this favorable situation for animals and plants are the great range of elevations within the park (from 2,000 to 13,000 feet) and the corresponding variety of living conditions that change with the elevation. Though inanimate, other natural objects and processes contribute to the ever-evolving Yosemite scene. Geological workings are constant, waterfalls ebb and flow, and meteorological forces add variety and life to the landscape. And because the setting has been so unchanged and undeveloped, Yosemite National Park is even more significant as a mountain laboratory of the natural world.

An erratic boulder transported to Olmsted Point by glacial ice

**There are differing views** as to the processes that shaped Yosemite, and most descriptions of Yosemite geology are rife with technical jargon, geological gobble-dygook, and scientific names. This is an attempt to make the processes that created Yosemite's landscape of granite and water more understandable for the layperson. And with it comes the promise that words like batholith, pyroclastic, and subduction will not be used.

Once upon a time, about 500 million years ago, sediment was deposited in layers on the ocean floor at the west edge of what would later become the continent of North America. This sediment was consolidated into rocks such as sandstone, chert, shale, and limestone. Neither the landmass of the developing continent nor the landmass covered by sedimentary rock under the ocean was stationary, however.

Time passed (about 300 million years or so) and the two landmasses moved toward each other and met, and then some exciting geology took place. The rock beneath the ocean was forced under the continental landmass with interesting results. The process caused the rock of the ocean plate to become very hot and liquefy into magma (which is the molten rock that shoots out of volcanoes). This hot liquid rose up under the edge of the continent to form volcanoes and, where it cooled and hardened before making it to the surface, great areas of granite rock.

This process occurred in a series of pulses over a period of some 150 million years. When it was complete, a mountain range had been formed that ran in a rough line parallel to the West Coast. Although it was largely covered by the continental crust (primarily sedimentary rock), this ancestral Sierra Nevada range was probably similar to the present Cascade Range of volcanoes. In some places the mountains may have been as high as 13,000 feet.

For approximately the next 55 million years, the main force at work in the ancestral Sierra was erosion (we all know what that is, right?). The volcanoes were worn away by wind and water, as was the continental crust that sat on top of the great granite mass created by the molten rock described above. The rock that eroded away was carried by rivers and streams into California's Central Valley. When this period of erosion was complete, what was to become the Sierra Nevada—now primarily exposed granite—stood only a few thousand feet high.

Everything was going along fine with the developing Sierra until, one day about 25 million years ago, the landmasses meeting along the present-day San Andreas Fault began to move again. The result was that the block upon which the Sierra sat was uplifted at its eastern edge and tilted toward the west. It is estimated that the tilt raised peaks on Yosemite's eastern edge as much as 11,000 feet.

Following uplift and tilt, river courses in the Yosemite region became steeper, and the erosive effect of their waters increased. The Merced River, for example, began to carve the granite much more sharply, and Yosemite Valley was deepened as a canyon. The Sierra Nevada began to show much greater surface relief and started to take on the form we know today.

About 2 or 3 million years ago, the earth's climate began to cool. Because of its extreme height, glaciers and ice fields covered the crest of the Sierra Nevada. At its most extensive, the ice covered more than half of Yosemite and sent glaciers down many of the valleys that had been created by erosion.

Glaciers tore loose large quantities of rock as they moved, carving U-shaped canyons and valleys, polishing rock faces, and breaking spires, domes, and various other rock formations along fractures, or joints. The glaciers carried the broken rock as rubble and deposited it along the edges of their paths.

This glacial period consisted of an unknown number of glaciations—perhaps as many as 10. The last glaciation reached its maximum between 20,000 and 15,000 years ago. At that point, the earth's climate began to warm again, glaciers receded, and nonglacial erosion became the main geological force working in Yosemite once more.

Yosemite Valley is one location in the park whose appearance has changed considerably since glacial times. Because glaciers dumped enormous quantities of rock and rubble at its western end, the Valley's outflow was stopped and water covered its floor. Geologists call this ancient body of water Lake Yosemite. Over a period of 10,000 years, sediment and silt washed down from the park's higher regions and filled the lake, creating the flat, dry valley floor we know today.

Yosemite's landscape continues to change even now. While the geological processes are not dramatic (some changes take millions of years), erosion continues, avalanches occur, and rockslides are common. The geologic story goes on in Yosemite and provides us with a better understanding of the extraordinary scenery that has made the park famous.

Glaciers carved the U-shaped Yosemite Valley

**Nineteenth-century** scientists were as puzzled by Yosemite Valley's origin as many first-time visitors are today. Their efforts to explain what they saw resulted in a variety of theories about the creation of the Valley's sheer walls and spectacular waterfalls.

Josiah D. Whitney, California's state geologist and director of the California Geological Survey, made many of the first studies of Yosemite during the 1860s. In his view, Yosemite Valley had not been formed by erosion or glaciation or any other traditional geologic force. He believed that a valley so deep could only have been created by a collapse of the section of the earth below it. Because Whitney was an accomplished Harvard professor with quite a reputation as a scholar and scientist, his theory gained some acceptance.

At about the same time, mountain wanderer John Muir (see page 51) was making observations of his own. He, too, was fascinated with the geologic history of Yosemite Valley. Muir advanced the hypothesis that it was the action of glaciers, an "over-sweeping ice current," that had carved the Yosemite landscape. He worked to popularize the theory and it came to be known as "Muir's discovery."

Whitney was not impressed nor convinced. He characterized Muir's ideas as absurd and passed them off as the ravings of a "mere shepherd." Doggedly, Whitney defended his "cataclysm" theory for some 20 years, until his death.

While Muir was not correct in all the details of the work of the glaciers, he was remarkably close. Later studies proved the basic soundness of his theory and helped establish John Muir's reputation as a thoughtful and insightful student of the Sierra.

## Joints Shaped the Rocks

The variety of rock shapes and formations that occur in Yosemite is impressive. From blocks to domes to spires to arches to sheets, there is tremendous diversity in the granitic terrain. How did these structures come to be?

All of Yosemite's unusual landmarks (with but a few exceptions) resulted from the existence of fractures within their original rock structures. These fractures, called joints, are the lines upon which the rock has been broken. They create zones of weakness within the granite that yield to the action of glaciers and to the intrusion of water.

Joints occur both vertically and horizontally, and some are inclined (for example, the Three Brothers formation was created along inclined joints). Vertical jointing is most prevalent and produced features like the face of Half Dome and the Cathedral Spires. Where vertical and horizontal joints intersect, the result is rectangular blocks.

Half Dome and El Capitan are representative of very sparse jointing. Their resistance to erosion and glaciation has kept them practically unchanged for thousands of years. Incidentally, there probably was no other half of Half Dome. Geologists believe that only 20 percent of the dome's original size has been lost.

The type of jointing most dramatic in the evolution of Yosemite landforms is sheeting, which results in the concentric joints that lead to the creation of domes. As overlying rock falls away, pressure is relieved on the granite. It expands upward and fractures result. The concentric fractures break off like the different layers of an onion in a process called exfoliation.

Vertical jointing shaped Half Dome

**The collection of** waterfalls in Yosemite National Park is unequaled anywhere in the world. And nowhere else have so many spectacular waterfalls been concentrated in so small an area as Yosemite Valley. What's most remarkable is the number of park waterfalls that are free-leaping; they make their descent without being broken on intervening ledges or outcroppings. The park's glacial geology is responsible for this unique situation.

While the glaciers carved major water-courses like Yosemite Valley very deeply, lateral tributary ice streams cut much more slowly and less effectively. The result was "hanging valleys," and streams and creeks that previously had fed directly into primary rivers became routed over the brinks of lofty precipices into the more deeply carved canyons below them. Today these waters still leap into space over sheer walls as Yosemite's waterfalls. Bridalveil Fall is a great example of a waterfall originating from a hanging valley.

Other waterfalls were created as the glaciers moved along and dislocated large blocks of granite from streambeds. The rock gave way along joints and took on shapes like steps in a staircase. This was the process responsible for Vernal and Nevada Falls, which drop in two major steps from Little Yosemite Valley. Known as the "Giant Staircase," this landform is well viewed from Glacier Point.

Yosemite's waterfalls are at peak flow during the months of April, May, and June, when 75 percent of the annual snowmelt occurs. May is usually the best single

Upper Yosemite Fall leaps from a hanging valley

month for waterfall watching. By July most of the surface runoff is gone, and many falls either dry up or are reduced to a trickle. Some falls (Bridalveil, for example) rarely dry up because the soil of their watersheds holds more water longer.

Not all the waterfalls in the park are large, spectacular, or permanent. Many cascades exist where streambeds were resistant to the glaciers but some gouging and polishing did occur. In those cases

## The Spirits of Yosemite Falls—An American Indian Legend

In the waters just below Cho'lok (Yosemite Falls) live the Po'loti, a group of dangerous spirit women. In the old days there was a village a short distance from the falls. A maiden from this village went to the stream for a basket of water. She dipped the basket into the stream as usual but brought it up full of snakes. She went farther upstream and tried again, but with the same result. She tried repeatedly, each time a little farther upstream, but always drew a basketful of snakes. Finally, she reached the pool at the foot of Cho'lok, and a sudden, violent wind blew her into it. During the night she gave birth to a child that she wrapped in a blanket and took home the next morning. The girl's mother was very curious and soon took the blanket off the baby in order to see it. Immediately a violent gale arose and blew the entire village and its inhabitants into the same pool. Nothing has ever been seen or heard of them since.

—from *Legends of the Yosemite Miwok*, compiled by Frank LaPena, Craig D. Bates, and Steven P. Medley (El Portal: Yosemite Association, 1993).

channels steepened, and now water spills over irregularly fractured granite or down gradual cliff faces. Other falls are ephemeral: they appear only during heavy thunderstorms or at the peak of the spring runoff. As abruptly as the rain ends, so do these fleeting displays.

In winter, park waterfalls have a different beauty. Because the snowpack prevents soil moisture from freezing, water continues to flow in the falls. But they become edged with ice, and droplets of water actually freeze as they descend through space. When this freezing occurs in a large volume, "frazil ice" is the result. Streams at the base of the waterfalls become filled with ice crystals that create ice slush. As it moves, the frazil ice adheres to any object below freezing and can clog streambeds.

The most famous winter waterfall phenomenon is the ice cone that builds up at the base of Upper Yosemite Fall. Ice slabs that have frozen at the fall's edges fall, freezing spray collects, and the ice cone grows, sometimes to a height of 300 feet, covering some 4 acres. The cone usually melts away by April.

## Waterfalls of Yosemite Valley

| | | |
|---|---|---|
| Yosemite Falls | 2,425 feet / 739 m | North wall, eastern end |
| Sentinel Falls | 2,000 feet / 610 m | South wall, west of Sentinel Rock |
| Ribbon Fall | 1,612 feet / 491 m | North wall, west of El Capitan |
| Staircase Falls | 1,300 feet / 396 m | South wall, behind Half Dome Village |
| Royal Arch Cascade | 1,250 feet / 381 m | North wall, west of Washington Column |
| Silver Strand Falls | 1,170 feet / 357 m | South wall, far west end |
| Horsetail Fall | 1,000 feet / 305 m | North wall, east side of El Capitan |
| Bridalveil Fall | 620 feet / 189 m | South wall, west end |
| The Cascades | uncertain | North wall, 2 miles west of Yosemite Valley |
| Nevada Fall | 594 feet/ 181 m | Eastern end of Merced River Canyon |
| Illilouette Fall | 370 feet / 113 m | Panorama Cliffs southeast of Glacier Point |
| Vernal Fall | 317 feet / 97 m | Eastern end of Merced River Canyon |

## The Twelve Highest Waterfalls in the World

| | | |
|---|---|---|
| Angel Falls | 3,212 feet / 979 m | Venezuela |
| Tugela Falls | 3,110 feet / 948 m | South Africa |
| Utigordsfossen | 2,625 feet / 800 m | Norway |
| Mongefossen | 2,540 feet / 774 m | Norway |
| Gocta Cataracts | 2,532 feet / 772 m | Peru |
| Mutarazi | 2,499 feet / 762 m | Zimbabwe |
| Yosemite Falls | 2,425 feet / 739 m | Yosemite |
| Espelandsfoss | 2,307 feet / 703 m | Norway |
| Ostre Mardalsfoss | 2,151 feet / 656 m | Norway |
| Tyssestrengene | 2,123 feet / 647 m | Norway |
| Sentinel Falls | 2,000 feet / 610 m | Yosemite |
| Cuquenan Falls | 2,000 feet / 610 m | Venezuela |

Source: infoplease.com/world/world-geography/highest-waterfalls-world

## Fires

Fire has long played a role in Yosemite's natural world. It is a major ecological force, with impacts similar to those of other natural phenomena such as floods, earthquakes, and hurricanes. Wildland fires, defined as all fires that burn in natural environments, greatly influence park ecosystems. Prior to the appearance of humans here, the ingredients for fire were largely controlled by climate. With the arrival of human beings, sources of fire and fuels were modified as people changed their environment.

Natural fire fosters new plant growth, expands wildlife populations, and removes dead trees and litter from the forest floor. Also, fires kill shrubs and trees that are invading grasslands. Following fire, healthy regrowth occurs. Accordingly, fire is recognized as an instrument of change and a catalyst for biological diversity and healthy ecosystems.

On occasion, wildfires (unwanted fires in the natural environment) affect national parks by burning forests, towns, or homes with devastating results. Because of these negative impacts, people often mistakenly consider all fires to be destructive forces. However, properly managed fire, referred to as prescribed fire, is an effective natural resource management tool.

In Yosemite, fires usually are classified as either natural or human caused. Natural fires are usually started by lightning. Natural fires may be monitored and allowed to burn under prescribed conditions; wildfires are those that humans seek to extinguish. Prescribed fires are initiated by humans under predetermined conditions and are used to manage certain types of landscapes, by reducing fuel buildup around campground areas or providing proper soil conditions for the germination of such species as the giant sequoia. Among the other benefits of prescribed burning are:

- Insect pest control
- Removal of undesirable plants that compete with wanted species
- Addition of nutrients, from ashes that remain after a fire, for trees and other vegetation
- Removal of undergrowth so that sunlight reaches the forest floor, to encourage growth of native species

A controlled burn in Yosemite

- Clearing of congested forest areas to prevent the accumulation of fuels

## The Fires of 1990

In August 1990, lightning from intense thunderstorms along the west side of Yosemite ignited about 40 different fires. Because the fires threatened human life and property, park staff immediately began to suppress them.

But two of the fires, known as the A-Rock and the Steamboat, quickly grew beyond control. A number of factors contributed to the severity of the fires, among them high winds, drought conditions, large amounts of available fuel, and steep terrain.

Containment and ultimate control of the two fires took some 2 weeks, more than 3,000 firefighters, and more than $13 million. The A-Rock fire eventually encompassed 18,100 acres (7,325 ha), while the Steamboat fire covered about 6,000 acres (2,400 ha). Damage was estimated at about $26 million and included the loss of homes (primarily in the park inholding known as Foresta) and the loss of income for concessioner and gateway community businesses.

More than 25 years later, the effects of the fires can still be seen. From the Big Oak Flat Road a few miles above Yosemite Valley, the Foresta region still appears starkly devoid of mature trees. Vegetation matures slowly, and it will be many more years before some semblance of the area's previous coniferous forest returns, especially since this area has been burned by subsequent fires. Along stretches of Wawona Road between Yosemite Valley and Chinquapin (the turnoff to Glacier Point) many acres of forest burned, and damage is visible along the roadway where wildfires swept through the area again in 2009, burning some of the same areas.

## The Rim Fire

The Rim Fire began August 17, 2013, in the Stanislaus National Forest and ultimately burned more than 255,000 acres (103,200 ha). Approximately 77,000 acres (31,200 ha) were in Yosemite National Park. The Rim Fire was among the largest

Burned pine trees in the Stanislaus National Forest 2 years after the Rim Fire

fires in California history and wreaked devastating damage on the forested areas along the Tuolumne River gorge and the Hetch Hetchy area of Yosemite. The Rim Fire threatened one of the park's famed groves of giant sequoias, the Tuolumne Grove in the Crane Flat area, but was stopped before it could destroy the ancient trees.

## The Fires of 2014

In the midst of a sustained drought in California, the summer of 2014 was a particularly difficult fire season for Yosemite. The situation was compounded by the large number of dead and dying trees, brought on by an infestation of bark beetles in the water-starved forest, providing fuel for the fires in the dry conditions.

The Meadow Fire started on July 19 as a result of lighting strikes, and burned almost 5,000 acres (2,000 ha). It was finally declared out at the end of September, through a combination of firefighting efforts and autumn rains. During the fire, portions of the famed John Muir Trail had to be closed, and hikers were evacuated by helicopter from Half Dome. The Meadow

Fire was visible from Glacier Point Road, with photographers and videographers providing the world with stark and surreal images of the flames against the night sky.

The El Portal Fire started on July 26 in the community of Old El Portal. Approximately 4,700 acres (1,900 ha) were burned in the El Portal Administrative Site, Yosemite National Park, and the Stanislaus National Forest.

The Dog Rock Fire started in early October and burned more than 300 acres (120 ha) along Highway 140 and in the communities of El Portal and Foresta.

## Floods

Since Yosemite was first occupied by those who recorded their experiences in writing, its natural watercourses have flooded periodically. In 1862, homesteader James Lamon was forced from his home by the rising Merced River, and in 1958 the Wawona Covered Bridge was damaged by the waters of the South Fork.

History has shown that flooding by the Merced, both in Yosemite Valley and downstream in the California Central Valley watershed area, is not uncommon—rather, it should be expected. Major floods in Yosemite Valley occurred in 1937, 1950, 1955, and 1964. Such events were the result of various factors, but the most common was warm winter rains falling on accumulated snow up to the highest elevations of the park—a natural phenomenon now referred to as an "atmospheric river" when it occurs on a large scale. When such conditions occur, the existing river channels cannot accommodate the huge quantities of runoff, and water flows into meadows, forests, and developed areas. Because of the relative regularity with which flooding occurs in Yosemite Valley, its floodplain has been carefully mapped.

## The Flood of 1997

In the early morning hours of January 1, 1997, rain fell on packed snow in Yosemite at elevations up to 9,500 feet (2,896 m). The deluge from the storm created a high volume of water rarely seen in the rivers and waterfalls of the park.

Runoff peaked in Yosemite Valley at about 11 p.m. on January 2, and streams and rivers overflowed their banks and carved new channels. More than 2,000 people (employees and visitors alike) were stranded in the Valley when all 3 access roads were closed. Evacuation finally took place after the water subsided, downed trees were removed, and road repairs were completed.

The effects of the flood were wide-ranging. Water channels were widened, riverbanks were scoured and eroded, and trees and shrubs were uprooted, but the flood's impact on the natural scene was not major. On the other hand, human-made structures and systems were seriously affected. Electrical service was shut down, mud and rockslides blocked roads and damaged power poles, sewer lines broke, and campgrounds, buildings, and roads were flooded. In some cases, large sections of roadway were washed away or underlying roadbeds were destroyed.

While initial repairs and recovery efforts were being made, Yosemite Valley was closed to the public for 3 months. For 2.5 years, repairs to Highway 140 continued, requiring regular road closures; unrestricted access to Yosemite Valley was finally achieved again in October 2000.

### 1997 Flood Statistics

- More than 1.4 miles (2.25 km) of riverbank and 550 acres (223 ha) of meadows were eroded in Yosemite Valley.

- About half of Yosemite Valley's 900 campsites were flooded. Many have since been eliminated and are not likely to be replaced.

- 9 road bridges in the Valley suffered damage and required repair. The footbridge at Happy Isles has been removed.

Spring flooding in Yosemite Valley

- A 300-foot (91-m) section of the 14-inch (36-cm) sewer line located beneath Arch Rock Road was destroyed, severing the Valley sewer system and contaminating the Merced River.

- More than 350 motel and cabin units at Yosemite Valley Lodge were flooded and removed.

- More than 200 concession employee quarters were flooded, and 439 employees were displaced.

- At least 10 archaeological sites sustained heavy damage, and some cultural features and artifacts were completely removed.

- The estimated cost of recovering from the damage and effects of the flood is $178 million.

### Rockfall

More than 1,000 rockfalls—the separation and rapid descent of rock from the Valley's cliffs—have been recorded as occurring in Yosemite Valley in the past 150 years. There are many reasons why Yosemite's granites can crash to the ground, including the effects of glaciation, weathering, and bedrock fractures. A rockfall is a natural process that can be triggered by the freezing and thawing of water, large heat variations, tree roots, and earthquakes. Whether large or small, rockfalls are a dramatic event that can endanger people, animals, and structures. When the National Park Service determines that there is likely to be a rockfall, the agency moves to reduce the risk by removing or closing buildings, such as the closure of a number of cabins in Half Dome Village after a 2008 rockfall. Rockfalls have killed people in the park, and being aware of this potential hazard and of your surroundings is called for if you plan to spend time near any of the Valley cliff faces or talus slopes (large piles of debris at the base of cliffs). If you witness a rockfall, move toward the center of the Valley, and report the event to (209) 379-1420 or at any visitor center.

**There are more than** 1,500 different types of plants in Yosemite. They range from the grand sequoias to tiny fungi and lichen. What follows is a brief overview of Yosemite flora with information on how to find out much more.

## Trees

Both cone-bearing and broad-leaved trees appear in abundance within Yosemite National Park. Conifers, the trees that bear cones, do not shed all of their leaves or needles annually, and this has led to their designation as "evergreens." Most of the broad-leaved trees drop their leaves each year.

## The Conifers

At least 18 different species of conifers occur in the park. About half of them are pines. Most common at lower elevations are the ponderosa (or yellow) pine and the Jeffrey pine. The ponderosa, abundant in Yosemite Valley, has yellow-orange bark, needles in groups of three, bark scales that fit together like a jigsaw puzzle, and a trunk up to 6 feet (1.8 m) in diameter. The Jeffrey pine looks much like the ponderosa but grows at higher elevations (Glacier Point is a typical locality). The bark of both species smells sweet, a scent often described as vanilla or pineapple. Both pines have cones with barbs; if you get pricked by handling a cone, it is likely from a ponderosa as the barbs on those cones point outward.

The two typical high-elevation pines are the lodgepole and the whitebark. The lodgepole has needles in twos, yellowish bark, and small cones. The whitebark features needles in bunches of 5 and purplish, pitchy cones, and tends to be dwarfed at tree line.

Other notable conifers are the red and white firs. Large forests of these trees can be seen along Tioga and Glacier Point roads. White firs occur between 3,500 and 8,000 feet (1,067 and 2,438 m) and have 2-inch (5-cm) needles that twist off the branch and 3- to-5-inch (8- to 13-cm) cones. Red firs, in contrast, have shorter needles that curl upwards and larger cones (5 to 8 inches; 13 to 20 cm), and grow between 6,000 and 9,000 feet (1,829 and 2,743 m).

Black oak in autumn in Yosemite Valley

## Broad-Leaved Trees

With a few exceptions, these trees are deciduous: they lose their leaves in the fall. As the leaves die they take on different hues, such as orange, yellow, and brown. It is the foliage of the broad-leaved trees, then, that provides us with Yosemite's sometimes spectacular "fall color." The deciduous trees are less varied than the conifers in the park.

There are several different oak species in Yosemite. In the Valley, the California black oak is distinctive. It grows to heights of 75 feet (23 m), has dark gray to black bark, and produces large acorns that were a staple of the American Indian diet. One of the most common trees in Yosemite Valley is the canyon live oak, which has holly-like evergreen leaves that it keeps all winter long.

Other conspicuous broad-leaved trees are the mountain dogwood, which produces beautiful and delicate whitish-green flowers each spring, and the quaking aspen, known for its paper-thin white bark and the rustling of its often-colorful leaves with the slightest breeze.

Along streams and rivers, particularly at lower elevations, one will encounter cottonwoods (leaves are bright green on top and light below), willows (slender pointed leaves), and alders (dark green leaves with obvious veins and small teeth).

**The spectacular** geography of Yosemite, with its elevations ranging from 2,000 to over 13,000 feet (610 to 3,962 m), supports a wonderful wildflower garden, not to mention shrubs, grasses, sedges, rushes, ferns, and fungi. The differing temperatures, precipitation levels, and growing seasons ensure that a wide assortment of plants find conditions to their liking at locations throughout the park.

The blooming season is a long one in Yosemite. It starts in the foothills in late February and gradually moves upslope as the weather warms and the snow melts. It doesn't reach the park's highest elevations until August, when flowers make a brief 2-month appearance. All told, the wildflower season in Yosemite lasts a full 6 months!

For the student of botany, Yosemite is indeed a remarkable classroom. Within the park is some of the most distinctive vegetation in the world. Because natural processes have been allowed to continue and because little disruption of the physical environment has occurred, plant life is varied and rich.

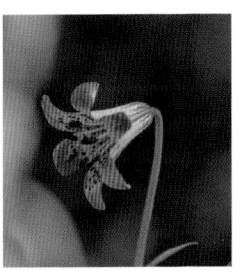
Alpine lily

Western azalea

Sneezeweed

Fleabane daisy

Henderson's shooting star

Lewis's monkeyflower

Leichtlin's mariposa lily

Western monkshood

Pussypaws

Alpine gold

Snow plant

Sierra stickseed

**After its granite** cliffs and domes and its spectacular waterfalls, Yosemite is best known for its famous big trees, the giant sequoias (*Sequoiadendron giganteum*). In fact, the 1864 Yosemite Grant set aside as a protected park only Yosemite Valley and the Mariposa Grove of Big Trees. These towering monarchs were recognized for their special qualities early in history, and they continue to inspire awe to this day.

The mature big trees can be recognized by their huge, columnar trunks that are free of branches for 100 to 150 feet (30 to 46 m) above the ground. The foliage is blue-green and individual leaves create rounded sprays, unlike the flattened branchlets of the incense cedar. The bark is quite fibrous, can be 4 to 24 inches (10 to 61 cm) thick, and is cinnamon brown in color. This bark covering is nonresinous and very fire-resistant. Sequoia wood is pink when cut, then darkens to red. It is amazingly resistant to decay (many downed trees remain intact on the ground for years). Cones are quite small (2 or 3 inches; 5 to 8 cm), are abundant, and produce several hundred seeds each.

The giant sequoias grow from these tiny seeds that are no larger than flakes of oatmeal. You would have to amass more than 90,000 seeds to produce a pound (nearly a half kilo) of them. Upon germination, a 1-inch (2.5-cm) seedling results, and these seedlings grow into young trees through the years. These youngsters are characterized by a fairly symmetrical, cone-shaped appearance with a sharply pointed crown.

At 700 or 800 years of age, sequoias are mature, have just about reached their maximum height, and have developed a rounded top. Some mature trees that have been burned are noted for their "snag tops." When fire damages the bases of the trees, water supply to their upper reaches is limited and the tops of the trees die. The trees remain healthy, but their appearance suggests the hazards they have survived and the effects of age.

Scientists believe that the giant sequoia is the largest living single-stem tree in the world (though this is sometimes disputed). The trees stop growing upward at about 800 years of age, but they continue to add bulk. Maximum height seems to be about 320 feet (98 m), and diameters vary depending on where the measurements are taken (there is quite a swelling at the base of each sequoia). Some trees at the base are more than 35 feet (10.7 m) in diameter, while at about 20 feet (6 m) above the ground, that size drops to about 20 feet (6 m).

It is hard to grasp the immensity of the sequoias. One example that provides perspective is the largest branch on the Grizzly Giant tree in the Mariposa Grove. It is more than 6 feet (2 m) in diameter. At that size it is larger than the trunks of the largest specimens of most trees in the eastern United States. It is also larger than many of the conifers in Yosemite.

Despite their longevity, giant sequoias are not the oldest living things. That distinction is reserved for the bristlecone pines, which may live to be 5,000 years old. Sequoias are known to live at least 3,200 years.

Giant sequoias occur naturally only in the Sierra Nevada, primarily at elevations between 5,000 and 7,000 feet (1,500 to 2,100 m). In Yosemite there are 3 groves: the Mariposa Grove (see page 116), the Tuolumne Grove, and the Merced Grove (page 130). Any visit to Yosemite should include a trip to see these impressive trees.

It is important to note that while the two species are related, sequoias are different from redwoods (*Sequoia sempervirens*). Redwoods live mostly on the misty Northern California coast and are relatively common there. They are the tallest trees in the world at almost 400 feet, but sequoias are more massive.

Giant sequoia

Approximately 90 species of mammals have been recorded in Yosemite National Park. What follows are brief descriptions of some of those mammals, particularly those that visitors are likely to see in the course of their stay in the park. As you travel through Yosemite by car, be especially careful to follow the speed limits. Each year several hundred animals are killed by motorists, especially along the Tioga and Glacier Point Roads. Large mammals are most active at dawn and dusk; drivers need to be aware and cautious at all times on park roads.

Black bear

## Black Bear

Many people react to the black bear with both fascination and fear. Because of the multitude of stories that are told about bears throughout the national park system, there are plenty of misconceptions that exist about these largest of park mammals.

Yosemite's black bear is often confused with the grizzly bear, a species that no longer exists in the park, nor in California. The grizzly once roamed the Sierra Nevada but was eliminated by hunters around the turn of the century. The last grizzly killing in Yosemite occurred in 1895, and the last authentic record of the killing of a grizzly in California is from 1922.

Grizzly bears are considerably more dangerous to humans than black bears. Occasional black bear incidents do occur, but those mainly result from improper food storage. Never feed the bears, and observe them at a distance (particularly when cubs are present)!

Despite their name, black bears can be brown, blond, cinnamon, or black. There are no members of the brown bear species (or any other) in Yosemite. Individuals range in size from 250 to 400 pounds (113 to 181 kg), although even bigger bears have been recorded.

Black bears can be observed throughout the park, particularly in the evenings. Many bears enter dens in winter for a period of sleep. Young are born in late winter and leave the den in spring to forage with their mothers.

## Black Bears and Human Food

Black bears are omnivores—they will eat practically anything. Typical fare is insects, small rodents, berries, acorns, and seeds. But human food, from hot dogs to cookies, also appeals to park bears; driven by their excellent sense of smell and enormous appetite, they are drawn to it. Once they have had a taste of it, they continue to seek it out from any possible source, including backpacks, picnic tables, ice chests, and cars. Their natural fear of humans fades, and some bears may become aggressive.

Aggressive bears often have to be killed. Each year black bears are killed in Yosemite as a direct result of human carelessness and improper food storage. In 2016, there were 38 bear incidents (down from nearly 500 in 2010), resulting in more than $5000 in damage; 2 bears had to be killed. No bear has ever killed a person in Yosemite National Park. The only way to prevent the continuing loss of bears is to make sure that all food and trash are stored properly.

"Food" includes any item with a scent, regardless of packaging. This includes canned goods, bottles, drinks, and items that you might not consider food, such as soaps, cosmetics, toiletries, perfumes, trash, empty ice chests, and unwashed food-preparation items.

### What If You See a Bear?

Never approach a bear, regardless of its size. If you encounter a bear in a developed area of the park or on a hiking trail, act immediately: yell as loudly as possible or, if necessary, throw small stones or sticks toward the bear from a safe distance with

## Bear-Aware Food Storage

**Parking areas** — Place food in food storage lockers if available, or in your hotel room or cabin (but not your tent cabin). Food must not be stored in vehicles after dark, even in trunks. Don't forget to clear vehicles of food wrappers, crumbs, and baby wipes. Food may be stored out of sight in vehicles with windows closed during daylight hours only, but bear lockers or trailhead bear boxes are still preferable.

**Campgrounds** — All food must be stored in latched food storage lockers without exception, day and night. Each campsite contains a food storage locker (bear box) measuring 33″ x 45″ x 18″.

**Tent cabins** — All food must be stored in food storage lockers, day and night. Never leave items with an odor in your tent.

**Hotel rooms and cabins** — All food must be kept inside your room or cabin. If you are not in your room, the windows and doors must be closed.

**Picnic areas and on the trail** — Do not leave food unattended; keep it within arm's reach at all times.

**Backpacking** — Bear-resistant food canisters are required for overnight hikers (see page 19). A list of allowed cannisters can be found on nps.gov/yose.

• • • • • • • • • • • • • • • • • • • • • • • • • • • • • • • • • • • • • • • • • • • • • • • • • • • • • • • • • • • • • • • • • •

the goal of scaring the bear (you don't want to injure it). If others are with you, stand together to present a more intimidating figure, but do not make the bear feel surrounded—you want the bear to run away! See page 19 for information on what to do about a bear in your campsite.

Use caution if you see cubs, as a mother may act aggressively to defend them. Never try to retrieve anything once a bear has it. If you follow these recommendations and act immediately, you should be successful in scaring bears away. Report all bear encounters to a park ranger as soon as possible in person or by calling (209) 372-0322.

## Keep Bears Wild

You can find out much more about Yosemite's bears—including their movements via GPS collars—at keepbearswild.org, developed by Yosemite Conservancy and the National Park Service. A special group of "Keep Bears Wild" products, including an enamel pin, patch, and stuffed animal, have been created, and proceeds from the sales of these items directly benefit park bears. One of the many programs supported is the bear canisters available for backpackers to rent.

## Mule Deer

Having experienced a life free of threat from humans, the mule deer in Yosemite seem almost tame. You are likely to spot one or more of these graceful creatures anywhere in the park, but they are especially obvious in Yosemite Valley and in the Wawona Meadow area.

Despite the fact that they seem unconcerned about humans, mule deer should be treated like any other wild animal. These deer should be given a wide berth and not be fed (nor should any other park animal); injuries have been caused to visitors who have disturbed these animals in the course of offering them human food. Even deaths have resulted from gorings and from the blows delivered by the surprisingly sharp hooves of the mule deer.

Mule deer

The mule deer takes its name from its large, mule-like ears. Weighing up to 200 pounds, it is primarily a browsing animal, eating leaves and tender twigs from trees, grass, and other herbs. The male mule deer (the buck) grows antlers each year for use in the mating season, or "rut," each fall. Despite popular belief, the age of a given buck cannot be determined by counting the number of antler points he sports.

Mule deer are very common in Yosemite, chiefly between 3,500 and 8,500 feet (1,100 and 2,600 m). They stay below the snow line in winter, often dropping into the foothills that border the west side of the park. Common predators of the mule deer are the mountain lion and the coyote.

Mule deer, like other large mammals in Yosemite, are susceptible to death by car. It is vital to park wildlife that drivers be aware of their surroundings and rate of speed.

### American Pika

You need to be lucky and adventurous to see a pika in Yosemite. These shy little animals live far from people, in rocky slopes high up near the Sierra crest, along the eastern boundary of the park. Even if you make it up there, you'll need to keep a sharp eye out—pikas are only a few inches long and have gray fur that blends into their rocky home. You are more likely to hear one than see it. If you hear a squeak and cannot identify the animal that made it (marmots and ground squirrels squeak too, but you should be able to see them without too much trouble), look carefully among

Pika

the rock piles. Pikas look a lot like voles or mice but are actually small rabbits with short ears. Good luck.

If you do find a pika you are seeing one of the most remarkably adapted and scientifically important animals in the Sierra Nevada. Despite living in some of the coldest, windiest parts of the range, they do not hibernate. They stay awake and alive through the winter by making hay. In the summer months, pikas cut pieces of grass and sedge from the area around their dens and leave them on rocks to dry in the sun. Once the hay is ready, they store it in a larder that sustains them all winter. Any pika you do see is probably making hay while the sun shines. If you sit still long enough, you may see one busily scampering back and forth between its plants and its den.

In response to climate change, the lower end of the pikas' range has moved uphill by at least 500 feet (150 m). At present, the easiest place (relatively speaking) to see a pika is along the path up Mount Dana, south of Tioga Pass.

## Tricks for Observing Animals

Try strolling down a forest trail, or walk along the edge of a meadow. Avoid groups of people, as most animals are easily frightened. Consider the color of your clothing and don't wear white—it makes you too conspicuous. Darker shades are better. Walk slowly. When you see an animal, don't make quick movements. If you should come upon one, such as a deer or a squirrel, continue slowly so as not to alarm it. Stop to watch it when you are still some distance away. If you want to see an animal that has disappeared into a burrow—a marmot, ground squirrel, or mouse—find a comfortable place to sit and remain quiet. Usually it will reappear in a short time to see where you are and what you are doing. Watch for evidence of mammal activities, such as dens, trails in the grass, or kitchen middens where squirrels have cut away and piled the scales of pine cones. Watch, too, for holes dug where pine nuts or acorns have been buried.

—from *Discovering Sierra Mammals* by Russell Grater
(El Portal: Yosemite Association, 1997)

## Mountain Lion

Terror-inducing stories abound about these large members of the cat family, but although they are present in Yosemite, they are almost never seen and rarely interact with humans. Also know as cougars, panthers, or pumas, mountain lions prey on other mammals, primarily deer. They are wary of people and go out of their way to avoid contact with park visitors; they are not normally a serious threat to human safety.

Besides deer, the mountain lion also will eat a number of small mammals, including marmots, rabbits, foxes, coyotes, and raccoons, and even porcupines and skunks when the pickings are slim. Because they help to keep Yosemite's deer population in check, mountain lions are considered an important component of the park ecosystem.

Mountain lions can weigh from 75 to 275 pounds (23 to 84 kg). They are 6 to 9 feet (1.8 to 2.7 m) long including the tail. They are recognized by their size, solid tan color, and extended tail. Females give birth to a litter of 1 to 6 cubs in midsummer every other year. Mountain lions produce a number of catlike sounds, including hisses, growls, and yowls, and their mating call has been likened to the screams of a woman.

## Humans and Mountain Lions

While mountain lion attacks on humans are extremely rare, they are possible. Generally, mountain lions are calm, quiet, and elusive. If you spot one, consider yourself privileged! The National Park Service offers the following safety recommendations:

- Do not leave pets or pet food outside and unattended, especially at dawn and dusk. Pets can attract mountain lions into developed areas.

- Avoid hiking alone. Watch children closely and never let them run ahead of you on the trail. Talk to children about mountain lions, and teach them what to do if they meet one (see below).

- Store food according to park regulations.

### What If You See a Mountain Lion?

- Never approach a mountain lion, especially if it is feeding or with kittens. Most mountain lions will try to avoid a confrontation. Always give them a way to escape.

- Don't run. Stay calm. Hold your ground, or back away slowly. Face the lion and stand upright. Raise your arms and do all you can to appear larger. If you have small children with you, pick them up.

Mountain lion

Coyote

- If the lion behaves aggressively, wave your arms, shout, and throw objects at it. The goal is to convince it that you are not prey and may be dangerous. If attacked, fight back!
- If you do see a mountain lion during your visit, you can report it to park rangers in person or by calling (209) 372-0322.

## Coyote

Normally a very shy mammal, the Yosemite coyote has become accustomed to the human presence and is commonly seen here, particularly in Yosemite Valley. In winter these dog-like creatures often can be viewed hunting in snow-covered meadows.

The coyote is one mammal that makes its presence known by its call. There is nothing more haunting (some would contend frightening) than the late-night howling and barking of a group of coyotes.

Weighing 25 to 30 (11 to 14 kg) pounds, coyotes live on small animals (primarily rodents), although fawns and an occasional adult mule deer are taken. Coyotes can be identified by their long, grayish fur (which is lighter on the underside) and a darkish tail.

There are no wolves in Yosemite. If you meet someone who swears that they have seen a wolf in the park, they are mistaken.

## Squirrels and Chipmunks

A variety of squirrels and chipmunks are present in Yosemite. Most visitors, particularly campers, will encounter one or more species of these active rodents.

The common squirrels are the western gray squirrel (all gray with a long bushy tail, often seen in trees), the Douglas squirrel or Sierra chickaree (a dark gray tree squirrel that chews on pine cones and squeaks a lot), the golden-mantled ground squirrel, and the California ground squirrel (a brown animal, speckled with white, which lives in burrows in the ground). The California ground squirrel is widespread throughout the state. The ones in Yosemite tend to be grayer than their counterparts in San Francisco. At higher elevations, the common ground squirrel is the "picket pin" (or Belding ground squirrel), which when seated in its erect posture looks like a stake driven into the ground.

There are at least 5 different species of chipmunks in the park. They are generally reddish brown in color, smaller than the squirrels, and wear 4 light-colored stripes separated by dark on their backs. These chipmunks are remarkably animated and quick. They dig burrows in stumps or the ground that are very hard to find.

**Western gray squirrel**

Yellow-bellied marmot

## Marmot

A common sight in the park's higher elevations is the yellow-bellied marmot; watch for these rotund fellows at Olmsted Point on Tioga Road. Actually members of the squirrel family, marmots resemble woodchucks, for which they are sometimes mistaken. They regularly sun themselves on subalpine rocks. They behave tamely at certain roadside turnouts. Please do not feed them.

Marmots are about 15 to 18 inches (38 to 46 cm) long and weigh about 5 pounds (2.3 kg). They are yellowish brown, live in dens under rock piles or tree roots, and hibernate during the winter. Their shrill warning note is distinctive.

## Bighorn Sheep

Native to the Yosemite area, Sierra Nevada bighorn sheep were eliminated here around 1900 as a result of hunting and diseases spread by domestic animals.

Concerted efforts to restore the bighorn sheep took place when 3 herds were released in the Yosemite area between 1979 and 1988. Since then, additional groups have been reintroduced to specific areas of Yosemite and the surrounding mountain range, including the 2015 release of what is known as the Cathedral herd. Data from GPS collars and field surveys are helping biologists monitor the endangered, iconic mammal.

Bighorn sheep are remarkable rock climbers, able to ascend and descend amazingly steep terrain. Some sheep weigh up to 200 pounds (90 kg) and are 3 feet (1 m) high at the shoulder. They are gray or buffy brown in color and grow hard, permanent horns. The males' horns sometimes spiral back into a full circle, while the females have small, slightly backward-curving horns. Watch for these beautiful animals in the mountainous regions around Tioga Pass.

Bighorn sheep ewe

Because Yosemite plays host to more than 260 different kinds of birds, it is not practical to provide an exhaustive bird list here. To learn more about Yosemite's birds, visit nps.gov/yose, try a ranger-led bird walk, or pick up a pair of binoculars and see what there is to see. The following highlights the species you are likely to encounter in the course of a visit.

## Steller's Jay

This is one bird that just about everybody notices in Yosemite. The jay is bright blue with a dark head and a very prominent crest. Unfazed by humans, it boldly alights on tables and other perches close to food, all the while screeching its disagreeable screech. Surprisingly, the Steller's jay also is capable of producing a soft, warbling song. When a group of jays encounters a hawk or owl, the raucous cacophony of shrieks and calls that goes up is almost overpowering.

Acorn woodpecker

## Acorn Woodpecker

In Yosemite Valley, the acorn woodpecker is the woodpecker you are likely to see. Colored black and white with a red head marking (sometimes there's yellow also), these industrious birds drill holes in trees, telephone poles, and buildings and fill them with acorns that they eat later (along with the bugs that have entered the acorns). Their flight is a distinctive series of shallowly U-shaped glides. They are exceptionally noisy, making a "wack-up, wack-up" call most often. Wherever you find oaks, you will find acorn woodpeckers.

## Belted Kingfisher

Along the Merced River and other bodies of water in the park, this striking blue bird can be seen flying low or perched on branches and snags, watching for fish and aquatic insects. If you're lucky, one will plunge into the water and emerge with dinner in its beak. There is a noticeable crest and a reddish band on the female's chest. You'll know it's a kingfisher if you hear a loud, rattling, clicking call.

American dipper

## American Dipper

Another water bird, the dipper, is truly phenomenal. Though gray and nondescript, these acrobatic creatures are named for their habit of bobbing up and down almost constantly. What's so phenomenal about them is their ability to fly into a stream or river and walk upstream, underwater, clinging to rocks on the bottom as they search for food. They have natural goggles—a translucent ocular membrane that covers their eyes while they hunt. As you stroll beside a stream or river, keep a close eye out for the amazing dipper!

## Clark's Nutcracker

The high-country counterpart of the Steller's jay is the Clark's nutcracker. Also known as the "camp robber," this white, gray, and black bird with a prominent beak

Clark's nutcracker

has a harsh, cawing voice. Very conspicuous in areas around Tuolumne Meadows, the Clark's nutcracker does crack and eat pine nuts, but it is not averse to cleaning up around your campsite either. You'll see these birds typically above 9,000 feet (2,750 m).

Black-headed grosbeak

### Black-Headed Grosbeak

While picnicking or camping, you may see this other common Yosemite Valley resident. The grosbeak is characterized by its black, white, and orange markings and by its "gross beak" that is used for opening seeds. Oftentimes woods echo with the grosbeak's delightfully lyrical song, a rich warble. The black-headed grosbeak is a sure sign of spring.

Great horned owl

### Great Horned Owl

You may never get a glimpse of this bird, but chances are good you will hear one. This nocturnal dweller in most of the park's life zones is active from dusk until dawn. Most of that time it issues a series of deep, sonorous hoots. If you happen to hear the horned owl, see if you can locate its perch.

These owls are excellent ventriloquists, so don't be surprised if you fail. If you see a bird with large ear tufts, it's a sure sign you're looking at a great horned owl.

### Yosemite's Ten "Most Wanted" Birds

Serious birdwatchers (or "birders") often keep a list of every bird known to occur in North America and beyond, and when they see a bird they've never seen before, they will check it off this personal "life list." The goal is to see every single species on the list. There are several birds in Yosemite that are rarely seen or seen in few other places.

Peregrine falcon

These "most wanted" birds are feverishly sought by many zealous birdwatchers for their life lists.

1. Great gray owl
2. Gray-crowned rosy-finch
3. Peregrine falcon
4. Black-backed woodpecker
5. Flammulated owl
6. Northern goshawk
7. Pileated woodpecker
8. Williamson's sapsucker
9. Northern pygmy owl
10. Black swift

**Lizards, frogs, and** snakes are all members of this category. Thirty-four different species of amphibians and reptiles are known to have established populations in the Yosemite Sierra, and there are no doubt more.

Amphibians (such as frogs and salamanders) lay their eggs in the water and breathe underwater through gills before reaching maturity, at which point they breathe air. Reptiles (such as snakes and lizards) breathe air.

All of the lizards in Yosemite are harmless. Because they prefer warm locations, they are found primarily in the lower elevations of the park (Yosemite Valley and below). Most commonly seen is the western fence lizard, which is black or blotched brownish-gray on top with a blue throat and belly.

At least 13 different types of snakes inhabit the park. With the exception of the western rattlesnake, none are poisonous. The most regularly seen species is the garter snake, which frequents meadows, ponds, streams, and lakes (it's a remarkably good swimmer). The garter snake is black, gray, or dark brown with a cream-colored stripe down its back and usually has red blotches on its sides.

The rattlesnake is Yosemite's only venomous snake but rarely bites people. The rattler varies from cream to black in color with a variety of blotches. The head is broad, flat, and triangular, and when surprised, the snake will coil and shake the rattles it sports at the end of its tail. The

Sierra Nevada yellow-legged frog

result is a buzzing sound that is a warning to stay away. They're pretty rare above 5,000 feet (1,500 m).

Frogs and toads are abundant in Yosemite; there are a minimum of 8 different kinds. You are more likely to hear from these denizens of the park than to see them. Most abundant is the Pacific tree frog, a small, green, gray, or brown fellow with a black mask and a constantly heard, year-round song. The Sierra Nevada yellow-legged frog, once quite common, has not been documented in the park in years. Efforts are underway to restore this and other frog species to high-country lakes free of nonnative predator fish.

The last of the amphibians are the salamanders and newts. These small, slimy creatures like it moist and dark. That's why they're rarely seen. Most likely to be discovered is the California newt, the brownish-orange newt that is often spotted after a heavy rain. Two species of salamander are found almost nowhere else but in the Yosemite region: the Mount Lyell and the limestone salamanders.

Sierra fence lizard

**When the glaciers** moved through Yosemite during the last ice age (more than 12,000 years ago), native fish populations were eliminated and all of the park's lakes and streams above the Yosemite Valley floor were left fishless. One job of the US Army in Yosemite National Park between 1890 and 1914 was to plant new fish species in the high country and provide greater opportunities for sport fishers. Nonnative species that were introduced and now occur in the park are the cutthroat trout, the golden trout, the brown trout, and the brook trout. The brook and brown trout have adapted best. Rainbow trout are the only game fish that naturally occur in Yosemite in the lower Merced River (Yosemite Valley floor and below), but they do not naturally occur in high alpine lakes and rivers. There are 5 other native species that occur naturally in the lower Merced, but they are relatively uncommon and are not game fishes (the Sacramento sucker, the Sacramento squawfish, the hardhead, the California roach, and the riffle sculpin).

Fish introduction has been very unfortunate for the other animals that inhabit Yosemite's high lakes and streams above the Yosemite Valley floor. Trout are predators, and their sudden introduction has devastated these ecosystems, including predating and competing with a federally endangered, endemic species of frog, the Sierra Nevada yellow-legged frog. In 2007, the park began removing fish from some high-country lakes and reintroducing frog species to these fragile environments. Two of these lakes are Budd Lake and Roosevelt Lake.

For information about fishing in Yosemite, see page 91.

For information about fishing in Yosemite, see page 91.

. . . . . . . . . . . . . . . . . . . . . . . . . . . . . . . .

**Q: How do I safely enjoy Yosemite's waterways?**

**A: Every year, people die in Yosemite due to water-related accidents. Most victims were not attempting to swim. Some were "merely" wading, some simply standing on shore when they slipped in. The good news is that Yosemite's waters are safe when viewed from the security of the trail or other developed areas. Stay far enough away from the water that you could never fall in if you slip. Be sure to check the park's website nps.gov/yose for allowable seasons and locations before boating. Always wear a Coast Guard–approved personal flotation device when boating or floating.**

Rainbow trout

Northern Pacific rattlesnake

**The relatively** undeveloped landscape of Yosemite Valley and the vast regions of wilderness around it are home to plants, animals, and other organisms that may in one way or another be hazardous to your health. The threat from these sources is generally not serious, and there are a number of precautions you can take and signs to watch for to avoid problems. Whatever you do, don't become frightened by the following list.

## Rattlesnakes

These wriggly reptiles are the only poisonous snakes in Yosemite. Out hiking, you will rarely encounter a rattler, and if you do it will almost always buzz its rattles when threatened. If you happen upon a rattlesnake, keep a safe distance and leave. Do not try to kill it or scare it away. It's always a good idea to watch carefully where you walk, where you put your hands, and where you sit.

## Scorpions

In Yosemite's lower elevations, this threatening-looking insect hides by day and becomes active at night. The sting delivered by this scorpion is painful but not at all dangerous to humans. Sierran scorpions are quite different from the more serious desert scorpions found in places like Arizona. Scorpions hide under rocks and logs, so be cautious when you're lifting or rolling such objects.

## Giardia lamblia

This funny-sounding creature is a protozoan that causes an intestinal disease called giardiasis. Its symptoms are chronic diarrhea, abdominal cramps, bloating, fatigue, and weight loss. Because giardia has been found to be present in park lakes and streams, you should purify any drinking water that is not from the tap. Either boil it for 3 minutes, use an iodine-based purifier, or use a giardia-rated water filter.

## Mosquitoes

These delightful insects have been characterized by one writer as the "most bothersome of the animal life in the High Sierra." Though relatively benign individually, roving bands of mosquitoes can make the lives of visitors, particularly in certain areas of the wilderness, totally miserable. They breed in locations with standing water, so they are common wherever there is snowmelt. Typically, that means 4,000 feet (1,200 m) at the end of May advancing upwards to 10,000 feet (3,000 m) by late July. What can be done about these pesky pests? Try repellents, long pants and long-sleeved shirts, and mosquito-net hats and tents. If you're backpacking, locate your camp to take advantage of any breeze and away from areas of moisture.

## Ticks

Some park ticks, the small bugs that suck blood from a variety of mammals, carry an illness known as Lyme disease. Not every tick, however, is a carrier. Symptoms of the disease in its advanced form can include arthritis, meningitis, neurological problems, and cardiac problems. If it is detected early, treatment can cure or lessen the severity of the disease. If you think you might have been bitten by a tick, watch for a rash at the spot of the bite and for symptoms of the flu. If you contract Lyme disease and you believe its source was Yosemite, please call the Park Sanitarian at (209) 379-1033.

Poison oak: leaves of 3, let it be!

## Poison Oak

This is one of the most widespread shrubs in California, and it's quite abundant in Yosemite's lower reaches. Fluids from the plant produce an irritating rash on the skin of humans and it can sometimes be very severe. Sufferers itch terrifically and can experience swelling. If you think you've been in poison oak, wash your body and clothes thoroughly to remove the oily fluid.

## Spiders

There are a couple of interesting critters in this category. The single truly dangerous spider in Yosemite is the black widow. With its black, orb-shaped body featuring a red "hourglass" marking on its underside, this arachnid is easy to identify. The black widow is not aggressive, but when disturbed may bite and inject a nerve poison that can cause severe symptoms and even death. If bitten, see a physician quickly.

Black widow

Much more fearsome in appearance is the tarantula, but this big, woolly critter is fairly benign. Up to 4 inches across, tarantulas are active at night and don't bite unless provoked. The bite is painful but not dangerous. Relatively common in the foothills, they are rarely seen in the park.

## Hantavirus

Hantavirus Pulmonary Syndrome (HPS) is a rare but serious respiratory disease that can be contracted through contact with infected rodents or their urine, saliva, blood, or droppings. The deer mouse is the primary reservoir for the strain of hantavirus responsible for the human cases in Yosemite National Park, and this little rodent is found throughout the United States. About 12 percent of deer mice carry hantavirus and in 2015, the CDC counted 18 cases of hantavirus in the United States. The virus is mainly transmitted to people when they breathe in air contaminated with the virus. If you observe evidence of rodent activity in your lodgings, do not try to clean it up yourself; notify housekeeping staff. If you are camping, do not pitch tents near rodent burrows or droppings.

Symptoms of hantavirus generally begin from 1 to 8 weeks after exposure and often include fever, fatigue, chills, muscle aches, and sometimes headaches, nausea, vomiting, dizziness, and abdominal pain. Four to 10 days after initial symptoms, symptoms

Deer mouse

may progress to include coughing, shortness of breath, and difficulty breathing. If you or someone you know develops any initial symptoms after a potential exposure, seek medical help immediately, as early intervention is extremely important. Be sure to inform the health provider of your visit to Yosemite. There is more information available at nps.gov/yose or at the Centers for Disease Control (CDC) website, cdc.gov/hantavirus.

## Plague

Plague is a rare but serious bacterial disease that is most commonly contracted from the fleas of an infected rodent. Occasionally, it is transmitted through contact with tissues from an infected animal, or rarely through contact with infectious respiratory droplets, from coughing or sneezing. Plague has been identified throughout California and the Sierra Nevada, including Yosemite. In California and Yosemite ground squirrels and chipmunks are the rodents most commonly associated with plague, but any mammal can potentially be infected—even domestic dogs and cats, which can then transmit the disease to their owners.

To minimize your exposure to the plague bacteria, never feed wildlife, avoid dropping food scraps outside, do not disturb rodent burrows, wear insect repellant with DEET, and tell a ranger if you see a dead animal. While plague is very serious, to put this in a little perspective during your visit to Yosemite, in 2015, the CDC counted 16 human cases of plague in the western United States.

There are 3 forms of plague: bubonic, septicemic, and pneumonic. Initial symptoms develop 2 to 6 days after exposure and can include nausea, vomiting, fever, chills, muscle aches, headache, and weakness. Additional symptoms include swollen lymph nodes (bubonic, the most common form); high fever, fatigue, weakness, bleeding (septicemic); and difficulty breathing, coughing, and blood-tinged saliva (pneumonic, which can be spread from person to person). If you develop any of these symptoms, seek immediate medical attention, and tell your healthcare provider that you may have been exposed to rodents and fleas. There is much more information about plague at nps.gov/yose and cdc.gov/plague.

California ground squirrel

Peregrine falcon

**While Yosemite** National Park is abundant with varied plant and animal life, several indigenous species have been lost to extinction over the years, and threats to park life-forms persist despite the National Park Service's best efforts to protect them. Grizzly bears were once residents of the Sierra, and other birds, mammals, and plants have been lost as well.

Some species of plants and animals, though still present, have undergone local, state, or national declines, raising concerns about their possible extinction if protective measures are not implemented. The US Fish and Wildlife Service, California Department of Fish and Wildlife, and Yosemite National Park have established categories for these species that reflect the urgency of their status and the need for monitoring, protection, and implementation of recovery actions.

Not all threats to park wildlife can be controlled. Take the peregrine falcon. These impressive flyers eat birds that migrate to Central and South America each winter. Use of pesticides is much more common in these wintering areas, and DDT has found its way into the systems of many Yosemite peregrines. The result is that their eggs became thin shelled and subject to breakage. Nesting success dropped dramatically, and park officials feared that peregrines might be lost for good.

But through a fairly complicated augmentation procedure, the National Park Service has seen a growth in peregrine numbers and nests. During the nesting season, climbers were employed to reach peregrine nests and remove the fragile eggs. They were replaced with plastic phonies. Captive-raised chicks were later placed in the nests, and the parents adopted the newcomers without hesitation. Work continues to encourage other countries to limit their use of harmful chemicals.

Other significant programs have involved the restoration of meadows, oak

Bighorn sheep herd

woodlands, and other park areas. A number of revegetation efforts are underway to reclaim portions of Yosemite that have been overused and stripped of plant life. Watch for evidence of this important work as you travel throughout the park, and be sure your use of Yosemite is consistent with the protection of the plants and animals here.

Sierra Nevada yellow-legged frog

Bald eagle

Willow flycatcher

## Yosemite Species Listed as At Risk by the US Government

### ENDANGERED

Sierra Nevada bighorn sheep
Sierra Nevada yellow-legged frog

### THREATENED

Valley elderberry longhorn beetle
California red-legged frog
Yosemite toad

### PLANT SPECIES OF CONCERN

Bolander's clover
Congdon's lomatium
Slender-stemmed monkeyflower
Three-bracted onion
Tiehm's rock-cress
Yosemite woolly sunflower

## Yosemite Species Listed as At Risk by the State of California

### ENDANGERED

Bald eagle
Great gray owl
Willow flycatcher

### THREATENED

California wolverine
Sierra Nevada red fox
Sierra Nevada yellow-legged frog

### RARE PLANT SPECIES

Congdon's lewisia
Congdon's woolly sunflower
Tompkin's sedge
Yosemite onion

Yosemite Falls as seen from a meadow in Yosemite Valley

# 4 | YOSEMITE VALLEY

**Yosemite Valley is** truly the heart of the park. With its granite monoliths, towering waterfalls, and peaceful meadows, the Valley is unique in the world for its remarkable scenery. Its 7 square miles make up only a small fraction of the park's entire area, but 75 to 80 percent of the visitors to Yosemite spend their time there.

Not surprisingly, this results in crowded conditions on weekends and during the summer and any vacation period. Campgrounds fill, concessioner accommodations become completely reserved, and day users clog Valley roads and parking lots. Efforts have been made to reduce the congestion caused by such heavy use; however, be prepared for delays by carrying food and water and using restrooms when they are available. Consider riding public transportation to Yosemite (see page 148) or parking your car during your stay and riding the free shuttle buses around the Valley. If possible, visit Yosemite in beautiful spring, fall, and winter seasons and midweek.

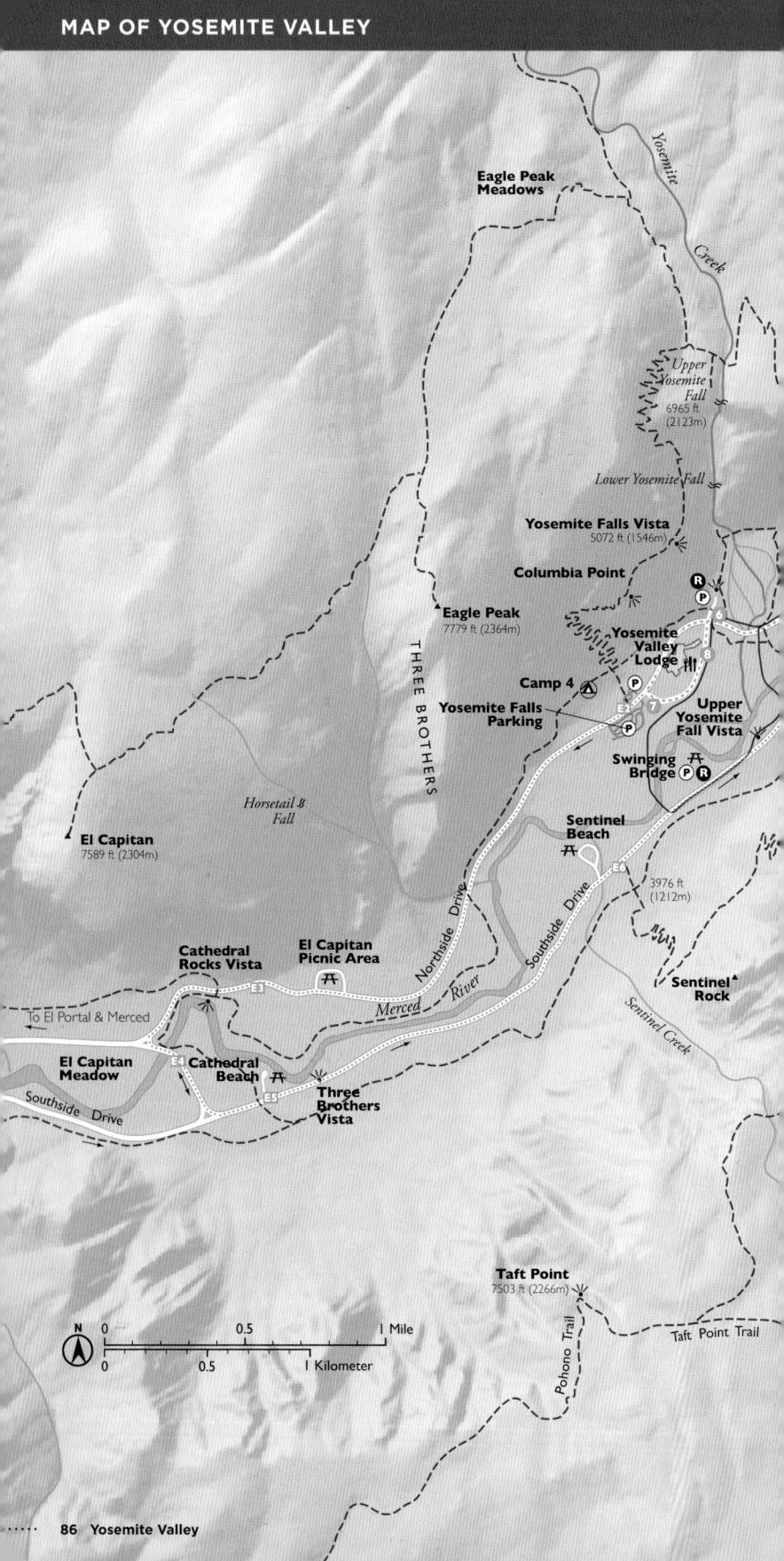

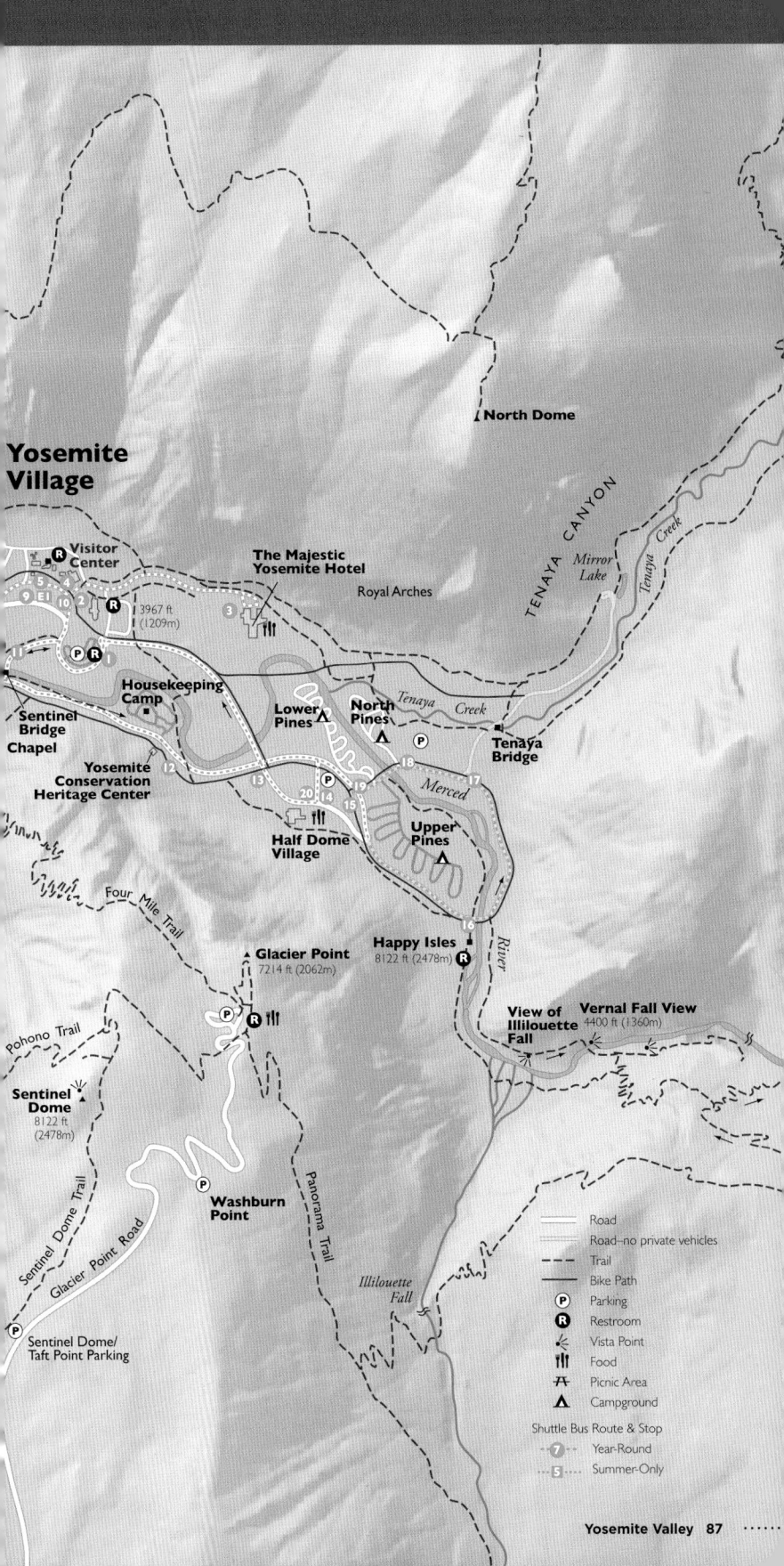

# Yosemite Village

**Visitor Center**

**The Majestic Yosemite Hotel**

Royal Arches

**North Dome**

TENAYA CANYON

*Mirror Lake*

*Tenaya Creek*

3967 ft (1209m)

**Housekeeping Camp**

**Sentinel Bridge Chapel**

**Yosemite Conservation Heritage Center**

**Lower Pines**

**North Pines**

*Tenaya Creek*

**Tenaya Bridge**

*Merced*

**Half Dome Village**

**Upper Pines**

Four Mile Trail

**Glacier Point**
7214 ft (2062m)

**Happy Isles**
8122 ft (2478m)

*River*

Pohono Trail

**Sentinel Dome**
8122 ft (2478m)

**View of Illilouette Fall**

**Vernal Fall View**
4400 ft (1360m)

Sentinel Dome Trail

Glacier Point Road

**Washburn Point**

Panorama Trail

*Illilouette Fall*

**Sentinel Dome/ Taft Point Parking**

| | |
|---|---|
| | Road |
| | Road–no private vehicles |
| | Trail |
| | Bike Path |
| Ⓟ | Parking |
| Ⓡ | Restroom |
| | Vista Point |
| | Food |
| 🛆 | Picnic Area |
| Ⓐ | Campground |

Shuttle Bus Route & Stop

7 Year-Round

5 Summer-Only

# CAN YOU FIND THE VISITOR CENTER?

**Lots of visitors** come to believe, after hours of searching, that the Yosemite Valley Visitor Center has been purposely hidden from them. In many national parks, the first place you are directed to, by prominent signs, is the parking lot right smack in front of the visitor center. Not so in Yosemite Valley. Here you must either possess a doctorate in nuclear physics or have experience as a Green Beret to make your way to "Information Central."

The Yosemite Valley Visitor Center

It really is worth taking the time to find the visitor center, because it's the ideal place to start your visit. There you will find an impressive orientation film, information services provided by knowledgeable rangers, the Yosemite Conservancy bookstore, and excellent exhibits that cover Yosemite's natural and cultural history. Near the visitor center are an Indian Cultural Exhibit and Indian Village, plus the Yosemite Museum.

You can get to the visitor center by shuttle bus, on bicycle, or on foot. Here's how to manage it from selected Valley locations.

## From Yosemite Village Parking

Park your car and board the free shuttle bus headed to the Yosemite Valley Visitor Center (bus stop 1). If you'd rather walk, there's a map available at the information station there that will guide you. It's about a .3-mile (.5-km) walk.

## From Yosemite Falls Parking near Camp 4

Park your car in the visitor parking lot across the street from Camp 4, and board the free shuttle bus (bus stop 7). If you'd rather walk, it is a little over 1 mile (1.6 km), flat, and pleasant with views of Yosemite Falls from the path.

## From the Pines Campgrounds

Jump on a shuttle bus at the stop nearest to you (bus stops 15 and 16 are close) and disembark at Yosemite Valley Visitor Center (bus stop 5). The visitor center is 50 yards (46 m) from the bus stop, on your right.

## From Housekeeping Camp

The shuttle bus stops right in front of the entrance to the camp (bus stop 13). Take it and get off at Yosemite Valley Visitor Center (bus stop 5). The visitor center is 50 yards (46 m) from the bus stop, on your right.

Columbia Point

THREE BROTHERS

Camp 4

Ribbon Fall

El Capitan

Sentinel Beach

El Capitan Picnic Area

Cathedral Rocks Vista

Northside Drive

Merced River

Big Oak Flat Road To Tioga Road & Manteca via (120)

Rainbow View

rockslides

El Capitan Vista

El Capitan Meadow

Southside Drive

Three Brothers Vista

Pohono Bridge

Valley View

Arch Rock Road To El Portal & Merced via (140)

Tunnel View

Bridalveil Fall

Cathedral Rocks

Cathedral Beach Picnic Area

To Glacier Point, Wawona, Oakhurst & Fresno via (41)

Bridalveil View

Stanford Point

Dewey Point

Bridalveil

N

0        0.5        1 Mile

0        0.5        1 Kilometer

Creek

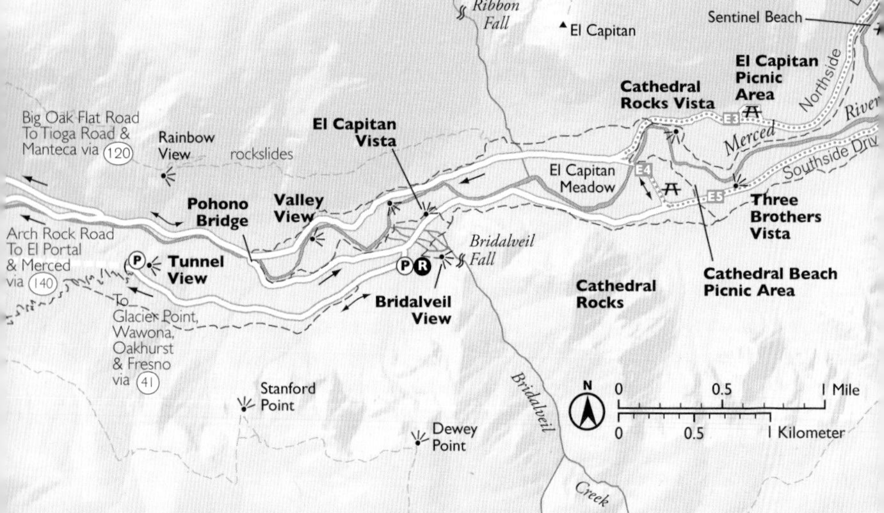

## From The Majestic Yosemite Hotel (formerly The Ahwahnee)

It's about a 15-minute walk along the Ahwahnee Meadow and past the Church Bowl to the visitor center. Or take the free shuttle bus from in front of the hotel (bus stop 3) and get off at the visitor center (bus stop 5).

## From Yosemite Valley Lodge (formerly the Yosemite Lodge)

Catch the free shuttle bus in front of the lodge registration area (bus stop 8). It will drop you off a few yards (a few meters) from the visitor center's front door (bus stop 9). The walk to the visitor center is less than a mile (1.6 km), flat and easy, and affords lots of good views along the way.

## From the Parking Area behind the Village Store

Walk around or through the Village Store to the pedestrian mall on the other side of it. Turn to your right and walk approximately 200 yards (180 m) up the mall to the visitor center, which is located at the mall's west end. If you're on your bicycle, follow the well-marked bike trails and watch for signs directing you to Yosemite Village and the visitor center.

## Free Shuttle Bus Rides

The easiest way to get around in Yosemite Valley (and to get out of your car and avoid traffic) is to ride, free of charge, the Yosemite Valley shuttle bus system. With stops at just about all locations in the eastern end of the Valley (and a stop at El Capitan in summer), the buses run every 10 minutes or so (somewhat less frequently in the winter) and access areas such as Happy Isles and Mirror Lake that are closed to private automobiles. In winter, shuttle service to several stops may be discontinued. Check in at the Yosemite Valley Visitor Center to find out which stops are working.

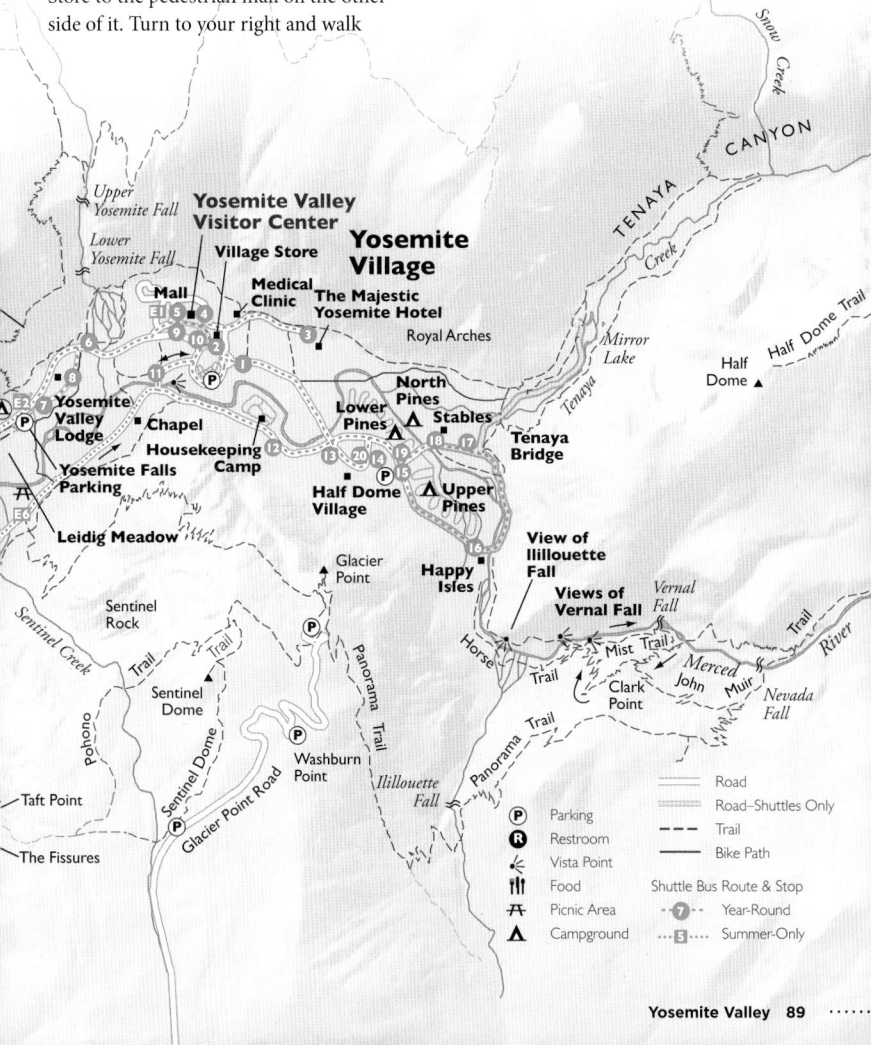

Lee Stetson as John Muir

### John Muir in Person

Noted actor Lee Stetson regularly portrays John Muir in dramatic presentations in Yosemite Valley. It's Yosemite Theater at its best. See page 92.

### A Browse through the Ansel Adams Gallery

This classy shop has been a leading Yosemite establishment since 1902. If you're a photographer, consider this your headquarters in the park. See page 52.

### The Hike to Vernal Fall

An amazingly popular trip, and for good reason. The short, strenuous hike on the Mist Trail is essential Yosemite: rock, light, and water at their most spectacular. See page 95.

### A Seat at Bracebridge Dinner

This lavish Christmas pageant is held annually at The Majestic Yosemite Hotel and features delicious food, seasonal music, elaborate costumes, and festive decorations. See page 23.

### Breakfast at The Majestic

It's a delight any time of the year to start your day with a casual yet luxurious breakfast in the grand dining room. See page 102.

### The Panorama from Tunnel View

This classic Yosemite viewpoint never ceases to amaze. From this spot the Valley's geologic origin couldn't be more evident. See page 105.

### A Visit to the Visitor Center Bookstore

Nowhere else in the universe has such a complete collection of books and other materials related to Yosemite and the Sierra Nevada been assembled in one place. See page 88.

### Lower Yosemite Fall in Springtime

When the snows of the Yosemite high country begin to thaw, Yosemite Falls are revitalized. Liquid thunder! See page 94.

Vernal Fall from the Mist Trail

## Enjoy an Interpretive Program

Throughout the year, park interpretive rangers and others present a wide variety of programs, walks, demonstrations, campfires, slideshows, films, and talks. There is usually no charge for these activities. Occasionally reservations are required. Consult the *Yosemite Guide* for the daily schedule.

## Visit Yosemite Valley's Eastern End

The free shuttle bus route takes visitors to the area of Yosemite Valley that is not accessible by private automobile. Happy Isles (the trailhead for hikes to Vernal and Nevada Falls and Half Dome) and Mirror Lake can only be reached by the shuttle bus or on bicycle or by foot. Excellent views of many landmarks, including Glacier Point, Half Dome, Tenaya Canyon, and Washington Column, are afforded from stops along the way. This section of the shuttle bus route may be closed in winter.

## Make a Circle Tour of the Entire Valley

Many of the park's famous spots, such as El Capitan, Bridalveil Fall, Tunnel View, Cathedral Rocks, and Sentinel Rock, are in west Valley locations. Shuttle service to El Capitan is available in summer, but at other times of year you may want to take a self-guided circle tour. Use the *The Road Guide to Yosemite* to develop your own route. It's packed with interesting information that will enhance your experience. Or let someone else do the driving. The park's concessioner offers a 2-hour guided tour. Available year-round, this open-air (in summer) or heated-coach (in winter) tour visits all of the Valley highlights. Learn more at travelyosemite.com, call (209) 372-1240, or visit any Yosemite Hospitality Tour & Activity Desk for reservations.

## Take a Bicycle Ride

Whether you've brought your bicycle or not, you can still see Yosemite Valley on two wheels. Bicycle rentals (with helmet) can be arranged at Yosemite Valley Lodge (bus stop 8; call (209) 372-1208), and at Half Dome Village (formerly Curry Village; bus stop 13; (209) 372-8435). Go to travelyosemite.com for more info. More than 12 miles (19 km) of paved bicycle paths separate bicycle traffic from autos, and bicycling is especially good on the closed sections of roadway in the Valley's east end. Try to avoid bicycling on busy Valley roads that are often flooded with automobiles. As a rule, sightseeing drivers are not particularly attentive to bicyclists. Apart from that, there are some strict rules for bicycle use in the Valley:

- Bicyclists should stay on paved bike paths and roads.
- No riding on walking trails and into meadows. Erosion and vegetation damage will result otherwise.
- Mountain and all-terrain bicycles are permitted in Yosemite Valley but not allowed on unpaved surfaces. Check at the Yosemite Valley Visitor Center for appropriate mountain bike routes.
- Ride to the right in single file.

## Catch a Fish

There are lots of trout in Yosemite Valley, but the Merced River is heavily fished. Stocking of trout is no longer done, and resident lunkers have developed a wariness of people and their multifarious fishing devices. Nevertheless, nice fish are caught every season by anglers of every skill level. Fishing in Yosemite is allowed in streams and rivers from the last Saturday in April to November 15. Fishing is allowed year-round in park lakes and reservoirs. Fishing from bridges and docks is prohibited. On the Merced River in Yosemite Valley, only catch-and-release fishing is allowed for rainbow trout. No natural or organic bait may be used, only artificial lures and flies with barbless hooks. The limit is 5 brown trout per day with 10 in possession. All persons 16 years of age and older must have a valid California sport-fishing license for fishing, which can be purchased online through the California Department of Fish and Wildlife. Fishing licenses may be available at the Mountain Shop in Yosemite's Half Dome Village, or at the Big Trees Lodge Store in Wawona at the south end of the park. Consult California Fish and Wildlife regulations for further Yosemite fishing rules.

## Paint a Picture

Art classes are available during most parts of the year at the Happy Isles Art and Nature Center (near bus stop 16). Artists working in many different media offer hands-on learning experiences to interested students regardless of skill level. There are beginner and children's classes as well, in the summer season. Class sessions are 4 hours in length and are scheduled from early spring through October and during holiday periods. For more information, call (209) 372-4207 or search under Art Center at yosemiteconservancy.org.

## Get Your Head Wet

While you should always be careful near Yosemite's waters, the Merced River provides some refreshing swimming spots during the summer months (it's too cold and fast flowing in the spring). Or try out Mirror Lake. If you must swim in a heated pool, in summer there's one at Yosemite Valley Lodge and another at Half Dome Village. A small pool is available only for guests at The Majestic Yosemite Hotel. Don't swim above the waterfalls! Yosemite has a short rafting season that varies from year to year during which rafts can be rented from the concessioner; find out more at travelyosemite.com.

## Indulge the Kids

The Happy Isles Art and Nature Center (near bus stop 16) is a great spot for parents and their children, open from spring until October (check the *Yosemite Guide*). You can purchase workbooks for the junior ranger and little cub programs, and there are exhibits of park animals, a children's corner, a night display, and much more. Kids can check out, free of charge, an Explorer Pack—a convenient-to-carry daypack filled with guidebooks and activities for the whole family.

## Go for a Hike

There's a price to be paid for Yosemite Valley's towering cliffs and sheer walls. Practically every hike leading out of Yosemite Valley is straight up and strenuous! But the Valley floor offers many enjoyable walks over flat terrain, and no matter what your hiking ability, you can find a trail to suit you. Several trails on the Yosemite Valley floor are wheelchair accessible. When you hike, be sure to wear sturdy, comfortable shoes and clothes that allow freedom of movement. Carry a flashlight and raingear. Rain (or snow) is a possibility in every season. Don't forget plenty of water (drinking from streams and rivers is not advised) and lunch and snacks. Dogs on leashes are allowed on fully paved trails on the floor of

Yosemite Valley, but nowhere else. Check out the Hike Smart tips on page 97.

## Take in the Yosemite Theater

Throughout the year, dramatic and musical performances are offered by the Yosemite Theater program. Modest fees are charged. Watch history come to life with actor Lee Stetson performing as John Muir and Ranger Shelton Johnson portraying a Buffalo Soldier in the early days of the national parks. Be inspired by the award-winning film *Return to Balance: A Climber's Journey* from the legendary rock climber Ron Kauk or learn about search-and-rescue missions from veteran park rangers. Tickets for the performances may be purchased at the Yosemite Valley Visitor Center up to 1 week in advance of performances. Learn more at yosemiteconservancy.org under Yosemite Theater.

Ranger Shelton Johnson as Elizy Boman, Buffalo Soldier

## Hear a Lecture

Each summer the Sierra Club operates the Yosemite Conservation Heritage Center, an educational center and library located across from Housekeeping Camp at bus stop 12. The Sierra Club built the lodge in 1903 in honor of Joseph LeConte, eminent University of California geologist. Berkeley architect John White designed the Tudor-style, rough-hewn granite building. Most evenings, lectures are presented here free of charge to interested visitors and Sierra Club members. Consult the *Yosemite Guide*, call (209) 372-4542, or visit the center for a schedule.

## Saunter in the Cemetery

Fascinating insights into Yosemite's history can be gained from a visit to the Yosemite Cemetery, located across the street from and just west of the Yosemite Museum. Several significant figures from the park's past are buried here, including a number of American Indians. First laid out in the 1870s, the cemetery houses the graves of such persons as James Mason Hutchings, Galen Clark, James Lamon, Sally Ann Castagnetto, Suzie Sam, and Lucy Brown. If you do visit the cemetery, remember that it is a sacred place for many and that proper respect should be shown.

## Accessibility

Many programs, facilities, and trails in Yosemite Valley (and throughout the park) are suitable for visitors in wheelchairs, with assistance. Also available are: assistive listening devices for programs, audio tours for the blind, many tactile exhibits, sign language interpreters (summer only), and a Braille brochure on Yosemite at the Valley Visitor Center. Brochures are also available in German, French, Italian, Chinese, Japanese, Korean, and Spanish. Information on accessible park programs, facilities, and trails can be found at park entrances or information stations, or you can contact the Accessibility Coordinator at (209) 379-1035, or Deaf Services at (209) 379-5250 or yose_deaf_services@nps.gov. You can also download the Yosemite Accessibility Guide from nps.gov/yose.

## Visit the Wilderness Center

Located in the Yosemite Village, not far from the Valley Visitor Center, the Wilderness Center offers a number of informative displays, a relief map of the entire park, information on planning your own wilderness trip, and maps, guidebooks, and selected backpacking items. It's also the place to pick up wilderness permits, make wilderness reservations (see page 17), and rent bear-resistant food canisters from spring to autumn. During winter, these services are provided at the Valley Visitor Center.

## Pack a Picnic

There are a number of fine spots for a picnic in Yosemite Valley. In the eastern end of the Valley, ride the bus to Happy Isles (bus stop 16) or walk to Mirror Lake. To the west, try El Capitan picnic area (on the right side of Northside Drive about 2 miles or 3.2 km west of Yosemite Valley Lodge), Bridalveil Fall parking area (intersection of the Wawona Road and Southside Drive), Cathedral Beach picnic area (on the left side of Southside Drive just past the El Capitan crossover), Sentinel Beach picnic area (on the left a mile or 1.6 km or so farther along Southside Drive), or Swinging Bridge picnic area (less than .5 miles or .8 km farther, on the left). See the map on pages 86–87 for locations. Please make sure that you leave your picnic site as you found it and pack out all your waste, even watermelon seeds and apple cores. You may not eat these, but animals will.

## Enjoy an Outdoor Adventure

Throughout the year, Yosemite Conservancy presents a series of outdoor adventures in Yosemite Valley and at other park locations. Courses cover such topics as botany, geology, natural history, photography, art, history and culture, and backpacking. Programs have been designed for all levels of experience, and Custom Adventure programs can be created for your visit. For more information, visit yosemiteconservancy.org, email adventures@yosemiteconservancy.org, or call 209-379-2317, ext. 10.

A Yosemite Conservancy Outdoor Adventure

**The floor of** Yosemite Valley is crisscrossed with many trails, and paths hug the base of both the north and south Valley walls. From about any point, there's good hiking. Wherever you walk, be sure it's not on one of the main roadways. Get out of your car and explore some of Yosemite's less-developed locales. You'll be amply rewarded for your effort.

Mirror Lake

## Mirror Lake

Take the free shuttle bus to the Mirror Lake Junction (bus stop 17; see page 89). During the winter you may have to walk from the Pines campgrounds (bus stop 19). From this point it's a relaxing .5-mile (.8-km) saunter over pavement to Mirror Lake. The trail beyond is also gentle as it follows Tenaya Creek eastward and then circles back. Walking up Tenaya Creek adds about 3 miles (4.8 km) to the total distance. Views of Half Dome, Mount Watkins, and Basket Dome are superb.

## Vernal Fall Bridge

This special vantage point is reached from Happy Isles (bus stop 16; see page 89). You may need to walk from Half Dome Village during the winter, when the shuttles may not run this way. Undoubtedly the most popular and busiest hike in Yosemite (you'll be elbow to elbow with lots of other people), the John Muir Trail leads .7 miles (1.1 km) to a bridge that allows a breathtaking view of Vernal Fall. The trail, while paved with asphalt, is not as easy as the other two hikes listed here. There is a moderate slope most of the way to the bridge, and there are a few ups and downs. But it's definitely worth the effort. If you're a strong hiker and still feeling hardy, the remaining hike along the Mist Trail to the top of the fall is about .5 miles (.8 km). Be warned, however, that it's all straight uphill over a very steep trail and a large number of granite steps. It's called the Mist Trail because it leads along the right flank of Vernal Fall, which, particularly in spring, blows heavy mist over trail and hiker alike. It can be like a monsoon. Most people wear rain gear, but even so, on this trail getting drenched is part of the adventure.

## Lower Yosemite Fall

Walk, bicycle, or ride the shuttle bus to the Lower Yosemite Fall trailhead near Yosemite Valley Lodge (bus stop 6; see page 89). It's no more than .25 miles (.4 km) to the base of the lower fall and its boisterous, watery display (at least most of the year). This, too, is a very popular excursion and it is wheelchair accessible. If you continue over the bridge and follow the trail, you will loop back to the trailhead in less than .5 miles (.8 km). On full-moon nights in April and May, take this walk and watch for beautiful "moonbows" in the lower fall—a phenomenon first written about by John Muir. You will have to check on the timing and location of the moonrise to get the full moonbow experience. It's worth staying up late (or getting up early) to see this spectacle.

**Each of the** major trails to the Valley rim is strenuous and requires an uphill hike of at least 3.5 miles (5.6 km) over switchbacks. Be sure you possess the requisite time, energy, footwear, and physical condition before you set off on any of these hikes. Also check the weather and turn back if rain clouds appear—even at a distance.

## Yosemite Falls Trail

This climb up the sheer north wall pays off with remarkable views of the falls and Yosemite Valley. The trail leaves from behind Camp 4, across the street from bus stop 7 at the day-use visitor parking lot, which is next to Yosemite Valley Lodge. The 3.6-mile (5.8-km) route gains 2,700 feet (823 m) in elevation as it passes Columbia Point, the top of Lower Yosemite Fall, and finally leads to the brink of Upper Yosemite Fall. When you reach the top, head back south toward the rim and find the walk down to the pipe railings. Be sure to stay behind the railings—it's a long way down the waterfall. Allow 6 to 8 hours for the round-trip. Strong hikers should consider continuing on to Yosemite Point or Eagle Peak (see pages 104–105).

## The Four-Mile Trail to Glacier Point

Perhaps most disappointing to hikers on this route is that the Four-Mile Trail is almost five miles (8 km) long. It's also a lot of work carrying yourself up 3,200 feet (975 m) only to be greeted by cars, lots of people, and a snack bar. But the views from Glacier Point are sensational and all the more satisfying for the exertion. The trailhead is on the right, below Sentinel Rock on Southside Drive and about a mile (1.6 km) before Yosemite Village. To drive to it you must make a loop on the Valley's one-way road system, crossing over at El Capitan (watch for signs returning you to Yosemite Village). One of the earliest trails built in the Valley, its location below and along the south wall means that it holds snow longer and opens later than the other trails, but also that it is cooler and shadier in the heat of July. This hike requires from 6 to 8 hours up and back.

## Tenaya Zigzags/Snow Creek Trail

This is a less-used 3.5-mile (5.6-km) route to the rim that actually originates in Tenaya Canyon, just east of Mirror Lake about 2.5 miles (4 km) from bus stop 17. It affords stunning views of the canyon, including Clouds Rest and Quarter Dome and, directly across from you as you ascend, of Half Dome. Once you've hiked the 108 switchbacks to the rim, the closest promontory is North Dome, which is another 3 miles (4.8 km; see page 104). If North Dome is your destination, allow 8 to 10 hours round-trip. The trailhead is at Mirror Lake, reached by taking a shuttle bus to the Mirror Lake junction (bus stop 17) and hiking .5 miles (.8 km) to the east. From the lake, the trail takes off to the north, up the canyon for 1.5 miles (2.4 km), and then turns left up the cliff.

## Vernal and Nevada Falls Loop Trails (the Mist Trail)

The walk to Vernal Fall over the Mist Trail is covered on the previous page, but the trail continues on to Nevada Fall above. Two different segments of the route lead to the same place—one restricted to stock use and one exclusively for people. The John Muir Trail (JMT) continues just past the Vernal Fall Bridge and is less steep, though longer (3.5 miles or 5.6 km to Nevada Fall).

The Mist Trail (foot traffic only) continues on past the top of Vernal Fall about 1.5 miles (2.4 km) over switchbacks to the rim. Ascending a gully to its left, hikers are treated to the world-famous profile view of Nevada Fall. From the top of the fall, trails lead to Little Yosemite Valley and Half Dome, and to Glacier Point over the Panorama Trail.

Hikers who go up the Mist Trail steps above Vernal Fall will avoid the congestion often present on the return trip and find their hike safer and more gentle, if a bit longer and higher, by making this a loop hike. Continue on just past Emerald Pool and take the Clark Point Cutoff Trail to the right. This trail is mostly a gentle climb to the JMT which loops back down to the Mist Trail just above the Vernal Bridge. Moreover, hikers who take the Clark Point Cutoff are rewarded with stunning views of the Merced River canyon and surrounding mountains and domes not seen from the Mist Trail. Depart from Happy Isles (bus stop 16, walk across the road bridge and find the trailhead on your right) and give yourself 6 to 8 hours for the round trip. Carry minimally 2 quarts/liters of water per person, snacks, and a rain shell, and wear sturdy footwear.

Hikers and Half Dome

**For many** the summit of Half Dome represents a hiking challenge they can't resist. For all its allure, the trip is long (about 17 miles round-trip; 27.4 km), steep (4,900 feet of elevation gain; 1,500 m), and physically demanding. It's rewarding, too, particularly the incredible views both along the way and at the top. The last 600 feet (183 m) up the back of the dome are steep enough to require the use of steel-cable handrails. Not for the faint of heart! Hold tight and keep moving.

If it sounds like too much of a grunt for one day, consider spending the night in Little Yosemite Valley (you'll need a wilderness permit) and make the ascent when you're fresh the next morning.

This busy trail (someone estimated that about 700 people scale Half Dome daily during the summer) begins from Happy Isles (bus stop 16). Allow 10 to 12 hours minimum for the round-trip.

Due to overcrowding on the trail, permits are now required to hike Half Dome, via a lottery system. For up-to-date information, check nps.gov/yose. To get a permit (plan ahead!), visit Recreation.gov or call (877) 444-6777.

The 10 Essentials for your daypack

If you're planning on hiking while in Yosemite, you will need to prepare for a range of situations, even during short day hikes. First and foremost, tell someone where you are going. Provide a map to a friend, showing your route, your goal, and when to call for help if you don't return. If no one knows you are missing, no one is going to be looking for you. Stay on the trail or developed areas; most serious problems occur when someone leaves the trail. Be mindful that steep trails, uneven terrain, altitude, and weather extremes make heading out in Yosemite likely more challenging than similar hikes elsewhere; be honest about your physical limits.

The majority of on-trail emergencies in the park involve ground-level falls, dehydration, or heat illness. Following these guidelines and carrying the 10 Essentials can help prevent these from happening to you. Last, Yosemite is a natural area, not a theme park; while there, you are responsible for your safety. More than 200 people each year require help from Yosemite rangers skilled in search-and-rescue techniques and prehospital medicine. A little preparation will help you enjoy your outdoor experience and help prevent you from becoming one of those unfortunates.

## Carry the "10 Essentials"

1. **Clothing:** to stay dry and warm during potential weather extremes.

2. **Sun Protection:** long-sleeved shirt and pants, sunglasses, sunscreen, lip balm, and a wide-brimmed hat.

3. **Water:** 1 quart/liter of water for every 2 to 3 hours of hiking or a water filter if you have a reliable water source.

4. **Food:** enough for an unplanned overnight, including salty snacks

5. **First Aid Kit:** for common injuries like blisters, wounds, sprains, and minor pain, and your personal medications

6. **Illumination:** a bright LED headlamp or flashlight (ideally 2 lights), and spare batteries

7. **Navigation:** compass and detailed topographic map (GPS optional)

8. **Repair Kit and Tools:** multifunction tool with a knife blade, duct tape, etc.

9. **Emergency Shelter:** a brightly colored, ultralight, pitchable tarp, bivy sack, or space blanket, plus parachute cord

10. **Fire and Signaling:** fire starter, cell phone with extra power pack, signal mirror, whistle, and brightly colored clothing, bandanas, and/or your shelter

## Lost the Trail?

There are only two kinds of hikers: those who have lost the trail and those who are going to lose the trail. Here are a few tips for when it happens to you:

- Expect to lose the trail. Whether you're hiking on trail or off, turn around frequently and check the route you've been following (your back trail). Remember landmarks as you hike, so that you can always go back the way you came.

- If you're not sure that you're still on the trail, stop! Look around—the trail is often only 50 feet away. But if you have no clue which way to go, choose a nearby feature as a point of reference. Now explore in any safe direction while keeping this reference point always in your sight. Start with your back trail, and if that doesn't work, return to your reference point and try another way, until you learn the area around you and can pick another reference point. Always be able to go back to your original reference point.

- Shortcuts in rugged country are almost always a bad idea. If you have the option of going down a slope that would be hard to climb back up, don't do it—it probably isn't the route you took before you lost the trail.

- Don't push on blindly. If it's getting dark, find a secure, sheltered, and comfortable spot to rest and wait for daylight.

- If nothing works, consider asking for help before you make your problem worse. (See page 98 for information on helping your rescuers.)

## Help Your Rescuers

If you are hopelessly lost or unable to return from your hike for any reason, your best option is to ask for help and to make it easy for others to find you.

- If you have a cell signal, first try a voice call (not text) to 911. If that fails, try voice or text to a friend. A 911 call usually provides the dispatcher with your location. If not, you may be able to use the phone's location app or simply consult your map.
- Move only to improve your safety and/or visibility or improve your cell reception.
- If possible, be out in the open.
- Whether or not you are visible, wear bright or contrasting colors and/or place brightly colored items where they can be seen from as many directions as possible, but especially from the air.
- Use rocks and sticks on the ground or tracks in the snow to spell a large "SOS" or "X."
- Wave your arms when a helicopter flies by. Movement will help you be spotted.
- Signal mirror: If aircraft are visible, or if you can see any place where people might gather, even miles away, use anything reflective (ideally, a signal mirror) to repeatedly reflect the sun's rays in their direction.
- Build a visible smoke column by piling green branches on a hot fire—but only if you are sure you can contain the fire and that fire conditions are safe.
- Use your light in continuous flash mode, or in groups of 3 flashes, or by waving it in a circle. In a pinch try your cell phone light or your camera flash, but remember that you might need to save your cell phone's battery for critical calls.
- Use your whistle frequently. It will save your voice.

**Q: My family is visiting Yosemite this summer. Can we cool off in the rivers?**

**A: Yes and no. Like swiftly moving waters anywhere, Yosemite's can be deadly. The best way to enjoy the park, while protecting yourself and those under your care, is to always stay on the trail or other developed areas.**

**Water-polished rock next to and in the water is slippery even when dry. River currents are stronger than they appear, even in shallow water, and are often powerful enough to push a car. You can't float in aerated (white) water, and the cold temperatures of Sierra Nevada waters can quickly sap your strength. Yosemite's waterways often contain submerged rocks and branches that can entrap swimmers. Be sure to obey posted signs—but don't assume an area is safe just because there is no sign.**

Snowmelt, whitewater, and boulders fill this Yosemite river

**There are about** 415 campsites in Yosemite Valley, most of them on the Recreation.gov system. Despite the fact that many of the campgrounds are practically void of vegetation and that campers are closely packed, these campsites are immensely popular. After all, it's Yosemite Valley.

It was in response to this popularity that the strictly structured reservation system was developed. While the need to reserve in advance does discourage spontaneity, it allows visitors coming from all over the US and the rest of the world to expect, with some certainty, that they will find a place to camp when they arrive. See page 15 for information on making a reservation.

For campers without reservations who find themselves in Yosemite Valley, sites can be found, but they are very difficult to obtain. You may put your name on a waiting list at the Half Dome Village campground reservation office in the back of the parking lot upon opening at 8 a.m. for any released cancellations or early-outs at 3 p.m.; you have to be present to get lucky.

## Camping Regulations

### CAMPING LIMITS

There is a 30-night camping limit within Yosemite National Park in a calendar year; however, May 1 to September 15, the camping limit is 14 nights, and only 7 of those nights can be in Yosemite Valley or Wawona. A maximum of 6 people (including children) are allowed per campsite. There is no limit on the number of tents (as long as they all fit into the campsite).

### CHECK IN AND OUT TIMES

Check-in time is noon, and sites may not be occupied before that time. You must check in prior to 10 a.m. the morning after the first night of your reservation, or your reservation will be cancelled. Campsites must be vacated by noon on the day of departure.

### BEARS

Yosemite Valley and other park locations provide excellent bear habitat. Bears are attracted by the same foods many campers enjoy—marshmallows, hot dogs, watermelon, etc. You are foolish if you do not store your food properly in your campsite (it's also a federal law). All of the Valley campgrounds feature bear-proof food lockers measuring at least 45"w x 18"h x 33"d that are very effective. Keep your bear locker closed and latched at all times. Food is not allowed in any parked vehicle after dark, and there is a fine of up to $5,000 for improper food storage. Remove all trash from your campsite and place it in animal-resistant trashcans or dumpsters.

### PETS

You may camp with your pets in all campgrounds except walk-in and group campsites. Pets must be on leashes (no longer than 6 feet) at all times, should never be left unattended, and are not permitted on trails off the floor of Yosemite Valley or any unpaved or semipaved trails.

### HOOKUPS

There are no recreational vehicle utility hookups in the park. Electrical extension cords may not be connected to campground restroom outlets. Sneaky, but no cigar.

### CAMPFIRES AND FIREWOOD

Campfires are permitted only between 5 p.m. and 10 p.m. May through September; they are allowed any time from October through April. Firewood collection is allowed only within campground boundaries. Firewood can purchased from the concessioner. Do not bring firewood into the park from other areas as such wood may be infested with microbial pests. Please use established fire rings and grates, and start your campfire with newspaper, not pine needles or cones. Use of chain saws is not permitted in the park.

### VEHICLE PARKING

Only 2 vehicles are allowed per site. All of your vehicles, including tent and utility trailers, must be parked on the parking pads. You can't just drive into your campsite. If you have more than 2 vehicles, you must park any extras outside the campground. The maximum length for recreational vehicles is 40 feet.

### DUMP STATIONS

No wastewater of any kind should be drained onto the ground. That's gross. Use utility drains at campground restrooms for dishwater and other gray water. Use the dump station at Upper Pines Campground for RV and other septic tanks.

## QUIET HOURS

Campers are expected to maintain quiet between 10 p.m. and 6 a.m. Generator use is allowed only from 7 a.m. to 9 a.m., noon to 2 p.m., and 5 p.m. to 7 p.m.

## SHOWERS

Unfortunately, there are no shower facilities in any park campgrounds. In Yosemite Valley, showers are available for a fee at Half Dome Village and at Housekeeping Camp.

## LAUNDRY

There is a public laundromat at House-keeping Camp.

## Valley Campgrounds

The following campgrounds are located at an elevation of 4,000 feet (1,200 m) in the eastern end of Yosemite Valley. Most require reservations (see page 15) and have a nightly fee of $26 per site (unless otherwise indicated). Some creative person decided to include "pines" in the name of practically every Valley campground, so be sure to take note of the location you've been assigned, or you may spend hours trying to find your way home. As dates of operation are subject to variation, check with NPS for details.

Setting up the tent

## NORTH PINES

This set of 81 campsites is located adjacent to the stable and next to the Merced River. Both recreational vehicles and tents are accommodated here from April through October. Pets allowed. Reservations required.

## UPPER PINES

The easternmost campground and the largest in Yosemite Valley, Upper Pines is closest to Happy Isles and the trail to Vernal and Nevada Falls. There are 238 sites here, and some pets are permitted. Both RVs and tents are welcome, and a sanitary dump station is available. Open all year. Reservations required from March 15 through November.

## LOWER PINES

Lower Pines is across the river from North Pines, with several campsites near the banks of the Merced. The 60 campsites are available for both recreational vehicle users and traditional tent campers. Open approximately April through October. Pets allowed. Reservations required.

## CAMP 4

This campground is primarily for climbers and backpackers; traditional family campers would feel out of place here. Climbing headquarters for Yosemite Valley, Camp 4 attracts mountaineers from all over the world. It's located near Yosemite Valley Lodge, across the street from shuttle bus stop 7 and the day-use parking area on Northside Drive. Parking spaces are provided outside the camping area, and users must carry their equipment and food to their sites. The 35 campsites are communal in nature (6 campers are assigned to each); the nightly fee is $6 per person. Campsites are available on a first-come, first-served basis. Be sure to arrive early because the campground fills up by midmorning practically every day of the summer. These campsites are not wheelchair accessible. Open for walk-in campers all year round; no pets are allowed.

## BACKPACKER WALK-IN

Designed for backpackers leaving for or returning from the backcountry (be prepared to show your wilderness permit), and also for bicyclists and bus passengers, this area of 25 sites has no parking. All access is by foot and there is a 1-night maximum stay. Users should check in at North Pines Campground, where a ranger will provide directions. Open from April to October in a typical year. Campers are charged $6 per person per night on a first-come, first-served basis. No pets are allowed.

## Gas

There are no longer any service stations in Yosemite Valley and gas is not available. The nearest gas to be pumped is in El Portal on Highway 140 (13 miles; 21 km), next to the El Portal Market. There are also stations at Crane Flat on Big Oak Flat Road (15 miles; 24.1 km), and in Wawona on Wawona Road (27 miles; 43.5 km). Plan ahead and be sure you have plenty in the tank before you drive into the Valley. Gas in Yosemite is expensive. A repair garage is open all year behind the Yosemite Village Store. A towing service is available 24 hours a day by calling (209) 372-1060.

## Food: Restaurants

Though the cuisine is mostly American and waits can be considerable during the summer, there are plenty of places to eat in Yosemite Valley. The following is a location-by-location listing of Valley eating establishments. Check the *Yosemite Guide* for hours of operation.

### YOSEMITE VALLEY LODGE (FORMERLY THE YOSEMITE LODGE)

**Food Court:** Open for breakfast, lunch, and dinner year-round. Quick and perfect for families. Many different choices, plus a good coffee bar. Inexpensive.

**The Mountain Room:** Offering dinner only, daily from spring to fall, and on weekends and holidays in winter. This is Yosemite's "steakhouse," with other entrées including salmon and pasta. The Mountain Room offers lots of local, organic, sustainably produced meat and produce. A view of Yosemite Falls can be seen from most tables. Reservations can be made for groups of 8 or more by calling (209) 372-1281. Open from 5 to 10 p.m., and Sunday brunch 9 a.m. to 1 p.m. Moderate to expensive.

**The Mountain Room Lounge:** Besides beer, wine, and cocktails, this facility offers a small selection of appetizers and entrées. Hours vary, but it's usually open from 4:30 to 11 p.m. weekdays, and weekends 12 to 11 p.m. Inexpensive to moderate.

### YOSEMITE VILLAGE

**Degnan's Kitchen:** Open year-round for sandwiches, coffee, snacks, salads, and picnic items. They will build a sandwich to your specifications, and you can piece together a nice lunch basket. There are also some breakfast options. There's limited outdoor seating, so plan on making yours a moveable feast. Hours may vary; in summer, expect about 7 a.m. to 6 p.m. daily. Inexpensive to moderate.

**Degnan's Loft:** Serving lunch and dinner, spring to fall. Located upstairs at the east end of the Degnan's building, the Loft offers pizza, appetizers, desserts, wine, and beer, with plenty of indoor seating. Hours may vary; in summer, expect about 12 to 9 p.m. daily. Moderate.

**The Village Grill Deck:** Fast-food breakfasts, lunches, and early dinners, spring to fall. Offerings include burgers, veggie options, sandwiches, shakes, and fries, with a morning menu, too. Located next to the Village Store with outdoor seating only. Inexpensive.

### HALF DOME VILLAGE (FORMERLY CURRY VILLAGE)

**Half Dome Village Pavilion Restaurant:** For breakfast and dinner, spring to fall. Breakfast items include yogurt, cereal, fruit, baked goods, and hot entrées. For dinner there's a variety of hot entrées, salad, and desserts. A family favorite, offering buffet service. Inexpensive to moderate.

**Meadow Grill:** Open spring through summer, this fast-food outlet has about the same offerings as the Village Grill. Hamburgers, hot dogs, chicken sandwiches, veggie burgers, salad, and soft drinks to go for consumption on the deck outside. Open 11 a.m. to 8 p.m. daily. Inexpensive.

**Pizza and Bar:** Open daily from spring to fall, this facility offers pizza and salad from January through November and during holidays when Half Dome Village is open. From March through November, it's open from 11 a.m. to 10 p.m. daily. Tables are outdoors on the deck. Inexpensive to moderate.

**Coffee Corner:** For the caffeine deprived; here you can find fresh-ground coffees, espressos, lattes, and baked goods. Open seasonally March through November, about 6 a.m. to 10 p.m. Located within the Half Dome Village Pavilion. Inexpensive.

**Ice Cream:** Open seasonally March through November, and located inside the Half Dome Village Pavilion at the Coffee Corner. Inexpensive.

### THE MAJESTIC YOSEMITE HOTEL (FORMERLY THE AHWAHNEE)

**The Majestic Dining Room:** Breakfast, lunch, dinner, and Sunday brunch, year-round. This regal dining room is a true delight. It's a joy to behold its beamed ceilings and impressive chandeliers. Perhaps breakfast is the most enjoyable meal here; casual attire is allowed and one experiences a feeling of relaxation and elegance as daylight filters through the massive windows. Dinner is the traditional, formal meal (though the views are obscured by darkness). Men must wear collared shirts and long pants, and reservations are suggested. The meals are superb, and like the Mountain Room, The Majestic offers an impressive array of locally grown, sustainably produced foods. Call (209) 372-1489. Expensive.

**The Majestic Bar:** Light fare and appetizers are served in the bar from 11:30 a.m. to 11 p.m. daily. A coffee bar located here is open 7 to 10:30 a.m. Moderate.

## Food: Groceries

Yosemite Valley has 4 outlets for groceries and camp supplies. They are open year-round with the exception of the Housekeeping Camp store, which closes in winter. Check the *Yosemite Guide* for hours of operation, or call the indicated phone number.

### VILLAGE STORE

If you can't find it anywhere else in Yosemite Valley, come here. Of particular note are the butcher shop and the fresh produce. Located at the east end of the Village Mall at bus stop 2. Phone (209) 372-1253.

### DEGNAN'S KITCHEN

This deli, included in the restaurant listings above, also has a decent selection of foodstuffs for picnics and snacks. West of the Village Store and next to the US Post Office on the mall. Phone (209) 372-8454.

### HALF DOME VILLAGE GIFT & GROCERY

A general store with convenience items and gifts, located in the Pavilion building next to the Hamburger deck at Half Dome Village. Phone (209) 372-8391.

### HOUSEKEEPING CAMP STORE

This is a convenience store catering to campers. It's open from spring to fall only. Located at Housekeeping Camp near bus stop 12. Phone (209) 372-8333.

## Lodging

The following is a list of lodging facilities, ranging from rustic to luxurious, in Yosemite Valley. Some rates are lower in winter, but overall there is little in the way of value lodging in the Valley. Information on rates can be found at travelyosemite.com. For information on making reservations, see page 14.

### YOSEMITE VALLEY LODGE (FORMERLY YOSEMITE LODGE)

Open all year, the Lodge offers traditional rooms and a few larger family rooms. Special value-season rates (both weekend and midweek) are available in late fall and winter. Yosemite Valley Lodge is preferred to Half Dome Village in winter because of its warmer location. The lodge is situated near and offers pleasant views of Yosemite Falls and the Merced River. Besides the dining options listed above, the following are available at Yosemite Valley Lodge: gift shops, tour/activities desk, post office, free wifi, ATM, outdoor amphitheater, swimming pool, bicycle rentals, and free shuttle service to various locations in the park. Rooms have fans, not air conditioning. Moderate to expensive.

### HALF DOME VILLAGE (FORMERLY CURRY VILLAGE)

Open from spring through late fall and on holidays and some weekends in winter. Originally designed to provide an economical lodging alternative in Yosemite Valley, Half Dome Village still features the least expensive accommodations. They are of 3 types: standard motel rooms with bath, cabins with bath, and canvas tent cabins without bath (both heated and unheated). Special value-season rates (both weekend and midweek) are available in late fall and winter. All cabins without bath utilize

A tent cabin at Half Dome Village

The Majestic Yosemite Hotel

communal bathrooms. Half Dome Village is cooler in summer than other Valley locations and is known for its informality. Nearby attractions are Happy Isles, the campgrounds, and the riding stable.

Other amenities include gift shops, showers, a mountaineering shop, a climbing school, a hiking guide service, swimming pool, an outdoor amphitheater, a tour/activities desk, free shuttle service to various locations in the park, and bicycle and raft rentals, plus an ice rink in winter. Inexpensive to moderate.

### THE MAJESTIC YOSEMITE HOTEL (FORMERLY THE AHWAHNEE)

Ansel Adams called this hotel "one of the world's distinctive resort hotels." Open year-round, this grand and imposing National Historic Landmark is definitely at the luxury end of the Yosemite lodging spectrum. Besides regular rooms in the main building, The Majestic features several cottages on the grounds. Rooms and cottages all have bathrooms.

The hotel's Great Lounge is a study in high style (afternoon tea offers a relaxing respite), and the dining room (see page 102) is without parallel. Located below the Royal Arches, The Majestic offers fine views of Glacier Point and the Valley's south wall.

Other guest services available are gift shops, a cocktail lounge, concierge service, a business center, and a swimming pool for guests of the hotel only. Expensive.

### HOUSEKEEPING CAMP

The experience at Housekeeping Camp is somewhere between camping out and staying in a rustic cabin. Guests are provided a developed "campsite" that features a covered shelter, a cooking and dining area, cots, a table, and a fire ring. You must bring your own linen (or sleeping bags) and cookware. Call it luxury camping, if you prefer, which differs from staying in a Half Dome Village tent cabin because you are able to prepare your own meals. The camp is open from spring through early fall only. Housekeeping Camp is located near the public campgrounds, across from Yosemite Conservation Heritage Center, and adjacent to the Merced River.

The camp offers public showers, a store, and a laundromat. Inexpensive.

## Glacier Point

Not only does the point provide an overwhelming panorama, but it's accessible by car (for better or for worse). The commanding views of Yosemite's high country, Half Dome, the Yosemite, Vernal and Nevada Falls, and the Valley below are unequaled.

## North Dome

This promontory allows the best view there is of Half Dome and Tenaya Canyon. Located on the north rim, it can be reached only by foot, either from Yosemite Valley (via the Yosemite Falls or Snow Creek Trails) or from Tioga Road (via the Porcupine Creek trailhead near Porcupine Flat Campground). All routes are very strenuous. See pages 95, 134.

## Eagle Peak

This lookout is actually the highest rock of the Three Brothers formation. About 3 miles (4.8 km) by trail from the top of Yosemite Falls, the peak offers impressive views of the entire Yosemite region, the Sierra foothills, and the Coast Range far beyond.

## Sentinel Dome

Lacking Glacier Point's glimpses of Yosemite Valley, this dome is almost 1,000 feet (300 m) higher. An unobscured, 360-degree vista presents itself to hikers who make the 1-mile (1.6-km) walk from Glacier Point Road. Particularly spectacular under a full moon.

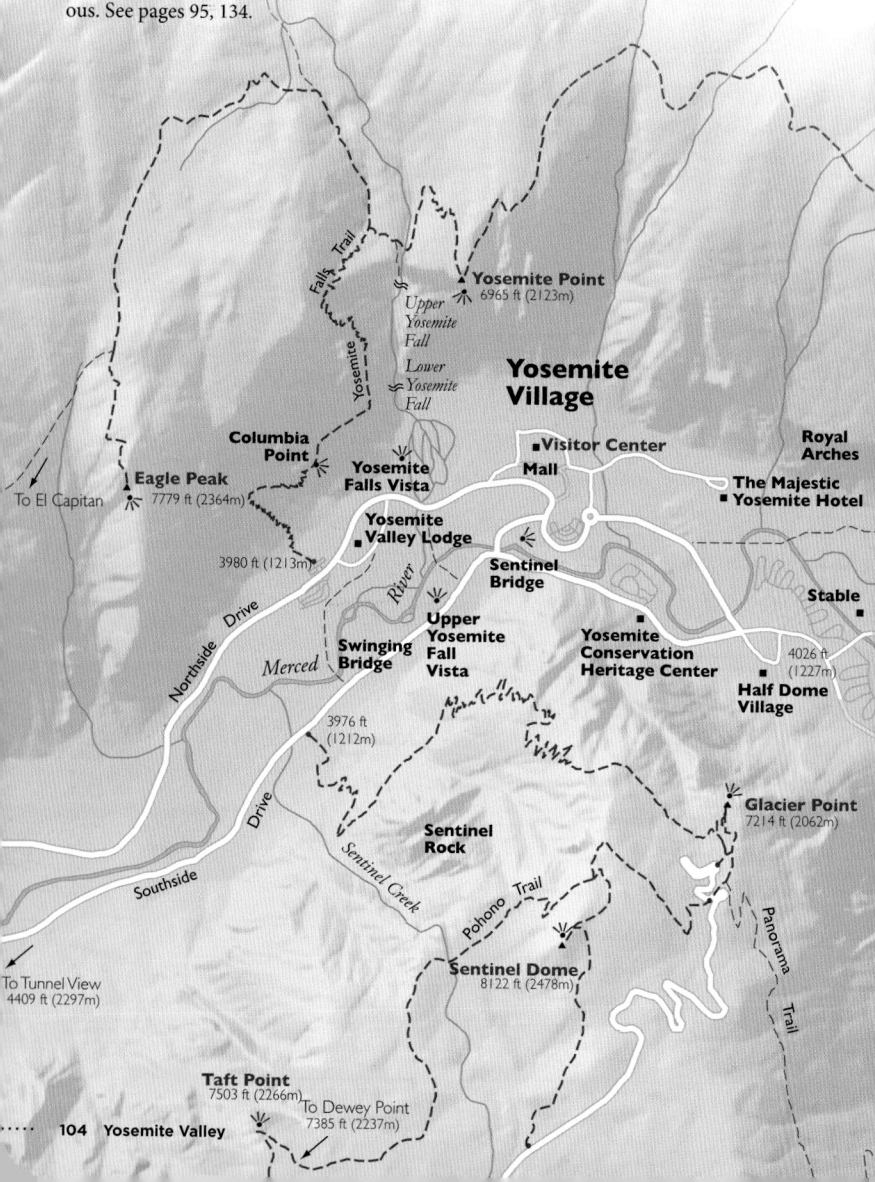

## Tunnel View

While only partway up the southwestern rim of the Valley, this viewpoint just below the Wawona Tunnel on Wawona Road is a Yosemite classic. More photos are shot at this location than anywhere else in the park, and for good reason. El Capitan, Bridalveil Fall, and Half Dome couldn't be more photogenic.

## Half Dome

The only drawback of a perch here is that the view doesn't include Half Dome! Something seems missing from the landscape when you're sitting on this enormous rock that has come to symbolize Yosemite more than any other landmark. The 8.5-mile (13.7-km) hike from Happy Isles is quite difficult, though hundreds of people a day undertake it each summer. See page 96.

## Yosemite Point

About .75 miles (1.2 km) to the east of the top of Yosemite Falls, the point is famous for its proximity to the Lost Arrow Spire, a remarkable freestanding shaft of granite. The view to the south rim is one of the best.

## Dewey Point

The series of viewpoints along the Pohono Trail on the south rim of Yosemite Valley is special. Dewey Point can be reached over the McGurk Meadow trail that heads north from the Glacier Point Road near Bridalveil Creek Campground. Both Dewey Point and Crocker Point (.5-miles or .8 km to the west) allow unusual perspectives on El Capitan and Bridalveil Fall. In winter, Dewey Point is a popular cross-country ski and snowshoe destination.

## Taft Point and the Fissures

Also on the Pohono Trail, these spots are accessed from the same trailhead on Glacier Point Road that heads to Sentinel Dome. An easy walk leads to Taft Point, with its view of the Cathedral Rocks and Spires and the north rim, and to the Fissures, which are deep clefts in the rock which drop a long way toward Yosemite Valley. Check out the echo here.

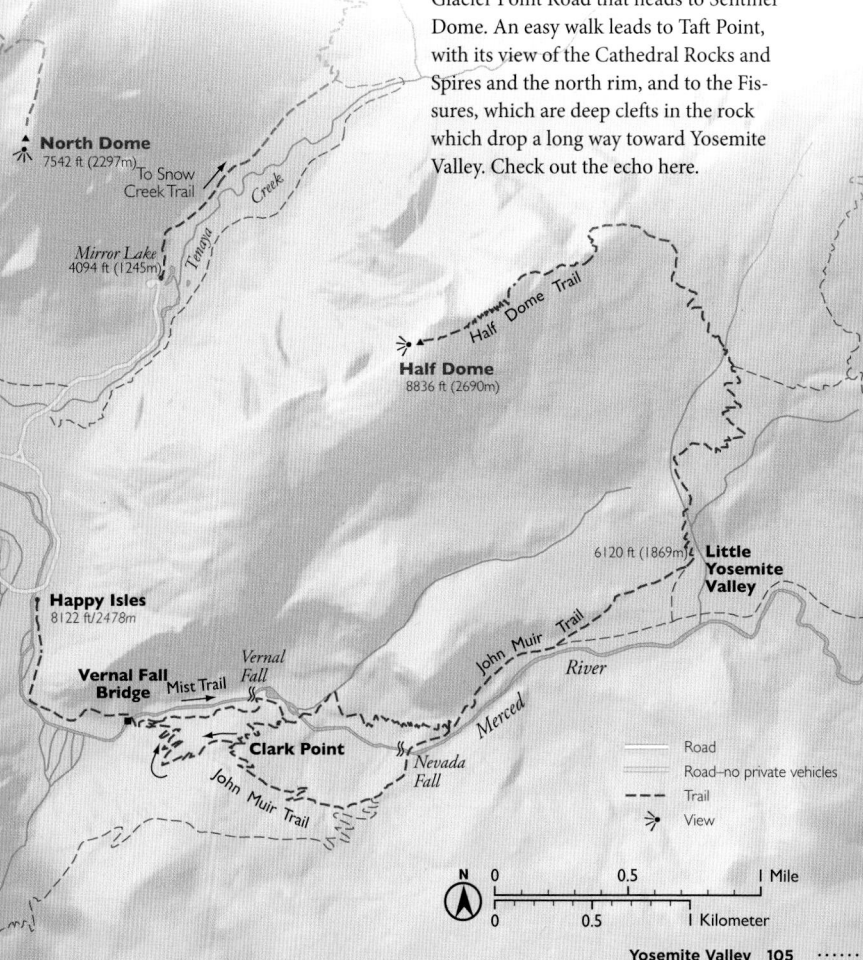

**North Dome**
7542 ft (2297m)
To Snow Creek Trail

*Tenaya Creek*

*Mirror Lake*
4094 ft (1245m)

Half Dome Trail

**Half Dome**
8836 ft (2690m)

6120 ft (1869m)  **Little Yosemite Valley**

**Happy Isles**
8122 ft/2478m

*Vernal Fall*

**Vernal Fall Bridge**  Mist Trail

John Muir Trail

*River*

**Clark Point**  *Merced*

*Nevada Fall*

John Muir Trail

Road
Road–no private vehicles
Trail
View

N   0              0.5              1 Mile
0              0.5              1 Kilometer

Mariposa Grove of Giant Sequoias

# 5 SOUTH OF YOSEMITE VALLEY

To the south of Yosemite Valley lies a part of the park that is less busy and noticeably more quiet. Known as the "Wawona District," the south end includes historic Wawona, the world-famous Mariposa Grove with its giant sequoias, and the road corridor that leads to Glacier Point. The main way to reach all of these locations is by car on Wawona Road, as only limited, seasonal shuttle bus service is available.

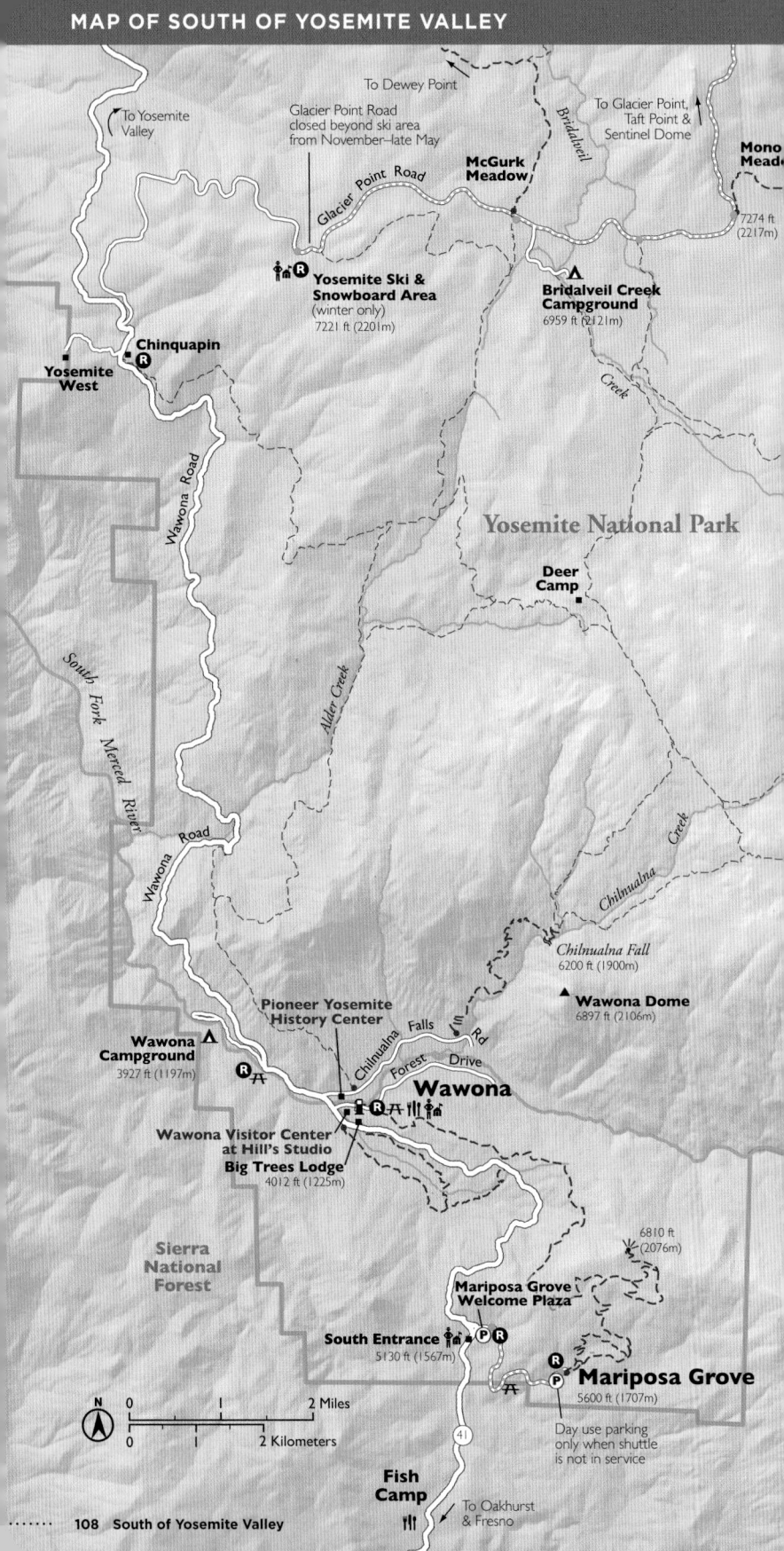

To Dewey Point

To Yosemite Valley

Glacier Point Road closed beyond ski area from November–late May

To Glacier Point, Taft Point & Sentinel Dome

Glacier Point Road

McGurk Meadow

Bridalveil

Mono Mead

7274 ft (2217m)

Yosemite Ski & Snowboard Area
(winter only)
7221 ft (2201m)

Bridalveil Creek Campground
6959 ft (2121m)

Chinquapin

Yosemite West

Creek

Wawona Road

Yosemite National Park

South Fork Merced River

Alder Creek

Deer Camp

Chilnualna Creek

Chilnualna Fall
6200 ft (1900m)

Wawona Dome
6897 ft (2106m)

Wawona Road

Pioneer Yosemite History Center

Chilnualna Falls Rd

Forest Drive

Wawona Campground
3927 ft (1197m)

Wawona

Wawona Visitor Center at Hill's Studio
Big Trees Lodge
4012 ft (1225m)

6810 ft (2076m)

Sierra National Forest

Mariposa Grove Welcome Plaza

South Entrance
5130 ft (1567m)

Mariposa Grove
5600 ft (1707m)

Day use parking only when shuttle is not in service

N

0    1    2 Miles

0    1    2 Kilometers

41

Fish Camp

To Oakhurst & Fresno

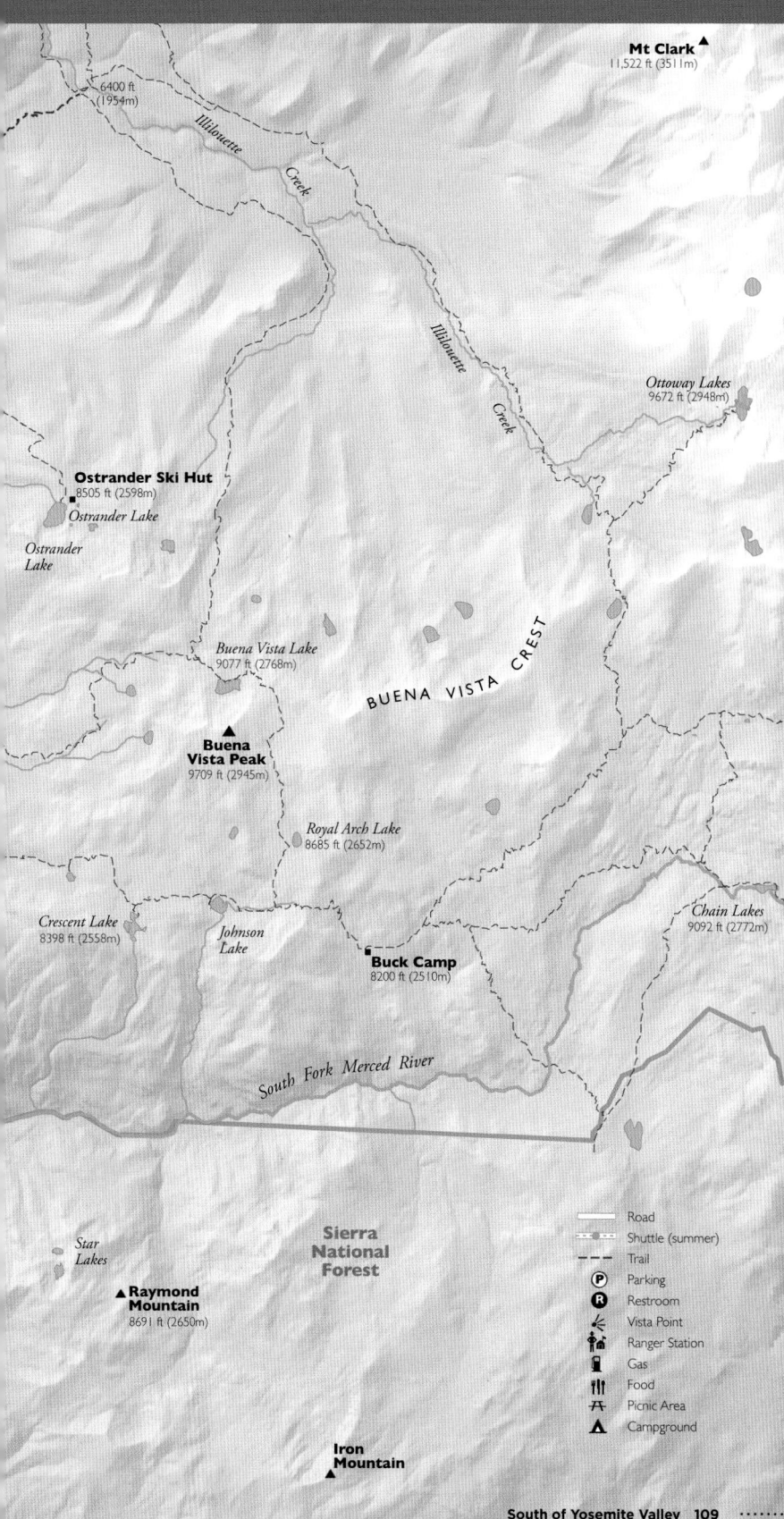

Mt Clark
11,522 ft (3511m)

6400 ft
(1954m)

Illilouette Creek

Illilouette Creek

Ottoway Lakes
9672 ft (2948m)

**Ostrander Ski Hut**
8505 ft (2598m)

*Ostrander Lake*

*Ostrander Lake*

*Buena Vista Lake*
9077 ft (2768m)

BUENA VISTA CREST

**Buena
Vista Peak**
9709 ft (2945m)

*Royal Arch Lake*
8685 ft (2652m)

*Crescent Lake*
8398 ft (2558m)

*Johnson
Lake*

**Buck Camp**
8200 ft (2510m)

*Chain Lakes*
9092 ft (2772m)

*South Fork Merced River*

*Star
Lakes*

**Sierra
National
Forest**

▲ **Raymond
Mountain**
8691 ft (2650m)

| | |
|---|---|
| ▬▬▬ | Road |
| ▭▭▭ | Shuttle (summer) |
| ▭ ▭ ▭ | Trail |
| Ⓟ | Parking |
| Ⓡ | Restroom |
| ⚞ | Vista Point |
| 👥 | Ranger Station |
| ⛽ | Gas |
| 🍴 | Food |
| ⛩ | Picnic Area |
| ▲ | Campground |

**Iron
Mountain**

### The Mariposa Grove of Giant Sequoias

No one comes away unimpressed by these towering sequoias. A world-class attraction. See page 116.

### The Walk to Wawona Point

Quiet, little visited, and offering a remarkable view, Wawona Point is the perfect destination for an excursion in the Mariposa Grove. See page 117.

### The Outdoor Barbecue at the Big Trees Lodge (formerly the Wawona Hotel)

On Saturday nights during the summer, enjoy a delicious meal on the lawn under the pine trees at this fine old hotel. Red-checked tablecloths in the wild. See page 115.

### The Slopes at Yosemite Ski & Snowboard Area (formerly Badger Pass)

Every winter, this area is transformed into a hub of skiing and snowboarding activity. Both downhill and cross-country opportunities abound. See page 22.

### The Pioneer Yosemite History Center

Explore this collection of historic structures and take the horse-drawn stage rides that depart from the History Center, making a short loop to the Big Trees Lodge. See page 110.

### The View from Glacier Point

From the railing at Glacier Point, you are lord or lady of all the Yosemite you survey. The view is unforgettable. See page 119.

### A Round at the Big Trees Lodge Golf Course

Play 9 holes at this exceptionally scenic and challenging course, or just take a walk once it has closed for the day. See page 114.

### Ostrander Ski Hut in Winter

A strenuous 9-mile ski from Yosemite Ski & Snowboard Area south of Glacier Point Road, the hut offers shelter and warmth to wilderness skiers. See page 23.

### Explore on Horseback

Take a ride on flat terrain, following the path that early Yosemite Euro-American pioneers took. See page 115.

The Bachelor and Three Graces

**Wawona is a** historic community nestled on a beautiful meadow adjacent to the South Fork Merced River about 27 miles south of Yosemite Valley. The area was settled very early in the park's history and became a stopover point on the stage route to the park. Galen Clark, a significant figure in Yosemite's past (see page 50), built Clark's Station there, and that cabin later grew to become the Big Trees Lodge (formerly the Wawona Hotel) we know today.

To the east of the main road on both sides of the river, a large number of private cabins and homes have been developed. This area, known as Section 35, was held privately for many years before it became part of Yosemite National Park. Known as an "inholding," much of the tract is still privately owned, although the National Park Service has purchased several homes and lots. Many of the residences are available as summer rentals (see the "Lodging" section on page 123).

For those seeking information, directions, or help, there is a visitor center in Wawona. To find it, turn off Wawona Road into the Big Trees Lodge grounds. The center is located within the Hill's Studio building, to the left of the fountain as you face the main hotel. If there's no parking available, park near the store (just past the gas station) and follow signs up the hill to Hill's Studio. The phone number at the Wawona Visitor Center is (209) 375-9531.

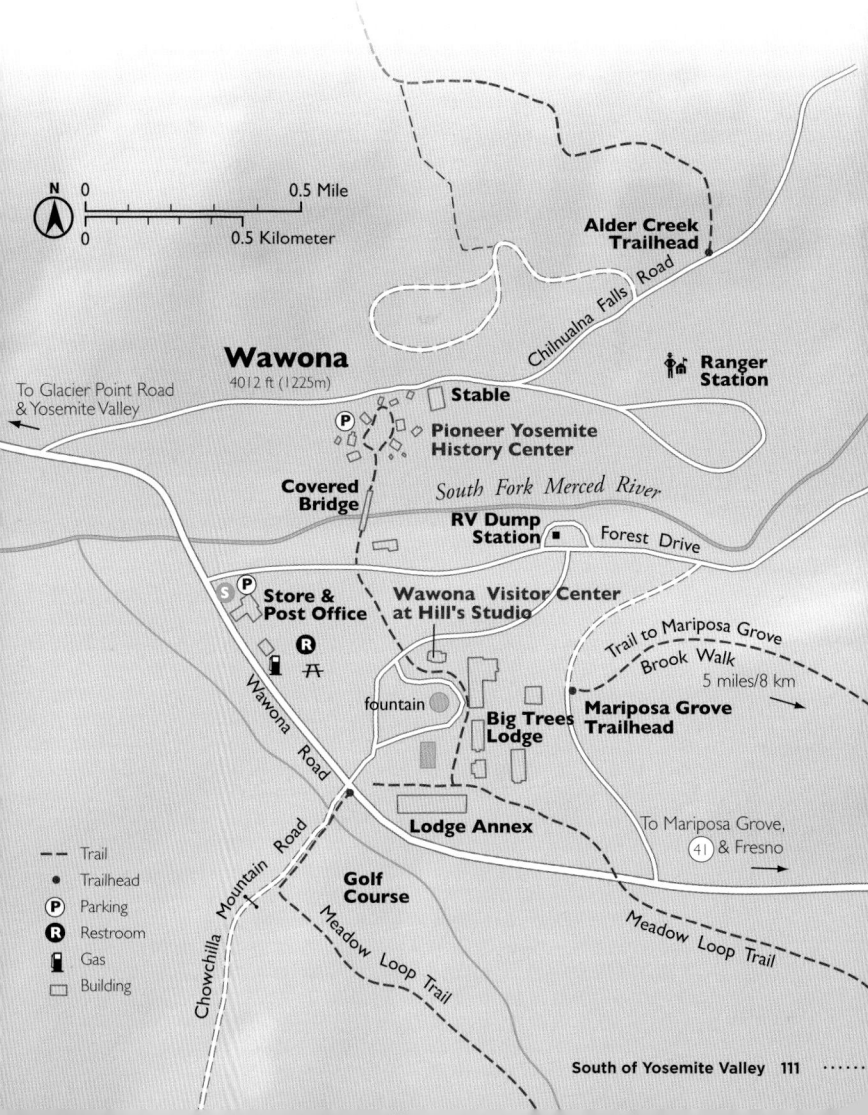

## The Wawona Shuttle Bus

During the summer, a free shuttle bus with a limited schedule may transport overnight guests of the Big Trees Lodge and the campground to the Mariposa Grove of Giant Sequoias. Check with the lodging sites for more information.

## Wawona History

Though probably not deliberately, when Yosemite pioneer Galen Clark (see page 50) settled on 160 acres in Wawona in 1856, he selected a spot almost exactly halfway between Mariposa and Yosemite on the developing route for visitors. Clark seized the opportunity and built a rustic lodging house for travelers that was known as Clark's Station.

Though Galen Clark recognized the potential of his way station, he proved unable to fulfill it. His management of Clark's Station was poor, and he invested considerable funds in completing the Mariposa stage road to Wawona. Financial pressure forced Clark to take on Edwin Moore as a full partner in 1869, and all signs indicated that Clark's fortunes had turned.

But over the next 5 years, ill-advised investments in mining ventures and land purchases along with the completion of the Coulterville and Big Oak Flat Roads into Yosemite Valley spelled doom for Clark and Moore. They were forced to sell their lodging house and related properties to the Washburn Brothers in December 1874.

The Washburns were an enterprising group of three brothers who had come to California from Putney, Vermont. They undertook a number of ventures in the Mariposa area before their purchase from Clark and Moore. It was their New England background that led them to cover the existing bridge over the South Fork Merced; it's the same bridge that leads into the Pioneer Yosemite History Center today.

At the same time they acquired the Wawona travelers' stop, the Washburns began work on the completion of the stage road from Wawona to Yosemite Valley. In this way they hoped to compete with the other routes. Four hundred Chinese laborers finished the job in June of 1875, and the Washburns' plan began to meet with success.

In 1876 the Washburns put up the long white structure that stands just to the right of the main hotel building today. And a year after the hotel burned in 1878, the two-story structure that is still used as the main hotel building went up. The inn was known as Big Tree Station until 1882, when it officially became the Wawona

US Cavalry at Camp A.E. Wood, 1896

The Wawona Tunnel Tree, 1929

Hotel (now Big Trees Lodge). Additional buildings went up over the years.

Congress established Yosemite National Park in 1890 and directed that the US Army should be responsible for managing it. Because Yosemite Valley and the Mariposa Grove of Big Trees had already been granted to the State of California and were not part of the national park, locating park headquarters became a challenge. Because Wawona was one of the few developed areas within the new park (though not part of it), among other reasons, it was selected as the summer command for army personnel.

Known as Camp A. E. Wood, headquarters were located on the site of the present Wawona Campground. For 16 summers, cavalry troops from the San Francisco Presidio occupied the camp and engaged in caring for the new park. Among their many activities were exploring and mapping, trail building, stocking fish, and enforcing antihunting and trespassing regulations. When the state grant and Yosemite National Park were combined in

1906, Camp A. E. Wood was abandoned and army headquarters were relocated to Yosemite Valley.

Over the years, changes to Wawona generally came with changes in transportation. Following the completion of the Wawona Stage Road, the Washburns' stage company flourished and visitation grew. In 1914 automobiles first navigated the road between Wawona and Yosemite Valley. The hotel management recognized that automobile travelers would want more recreational opportunities, and they proceeded to build a dance floor, soda fountain, croquet court, swimming tank, and golf course over the next 15 years.

As the hotel prospered, so did the community in Section 35 (the number assigned to the plot of land in its legal description), which included several homesteads and which housed workers for the hotel and for other support services. When most of the Wawona region was added to Yosemite National Park in 1932, only Section 35 remained in private ownership. It is in this area of Wawona that many private homes, cabins, and visitor rentals are located today (see page 123).

The top of Chilnualna Fall

## Step Back in Time

The Pioneer Yosemite History Center is a collection of historic buildings that have been moved from other locations within the park. The center is located near the Big Trees Lodge, just east of the gas station (prominent signs will direct you there). Each building represents a different time period in Yosemite's history. At times during the summer, park rangers and volunteers engage in "living history," which means that they dress in period costume and portray actual Yosemite residents from bygone days. You can try, but you'll have a hard time getting these old-timers to break character.

The Wawona stage coach

Interesting attractions are an exhibit of old horse-drawn vehicles, the covered bridge over the South Fork built in the 1870s that has been restored, and a blacksmith who actually practices his craft while you watch.

For a small fee, you can take a short ride on a horse-drawn stage to get a feel for what early trips to Yosemite must have been like. During parts of the year, regular ranger-led tours of the History Center may be scheduled (consult the *Yosemite Guide* for details).

### Hit the Links

A conspicuous adjunct to the Big Trees Lodge is the beautifully laid-out golf course nearby. Whether you're a golfer or not, a stroll around the 9-hole circuit is both relaxing and replete with scenic vistas. (If you're a nongolfer, take your walk after the course is closed, please!)

The golf course was built in 1917 and features some of the most magnificent golfing holes anywhere. While the layout is not particularly long, it features lots of rough and water hazards and is remarkably challenging. Watch out for deer grazing the fairways, particularly on the first hole. Golf clubs and carts are available for rent, and reserving a tee time is recommended; phone (209) 375-6572.

### Enjoy an Outdoor Barbecue

Every Saturday night during the summer and select holiday dates, an old-fashioned barbecue is served outdoors on the expansive lawn of the Big Trees Lodge. Red-checked tablecloths sport steaks, hamburgers, corn on the cob, western beans, and more. Check at the hotel desk for times and prices.

### Get in the Swim

The South Fork Merced River as it runs through Wawona is dotted with swimming holes and beaches. All swimmers should follow basic safety guidelines. Or try your hand at fishing. (See page 91 for general fishing information and regulations.) Guests at the Big Trees Lodge may use the small swimming pool on the grounds.

### Horse Around a Little

Guided horseback and mule rides are offered by Yosemite Hospitality at the Big Trees Stable in summer. No riding experience necessary, though children must be at least 7 years old and 44" tall. The stable is behind the Pioneer Yosemite History Center on Chilnualna Falls Road. Stop by for details, or call (209) 375-6502.

### Hike Some More

A variety of hiking awaits you at Wawona, from easy and flat to steep and strenuous. Be sure to check park hiking guidelines before you take off (see page 97). Give yourself plenty of time and don't undertake more than you're capable of.

### Range with a Ranger

From spring through fall, a program of ranger naturalist activities is presented free of charge to the public in the Wawona area. Check the *Yosemite Guide* for listings and times.

### Tour an Artist's Studio

The Thomas Hill Studio on the grounds of the Big Trees Lodge is open in summer as a visitor center and features a terrific exhibit on the work of Hill along with other art programs. Thomas Hill used the building as a summer studio from 1885 until his death in 1908, and his fine landscape paintings of Yosemite and elsewhere are critically acclaimed.

Getting ready for a ride at the Big Trees Stable

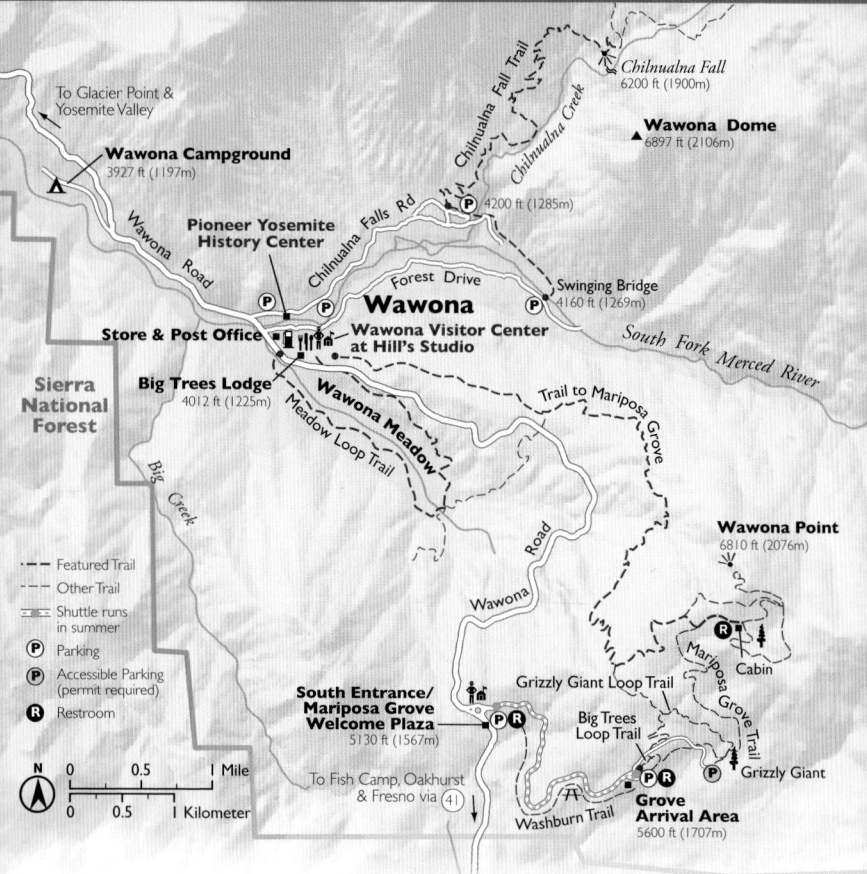

## The Meadow Loop

This pleasant walk begins directly across Wawona Road from the entry road to the Big Trees Lodge. Follow the gravel road about 50 yards (46 m) across the golf course just into the trees and take the road that leads off to the left. This almost entirely flat route skirts the edge of the Wawona Meadow and then circles back, crosses Wawona Road, and finishes up behind the Big Trees Lodge. Approximately 3 miles (4.8 km) total, the loop should take an hour and a half or less. The hike is easy, leisurely, picturesque, and dogs are welcome.

## Chilnualna Fall

The trail to this delightful cascade is fairly strenuous, gaining almost 2,500 feet (762 m) in approximately 4 miles (6.4 km). Start from the trailhead, which is located 1.7 miles (2.7 km) east of the main road on Chilnaulna Falls Road. There's parking space on the right for 25 to 30 cars. If the road turns to dirt, you've gone too far. The route is an enjoyable one through manzanita, deer brush, and bear clover,

and finally meets with Chilnualna Creek. The fall, instead of leaping and free-falling from some precipice, drops through a narrow chasm in a furious rush. Allow 6 to 8 hours for this 8-mile (12.9-km) round-trip. Start early in the morning, when temperatures are cooler, and carry lots of water in the summer, when the weather can be extreme.

## Mariposa Grove of Giant Sequoias

Starting behind the Big Trees Lodge is a long, uphill climb to the Mariposa Grove. Passing through forest most of the way, the trail offers excellent views of the Wawona Basin and Wawona Dome as it nears the big trees. The trail ends at the Mariposa Grove Cabin near the fallen Wawona Tunnel Tree. Because the elevation gain is 2,000 feet (610 m) in 5 miles (8 km), this hike is for the well-conditioned only. For an easier alternative, take the summer shuttle bus, if it's running to the Mariposa Grove and hike back to Wawona. Figure on spending 8 to 10 hours making the up-and-back trip of 13 miles (21 km).

**Located at the** southernmost end of Yosemite, the Mariposa Grove is the largest stand of giant sequoias (*Sequoiadendron giganteum*) in the park. These ancient monarchs are inadequately described with numbers, but how else do you do it? Sequoias can be 3,000 years old, reach almost 300 feet (91 m) into the sky, and measure more than 50 feet (15 m) around. A typical mature sequoia weighs in at over 2 million pounds (90,00 kg).

Among the many notable trees here are the Grizzly Giant, about 2 millennia old and 97 feet (30 m) around at its base, and the fallen Wawona Tunnel Tree, in which a hole was cut in 1881 that allowed thousands of automobiles and other vehicles to pass through and be photographed before the 2,100-year-old tree toppled in 1969. There are more than 500 mature sequoias here.

From about May 15 to October 15, from 8 a.m. to 8 p.m., a free shuttle bus transports visitors from the Mariposa Grove Welcome Plaza (a parking area next to the South Entrance Station) to the grove, a distance of 2 miles (3.2 km), where hiking trails lead out among the trees. Off-season shuttle service may operate in spring and fall from 9 a.m. to 5 p.m.; check availability at the Welcome Plaza and pick up a copy of *Ancient Sentinels: The Sequoias of Yosemite National Park* for insights and a self-guided tour. The road to the Mariposa Grove is often closed in winter when the snow is deep.

Visitors with valid accessibility placards may drive from the Welcome Plaza to the Grove Arrival Area and on to the Grizzly Giant. Small day-use parking areas are located in these two locations, and provide access to trails that meet standards for people with limited mobility, including a trail to the California Tunnel Tree. When the shuttle is not running and the road is open, anyone may drive to the Grove Arrival Area and park in the day-use lot.

For hikers, there are well-marked trails ranging from moderate to strenuous that meander through the incredible trees. Be sure to follow well-established trails and leave no trace of your hike. The Mariposa Grove Trail ends at Wawona Point,

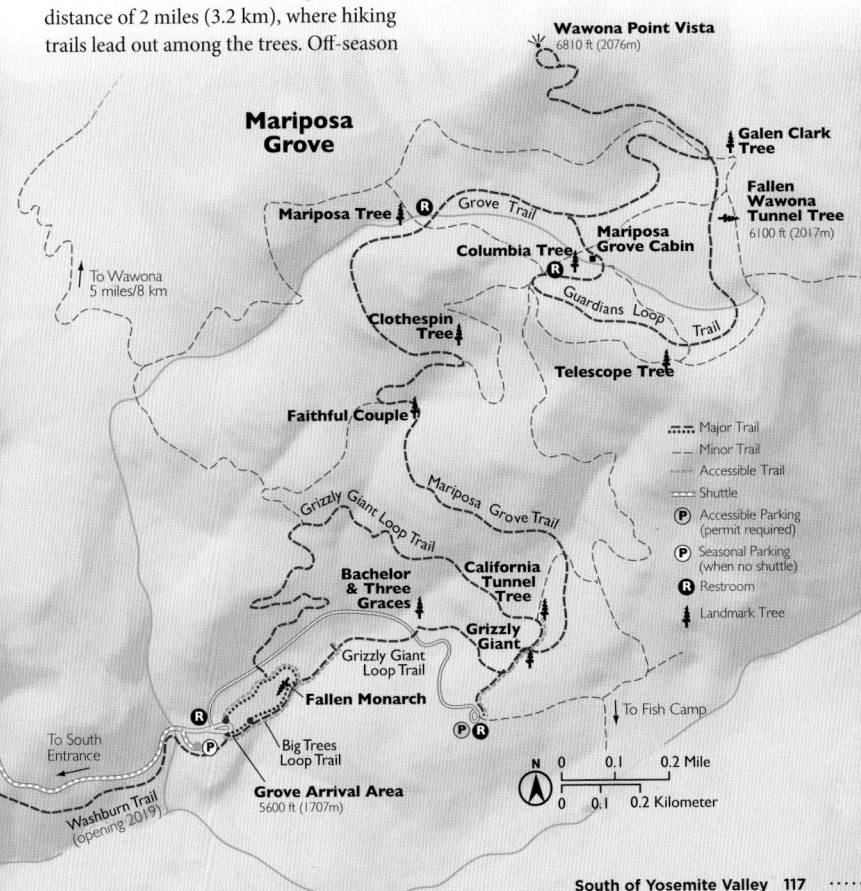

elevation 6,800 feet (2,073 m). While there are restrooms dotted along the main trails, there are no restrooms nor water at Wawona Point; plan accordingly.

Visiting the Mariposa Grove in winter is a remarkably peaceful experience available to well-prepared cross-country skiers and snowshoe hikers. Park at the Welcome Plaza (which has the only restroom near the grove open in winter), hike in to the grove Arrival Area, and look for trails marked for winter travel.

## Stroll to the Grove

Beginning in 2019, visitors may walk the 2 miles (3.2 km) from the grove Welcome Plaza to the Arrival Area along the Washburn Trail, a rustic route that follows a remnant of the historic Washburn Road.

## Walk in the Sequoia Forest

All trails into the Mariposa Grove of Giant Sequoias are uphill, except for the Big Trees Loop and the accessible trail from the small day-use parking area close to the Grizzly Giant. From the trailhead at the far end of the Grove Arrival Area, there is an elevation gain of about 1,000 feet (305 m) to where the fallen Wawona Tunnel Tree is located, a distance of about 3 miles (4.8 km). The going is gradual, however (22 children from Mrs. McDaniel's second-grade class made it up and back!), and walking is the best way to appreciate the majesty and serenity of these stately trees. Be sure to check park hiking guidelines before you take off (see page 97).

## Easier Hikes in the Mariposa Grove

### BIG TREES LOOP TRAIL

This short (.3 miles or .5 km), relatively flat, accessible trail passes the Fallen Monarch and features interpretive signs with information about giant sequoias. Allow 30 minutes for the loop.

### THE GRIZZLY GIANT

From the Grove Arrival Area it's only .7 mile (1 km) and a 400-foot (122-m) climb to the Grizzly Giant, one of the largest and oldest trees in the Mariposa Grove. Along the way you'll encounter lots of other sequoias and get a personal perspective on the mammoth scale of these trees. Allow from 1 to 2 hours for the round trip. The Grizzly Giant is just .13 miles (.2 km) from the small day-use parking area for visitors with accessibility placards.

### GRIZZLY GIANT LOOP TRAIL

Instead of turning around at the Grizzly Giant, extend your amble another 1.2 miles (1.9 km) past the California Tunnel Tree and loop back on the Big Trees Loop Trail. The total Grizzly Giant Loop Trail should take about 2 to 3 hours.

Q: If I lose my way while out and about in Yosemite, can I text to 911 for help?

A: As of this writing, there is no text-to-911 service in Yosemite, and in many places there is no text or cell service at all. If you have a cell signal, try a voice call to 911. If that doesn't work, try calling or texting a friend who can then contact rangers in Yosemite with your location. Use a map or location app to provide your coordinates, or, better yet, carry a map and compass and the knowledge of how to use them.

The Grizzly Giant

**The road to Glacier Point** leaves Wawona Road at Chinquapin junction, 9 miles (14.5 km) south of Yosemite Valley and 12 miles (19.3 km) north of Wawona. The route winds 16 miles (25.7 km) to Glacier Point, passing a variety of attractions, most of them short hikes from the road. From mid-May to September, you may be required to use a free shuttle from the Yosemite Ski & Snowboard Area to Glacier Point between 10 a.m. to 4:30 p.m. when the Glacier Point parking lot fills. The shuttle leaves every 20 minutes though wait times may be longer. If the shuttle operation is too full, the road may be closed to vehicle traffic. In winter the road is plowed only as far as the Yosemite Ski & Snowboard Area, 6 miles (9.7 km) from Chinquapin. Be sure to carry tire chains in your car if you're heading out Glacier Point Road during the off-season.

## Stare at the Stars

During the summer, ranger naturalists maintain a large telescope at Glacier Point and schedule regular evening programs that make use of it. There aren't many better spots for gazing at the heavens, plus you'll have the help of knowledgeable astronomers. Tickets are available at any tour and activity desk. Check the *Yosemite Guide* for other ranger-led programs at Glacier Point and Bridalveil Creek Campground.

## Hikes, Hikes, and More Hikes

Given its proximity to the south rim of Yosemite Valley, Glacier Point Road provides a series of natural trailheads for spectacular day hikes. And thanks to Yosemite Hospitality, you have the option of walking all the way down to Yosemite Valley without needing to go back and retrieve your car. During the summer, the concessioner operates a tour bus from the Valley to Glacier Point. The tours usually run 3 times a day, depending on road and weather conditions. For more information go to travelyosemite.com or call (888) 540-5794.

## Strap on Some Skis or a Board

Yosemite Ski & Snowboard Area, 6 miles (9.7 km) from Chinquapin out Glacier Point Road, is the center of Yosemite ski activity during the winter. Not only are there ski lifts, ski and snowboard rentals, and a lodge, but cross-country skiers are also encouraged to utilize the groomed tracks out Glacier Point Road (see page 22).

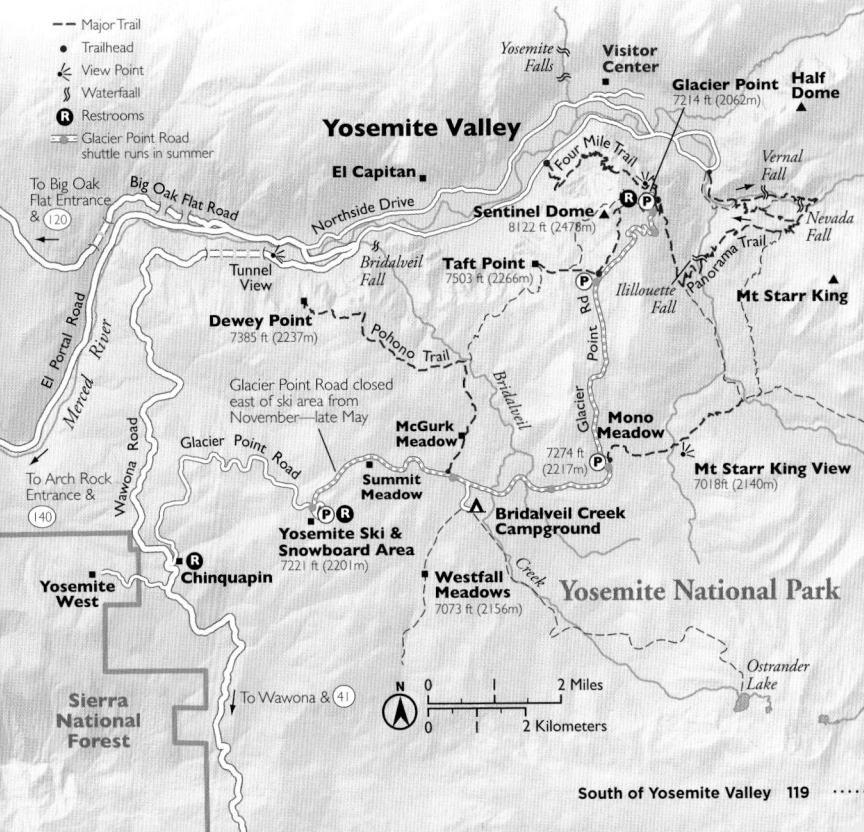

The view from Sentinel Dome

## Dewey Point

This commanding viewpoint (7,385 feet; 2,251 m) offers one of the most interesting perspectives on Bridalveil Fall and El Capitan. The trail starts .2 miles (.3 km) west of (before you get to) Bridalveil Creek Campground on Glacier Point Road (look for the sign at McGurk Meadow). There are trail markers on both sides of the road: you will want to head north. The route meanders through forest and meadows, intersects with the Pohono Trail (go left), then extends to the Valley rim. Here the rock abruptly falls away, leaving you on the edge of Yosemite Valley. Be careful! While there's not much elevation gain or loss, the round-trip is approximately 7 miles (11.2 km). Allow 4 to 6 hours for the out-and-back hike.

## Mono Meadow and Mount Starr King View

From the parking area 2.5 miles (4.0 km) beyond Bridalveil Creek Campground on Glacier Point Road, this trail leads to the east and to a terrific spot for admiring Mount Starr King, Half Dome, and Clouds Rest. You will drop steeply for .5 miles (.8 km) to Mono Meadow, then continue a mile (1.6 km) farther to an unmarked clearing and the view, which you can't miss. Stop short of the switchbacks down to Illilouette Creek. The 3-mile (4.8-km) round-trip (a little strenuous on the way back) should take about 3 hours.

## Taft Point

Unusual rock formations and an overhanging lookout point reward hikers on this short route. Start at the parking lot on Glacier Point Road about 6 miles (9.7 km) past Bridalveil Creek Campground (it's on the left, when you first catch a glimpse of Sentinel Dome). The trail is mostly flat and slightly downhill to the Fissures (wide gaps in the rock hundreds of feet deep) and Taft Point, where you'll be standing on the only solid object between you and the Valley floor below you. Take care not to fall! Be thorough in your investigation of the point, which offers up several unique views. It's just over 2 miles (3.2 km) round-trip; give yourself 2 hours.

## Sentinel Dome

The trailheads for this hike and the one to Taft Point are the same. Park on the left about 6 miles (9.7 km) past Bridalveil Creek Campground on Glacier Point Road (about where you first eye Sentinel Dome). The 1.1-mile (1.8-km) hike to the top is a small price to pay for the 360-degree panorama of Yosemite's unbelievable landscape. You'll be at 8,122 feet or 2,476 m (more than 4,000 feet or 1,200 meters above the Yosemite Valley floor); it's a good idea to have a park map for landmark identification. Try this easy hike at sunrise or sunset or on the night of a full moon (if you do, bring a good flashlight or headlamp). The round-trip requires about 2 hours.

## Yosemite Valley

Take the tour bus operated by the park concessioner (see page 119) or have someone shuttle you to Glacier Point and then walk back down to Yosemite Valley over the Four-Mile Trail (4.8 miles; 7.7 km) or via the Panorama Trail by way of Nevada and Vernal falls (8.5 miles; 13.7 km). The Four-Mile Trail begins to the left of Glacier Point and follows a series of switchbacks down the face of the south Valley wall. It terminates about a mile (1.6 km) west of Yosemite Village on Southside Drive. The Panorama Trail begins to the right (north) of the amphitheater, which is next to the concession building facing the view of Half Dome, then drops down and heads south to the top of Illilouette Fall, then back north and east to Nevada Fall. There are two routes to the Valley, either the John Muir Trail or the Mist Trail (see page 95) and trail's end at Happy Isles (bus stop 16). Figure on 3 to 4 hours to hike the Four-Mile Trail and allow 6 to 8 hours to travel the Panorama Cliffs route.

**The campgrounds** in this part of the park tend to be less busy and crowded than those in the Valley, though in summer they are full every night. Advance reservations are required for the Wawona Campground between May and September, but Bridalveil Creek Campground is operated on a first-come, first-served basis when it is open between July and September. In campgrounds where no reservations are allowed, visitors will do well to arrive as early as possible to arrange for a camping spot, because check-out time is noon.

Camping regulations are roughly the same as those for Yosemite Valley (see page 99). Pets are allowed in designated sites in both the Wawona and Bridalveil Creek campgrounds, and there are no showers in any park campground. The camping limit is 30 days per calendar year south of Yosemite Valley, but there is a 14-day limit at Bridalveil Creek Campground, and a 7-day limit at Wawona Campground, during summer.

## Wawona Campground

This popular spot is located at the 4,000-foot (1,200-m) elevation on the banks of the South Fork Merced River, approximately 25 miles (40 km) south of Yosemite Valley on Wawona Road. The daily fee for the 93 camping sites here is $26, and the campground is open all year (prepare for extreme cold and snow in the winter, however).

## Bridalveil Creek Campground

You'll find this group of 110 campsites 9 miles (14.5 km) out Glacier Point Road from Chinquapin (about 25 miles or 40 km from Yosemite Valley). Open from July through early September, the campground is much cooler than Yosemite Valley or Wawona, given its location at over 7,000 feet (2,100 m). The nightly fee is $18, first come, first served.

## Group & Horse Campgrounds

Sections of the Wawona and Bridalveil Creek campgrounds have been set aside for use by organized groups only at a rate of $50 per site per night. Reservations for group campsites are required all year, and can be made at Recreation.gov or by calling (877) 444-6777. Groups of between 13 and 30 people are allowed in each campsite, where only tent camping is allowed. Pets are not permitted in group sites. There are also horse camps at both the Wawona and Bridalveil Creek campgrounds. You must have a horse with you to use the horse campsites, no exceptions. Call (877) 444-6777 for information.

Kids love camping!

## Gas

The only gas station in this part of the park is located in Wawona, just north of the Big Trees Lodge on the main highway. The self-serve facility accepts major credit cards, is open year-round, and tire chains are available for purchase.

For towing services, call (209) 372-1060 at any time of the day or night.

## Food: Restaurants

For anything other than snacks and simple sandwiches, there's only one choice in the south end of the park—the Big Trees Lodge Dining Room. Within a half-hour's drive of the South Entrance, there are a number of good restaurants along Highway 41 between Fish Camp and Oakhurst. The following places to eat are open seasonally; be sure to check the *Yosemite Guide* for dates and hours of operation.

### BIG TREES LODGE DINING ROOM

Serving breakfast, lunch, and dinner from spring through fall and on holidays in the fall and winter. Located in the Victorian main building at the hotel, the dining room has retained a historic feel. The sepia-toned photographs by Carleton Watkins and the sequoia-cone light fixtures are perfect touches in this charming, multiwindowed facility. The food is fine, the wine list good, and there's a full bar. In summer there are a few tables on the porch for outdoor dining, and they also serve in the bar area. There's cocktail service on the verandas and in the lobby lounge. On Saturdays in summer try the outdoor barbeque on the hotel lawn. Reservations are advised for groups of 10 or more; call (209) 375-1425 for more information. Moderate to expensive.

### BIG TREES LODGE GOLF SHOP SNACK STAND

Open spring through fall inside the golf shop at the Big Trees Lodge. Cold drinks, hot dogs, prepackaged sandwiches, and other simple items are available for those in a hurry or in need of a light meal or snack. Moderate.

Big Trees Golf Course

### YOSEMITE CONSERVANCY DEPOT

From spring through fall, prepackaged snacks, books, and gifts are available at this store at the Mariposa Grove Welcome Plaza near the South Entrance Station.

### GLACIER POINT SNACK STAND

A summer and fall operation (10 a.m. to 5 p.m.) with a limited menu, primarily providing munchies for visitors to Glacier Point. Moderate.

## Food: Groceries

Campers, vacation home renters, and park visitors have the following two choices for groceries in the park south of Yosemite Valley. Check the *Yosemite Guide* for operating hours, or call the indicated numbers.

### BIG TREES LODGE STORE

Located adjacent to the gas station just off the main highway and north of the Big Trees Lodge.

### THE PINE TREE MARKET

You'll find this store in the heart of the community of North Wawona. It's less than a mile east of the main highway on Chilnualna Falls Road. Phone (209) 375-6343.

## Lodging

Wawona is the only area in the park where the majority of lodgings are not operated by Yosemite Hospitality, the park's main concessioner. The Big Trees Lodge is part of the Yosemite Hospitality system, and to reserve a room there, you should follow the steps which are detailed on page 14. You must contact each of the other lodging providers directly to reserve from them.

### BIG TREES LODGE (FORMERLY THE WAWONA HOTEL)

Open from spring through fall and on weekends and holidays through Christmas. This is the oldest resort hotel in California; the structure to the right of the main hotel building was built in 1879. The whitewashing, wide porches, well-kept grounds, and an old-fashioned bathing tank (we call them swimming pools now) all suggest another era in Yosemite's history. It's a remarkably peaceful and relaxing setting, but guests should keep in mind that some of the rooms are 100 years old. Rooms with a private bath rent for a bit more than those that share a community bathroom.

Big Trees Lodge

Besides the dining room, the hotel incorporates a golf course with pro shop and snack bar, tennis courts, and a cocktail lounge. Be sure to listen for beloved piano man Tom Bopp, who performs on select evenings during the year in the lobby.

### THE REDWOODS

Open year-round. This is a collection of about 130 privately owned vacation homes and cabins available for rental on a daily or weekly basis. Located in the privately held section of Wawona near the South Fork Merced (approximately 1 mile or 1.6 km out Chilnualna Falls Road), the rentals vary in size from 1 to 6 bedrooms and all have kitchens and fireplaces. Rates vary with the seasons and there may be a minimum night stay depending on the season. For information or to book go to redwoodsinyosemite.com or call (877) 753-8566.

### YOSEMITE'S SCENIC WONDERS VACATION RENTALS

Open year-round. Located in Yosemite West, just beyond the park boundary, but accessible only via park roads, these rental units are situated about halfway between Yosemite Valley and Wawona. Their proximity (8 miles; 12.9 km) to the Yosemite Ski & Snowboard Area has made the condos a favorite of winter visitors. But cool summer temperatures and the short drive to Yosemite Valley (about half an hour) make Yosemite West popular at other times of year as well. At 6,000 feet (1,800 m) above sea level, this area has snow into the sunny days of late spring, and you can have a snowball fight in a T-shirt. Rates vary depending on unit size and the season. Visit scenicwonders.com and yosemitewest.com for information on rentals managed by this company, or call (888) 967-3648 for more information. Moderate to expensive.

### YOSEMITE WEST RESERVATIONS

Open year-round. This company handles the rental of a collection of studios, apartments, townhouses, duplexes, individual cottages, vacation homes, and mountain homes in the Yosemite West development. These are located just west of the park, less than 1 mile (1.6 km) south of Chinquapin off the Wawona Road (15 miles or 24.1 km from Yosemite Valley and 8 miles or 12.9 km from Yosemite Ski & Snowboard Area). Rates range quite a bit and discounts are available for longer stays. For reservations and information visit yosemitewestreservations.com or call (559) 642-2211 for assistance. Moderate to expensive.

An autumn sunset in Tuolumne Meadows

# 6 NORTH OF YOSEMITE VALLEY

**More than two-thirds of** Yosemite National Park lies north of Yosemite Valley, much of that region being wilderness. The area is made accessible primarily by Tioga Road, the only trans-Sierra road crossing between Walker Pass, in Kern County, and Sonora Pass to the north. Spectacular high-country terrain, brilliant blue lakes, and astounding granite peaks are reached via this route that leads through Tuolumne Meadows, the largest subalpine meadows in the Sierra Nevada. The road crests the range at 9,945-foot (3,031-m) Tioga Pass.

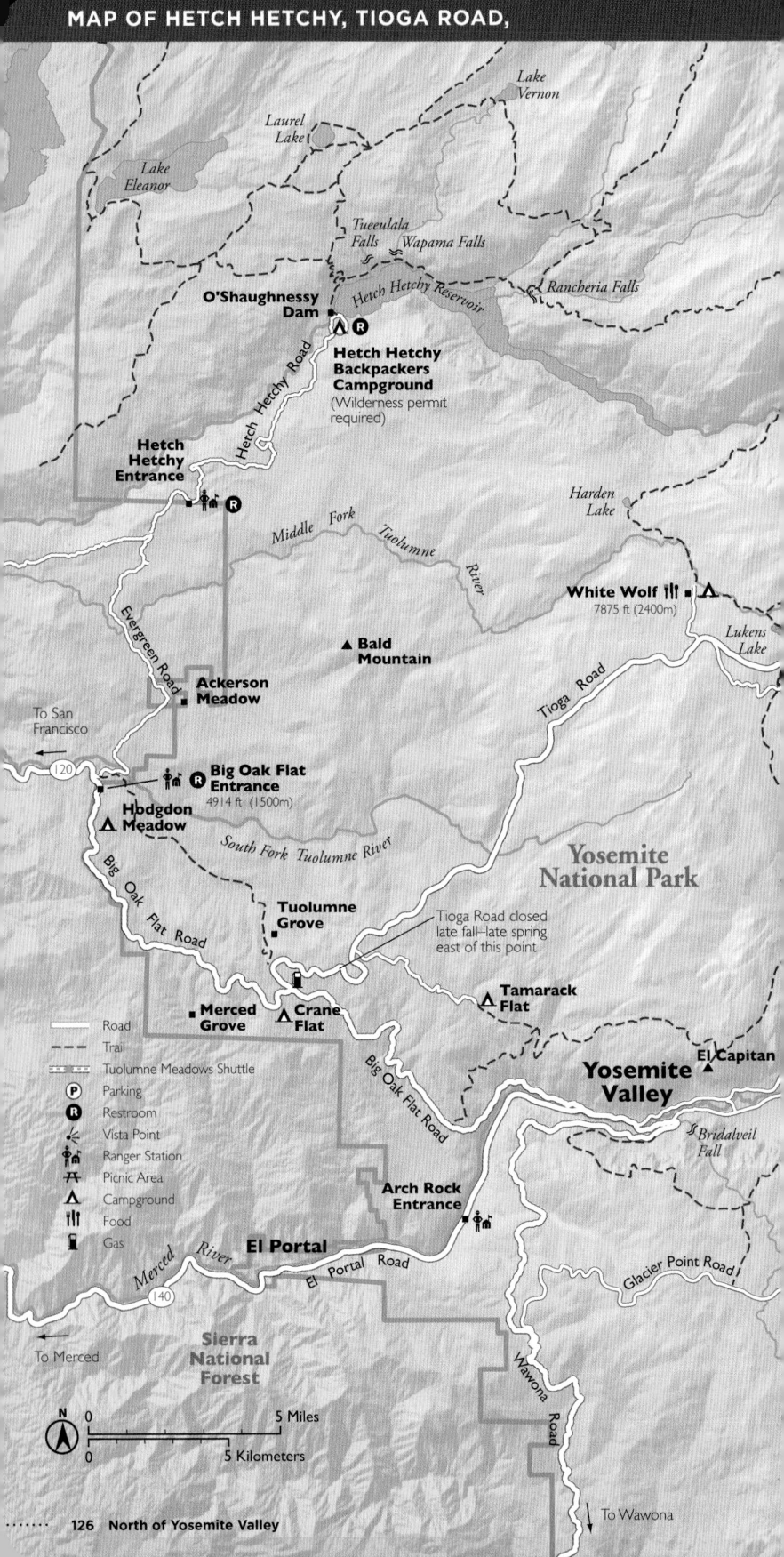

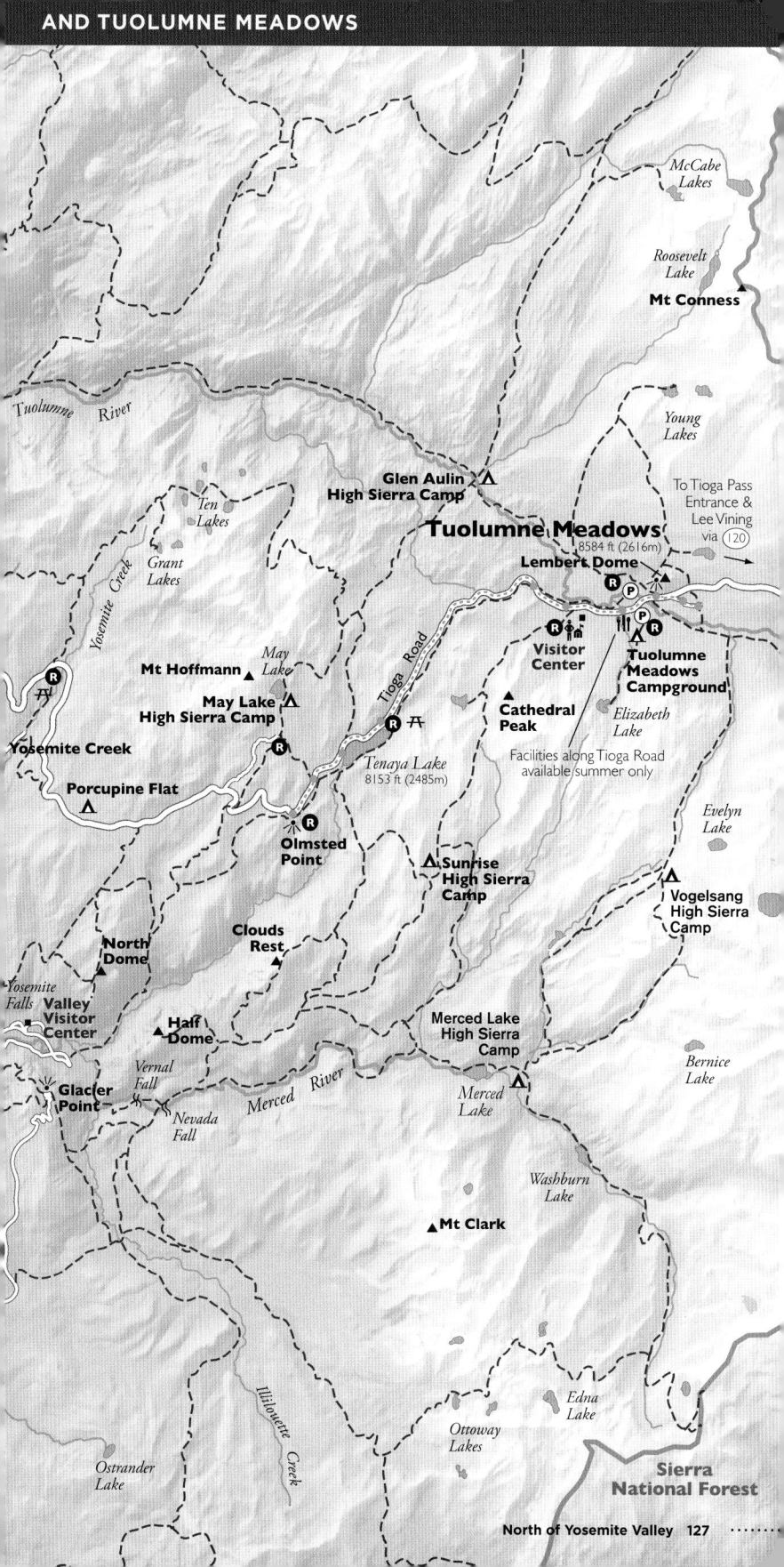

*McCabe Lakes*

*Roosevelt Lake*

**Mt Conness**

*Tuolumne River*

*Young Lakes*

To Tioga Pass
Entrance &
Lee Vining
via (120)

*Ten Lakes*

**Glen Aulin
High Sierra Camp**

**Tuolumne Meadows**
8584 ft (2616m)

**Lembert Dome**

*Grant Lakes*

*Yosemite Creek*

*May Lake*

**Mt Hoffmann**

**Visitor
Center**

**Tuolumne
Meadows
Campground**

**May Lake
High Sierra Camp**

**Cathedral
Peak**

*Elizabeth
Lake*

**Yosemite Creek**

Facilities along Tioga Road
available summer only

**Porcupine Flat**

*Tenaya Lake*
8153 ft (2485m)

*Evelyn
Lake*

*Tioga Road*

**Olmsted
Point**

**Sunrise
High Sierra
Camp**

**Vogelsang
High Sierra
Camp**

**North
Dome**

**Clouds
Rest**

*Yosemite
Falls*

**Valley
Visitor
Center**

**Merced Lake
High Sierra
Camp**

*Bernice
Lake*

**Half
Dome**

*Vernal
Fall*

*Merced River*

*Merced
Lake*

**Glacier
Point**

*Nevada
Fall*

*Washburn
Lake*

**Mt Clark**

*Illilouette Creek*

*Edna
Lake*

*Ottoway
Lakes*

**Sierra
National Forest**

*Ostrander
Lake*

Tenaya Lake

### The Summit of Mount Hoffmann

This is the geographic center of Yosemite, with extraordinary views in every direction. See page 135.

### The Beach at Tenaya Lake

Unbelievably fine on a warm day, a terrific spot anytime. Enjoy a picnic or a swim, or simply take a nap. See page 132.

### The Turnout at Olmsted Point

To see the vast expanse of glacier-carved granite is worth the stop alone. But there's much more—and marmots, too. See page 133.

### The Hike to the Merced Grove

Easy and quiet. Plus this is Yosemite's most remote and least-visited sequoia grove. See page 130.

### A Meal on the Porch of White Wolf Lodge

Breakfast and dinner are likely times to sit outside at this quaint spot and watch the White Wolf meadow do whatever meadows do. See page 145.

### A Visit to Hetch Hetchy Reservoir

This body of water occupies a valley that has been characterized as Yosemite Valley's little brother. It has retained much of its beauty and offers great hiking. See page 129.

### The Trail into Lyell Canyon

The Lyell Fork of the Tuolumne River is one of the park's most peaceful and inspiring settings. The trail leads to and along its course. See page 141.

### The High Sierra Camps

Whether you hike the full loop or visit just one of these 5 backcountry encampments, the experience will be unique. Stop for a mind-blowing meal, or pamper yourself by staying over. See page 136.

White Cascade near Glen Aulin High Sierra Camp

The **Hetch Hetchy** area of Yosemite, as it is called in this book, includes the portion of the park that is found on its western boundary along Big Oak Flat Road north of Crane Flat, and along Evergreen and Hetch Hetchy roads (see page 131). The region is best known for its two groves of giant sequoias (the Merced and Tuolumne Groves) and for the Hetch Hetchy Reservoir on the Tuolumne River.

National Park Service offices here are located at the Big Oak Flat Entrance, where there is a ranger station (209) 379-1899), a campground reservation office, a small visitor center and book sales area, a wilderness permit and reservation office, and public restrooms. If you've entered the park from the west over Highway 120, this is a good place to orient yourself; Yosemite Valley is still 25 miles (40 km) away. There's also the Hetch Hetchy Entrance Station, about 10 miles (16 km) from the Big Oak Flat Entrance on the way to Hetch Hetchy. This road is open during daylight hours only and sometimes closes for snow. Call the Yosemite information line for road conditions at (209) 372-0200 to check on it.

The route to Hetch Hetchy Reservoir is over Evergreen Road, located just north of the park off Highway 120. If traveling from the south, leave the park through the Big Oak Flat Entrance. The right turn onto Evergreen Road is 1 mile (1.6 km) past the entrance station. From the north, turn left on Evergreen Road 1 mile (1.6 km) before you reach the park on Highway 120. Hetch Hetchy is 16 miles (25.7 km) out on this road, which becomes Hetch Hetchy Road at Camp Mather (bear right at the intersection).

## Hetch Hetchy and the Dam

Many wonder how a feature like Hetch Hetchy Reservoir came to be sited within the boundaries of a national park. It wasn't easy or quick, but when the political struggle ended, the scenic qualities of Hetch Hetchy Valley had been "submerged" for the good of the citizens of San Francisco and their thirsts.

The city had been looking for a dependable supply of mountain water when, shortly after the turn of the century, Hetch Hetchy was proposed as the perfect location for a dam site. The notion of a reservoir in Yosemite was not universally attractive,

however, and John Muir, the Sierra Club, and others opposed the project and fought it for many years. On several occasions the Hetch Hetchy project was outright rejected. But the city fathers were persistent, and in 1913 the Raker Bill granting San Francisco permission to dam the Tuolumne River at Hetch Hetchy was passed in Congress.

Losing the fight to save Hetch Hetchy devastated Muir. Many believe that his efforts left him exhausted and contributed greatly to his death about a year later. On the other hand, the reservoir proved an enormous success for the city of San Francisco. Much of the Bay Area still relies on the project for the bulk of its water and power.

Hetch Hetchy Reservoir

O'Shaughnessy Dam (named for the chief engineer) was constructed beginning in 1919 and took about 4 years to finish. The resulting reservoir is 8 miles (12.9 km) long, has a capacity of more than 117 million gallons (443 million l), and covers 1,861 surface acres or 3 square miles (753 ha or 7.5 sq km). The dam itself is 410 feet high, 910 feet long, and 308 feet thick at its base (125 m high, 277 m long, and 94 m thick), which tapers to 24 feet (7 m) at the top. One interesting fact about the Hetch Hetchy project is that the water in the system pipelines flows all the way to San Francisco by gravity!

Bridge at Wapama Falls, Hetch Hetchy

**The Hetch Hetchy** area is best enjoyed in spring and fall. Hetch Hetchy Reservoir's setting is more foothill than montane, and gray pines, manzanita, and lower-elevation wildflowers are abundant there. The area's other attractions are much higher, averaging about 6,000 feet (1,800 m) above sea level. These higher elevations feature sugar pines, sequoias, and the most accessible winter hiking in Yosemite. Stop at the Big Oak Flat Information Station to get oriented.

## Walk through the Merced Grove

Yosemite's quietest stand of sequoias is the Merced Grove, accessible only on foot. It's a 2-mile (3.2-km) hike into the grove from the trailhead on Big Oak Flat Road. Located 3.5 miles (5.6 km) north of Crane Flat, or 4.5 miles (7.2 km) south of the Big Oak Flat Entrance, the trailhead is marked by road signs.

Follow the dirt road for about a mile (1.6 km), then take the left fork down into the grove. This is the park's smallest group of sequoias (about 20 trees). Look for the old Merced Grove cabin that was originally built as a ranger station.

These sequoias convey the silent majesty that has characterized them for thousands of years. The absence of motorized vehicles and the solitude are a real treat for hikers to the Merced Grove. Allow 3 hours for the 4-mile (6.4-km) round-trip.

## Hike the Tuolumne Grove

The former route of Big Oak Flat Road leads downhill from Crane Flat into the Tuolumne Grove, a cluster of about 45 sequoias. This dirt road drops steeply for about 1 mile (1.6 km) to where the first big trees can be spotted. Along the way, you will see reminders of the Rim Fire, which came dangerously close to the grove. An interesting attraction in the grove is the "Dead Giant" tree, a lifeless but still-standing partial tree that was tunneled out in 1878. There's also a self-guiding nature trail, .5 miles (.8 km) in length, that should take about thirty minutes to walk. Check out Dead Fred, a hollow fallen sequoia. Starting at the roots, you can crawl through the trunk for about 100 feet (30 m). It's a tight squeeze at the end, but there's an outlet halfway down.

The trail to the Tuolumne Grove takes off near Crane Flat. From the intersection of Big Oak Flat Road and Tioga Road, take Tioga Road 1 mile (1.6 km) to the east (toward Tuolumne Meadows). Turn left into the Tuolumne Grove parking lot. The route is obvious; the round-trip of about 2 miles (3.2 km) is relatively easy, though it's all uphill on the way back.

## Let Them Entertain You

In summer, National Park Service rangers conduct a variety of walks, programs, and campfires. Check the *Yosemite Guide* under Hetch Hetchy/Hodgdon Meadow/Crane Flat/White Wolf visitor activities

## Lookout for Fire

The Crane Flat Fire Lookout is staffed during the summer, when the National Park Service bases a helicopter crew here. You can visit the facility, which can be reached by a primitive road leading off to the east less than 1 mile (1.6 km) north of Crane Flat on Big Oak Flat Road. It's a .5-mile (.8-km) uphill trip to the lookout.

Watch for fire and other emergency vehicles along the way. The view from the lookout is special, with glimpses of the park in every direction. It's fun to cross-country ski or snowshoe here in winter.

## Hike Hetch Hetchy

Though the once beautiful valley of Hetch Hetchy might be lost forever, many of its scenic wonders can still be appreciated. Tueeulala and Wapama Falls still thunder from the north rim, Kolana Rock rises imposingly from the reservoir's southern shore, and a remarkable variety of plant and animal life populates the perimeter.

While Hetch Hetchy is at roughly the same elevation as Yosemite Valley, it's much warmer. In the middle of summer it's downright hot. Perfect months for day hiking are October through May. You'd be amazed at how warm the north side of the reservoir can be in the winter. The main trail at Hetch Hetchy leads over the dam, through a tunnel, and along the north edge. The undulating route passes Tueeulala Falls, Wapama Falls (about 2 miles or 3.2 km from the dam), and Rancheria Falls (6.5 miles or 10.5 km out). Hike as far as you like. In spring, be prepared at Wapama Falls for the high water and heavy mist that sometimes force closure of the trail. Retrace your steps back to the dam.

Fishing is allowed in Hetch Hetchy Reservoir, but swimming and boating are not. Backpacking is popular at Hetch Hetchy, especially in autumn and spring. The Rim Fire struck the Hetch Hetchy area hard; there are signs of significant fire damage throughout this part of Yosemite and along Evergreen Road and Mather Road as well.

**Originally a wagon** road across Tioga Pass built by the Great Consolidated Silver Company in 1883, Tioga Road literally splits Yosemite National Park in two. Improved to its present condition and alignment in 1961, the road opened up some of Yosemite's most stunning country and allowed access to previously remote high-country destinations. Today the Tioga Road corridor is rife with scenic and recreational opportunities.

For the purposes of this book, Tioga Road refers to the area of the park along Tioga Road (which extends from Crane Flat to Tioga Pass, some 46 miles or 74 km east) except for the Tuolumne Meadows area, which begins on page 137.

Visitors should be aware that Tioga Road is not open all year. Heavy snows require the National Park Service to close the road (from November until May or June, usually), though snow is a possibility in any season. Typically mild summer weather attracts both recreationists and travelers headed east in large numbers. There are plenty of options for fun along the road, with multiple campgrounds, trailheads, lakes, streams, and scenic views to choose from. For information and assistance, there is a ranger station at the Tioga Pass Entrance (as well as the Tuolumne Meadows Visitor Center, described on page 139).

Whether you're just passing through or making a leisurely trip along Tioga Road, your experience will be a better one if you know where you are and what you're seeing. A valuable aid in this regard is *The Road Guide to Yosemite*, available from Yosemite Conservancy, which is chock full of natural and human history, including information keyed to the markers you'll see along the road.

## Get In over Your Head

The best place to have a swim along Tioga Road is Tenaya Lake. The park's largest lake, it is located approximately 8 miles (13 km) west of Tuolumne Meadows, or 30 miles (48 km) east of Crane Flat. The inviting sandy beach on the eastern shore is a good bet, but be prepared for some cold water. Use the dressing rooms and bathrooms in the parking lot just east of the lake. If it's too cold to swim, have a picnic in this dramatic setting. If you're at Tenaya Lake in late summer, check out the tree trunks rising from the water—long ago there was a forest here, and the icy, oxygen-poor water preserves the trees to this day.

## Be Programmed

During summer, ranger naturalists offer free programs for visitors at various locations along Tioga Road. Check the *Yosemite Guide* for details.

## Hike All You Like

The territory stretching out to the north and south of Tioga Road is a veritable hiker's wonderland. From numerous points along the route, trails lead into a landscape unequalled anywhere in the world. Hikes range from easy to very strenuous, becoming more difficult with increased elevation. Follow basic hiking precautions (see page 97), and in this high-country setting, stay hydrated by drinking lots of liquids. The most common hiking-related ailment is altitude sickness; consider spending a day or so getting acclimatized before starting to hike.

For those hikers who travel to Yosemite without a car or who wish to leave their vehicles in Yosemite Valley, Yosemite

Cathedral Lake and Peak

**The view from Olmsted Point**

Hospitality operates a hikers' bus that traverses the length of Tioga Road at certain times each day from approximately late June to Labor Day. You can arrange to get off at trailheads along the way. The bus departs from several locations in Yosemite Valley and along the Tioga Road each day. There is a nominal fee and it is recommended to book a seat in advance. Go to travelyosemite.com or call (209) 372-1240. YARTS also provides service along Tioga Road. For information, call (877) 989-2787 or visit yarts.com.

In addition to the hikers' bus between Yosemite Valley and Tuolumne Meadows, there is a small shuttle bus service that operates only in the Tuolumne Meadows area roughly June through mid-Sepember, allowing visitors to leave their car at one of the parking lots and ride the bus to points of interest and trailheads. There is a nominal fee for this service, and the seasonal schedule is posted at bus stops or at nps.gov/yose.

### Wet a Line

Fishing can be amazingly good along Tioga Road. Spots like Lukens Lake, Harden Lake, Tenaya Lake, and May Lake (all described in this chapter) are home to many feisty, if somewhat small, trout. Yosemite Creek and the Dana Fork of the Tuolumne River can also yield up a fish or two. The general park fishing regulations apply (see page 91); check with a park ranger for any special rules.

### Check Out Half Dome's Back Side

One of Yosemite's most remarkable scenic overlooks is found at Olmsted Point, and it shouldn't be missed. This major pullout is located 2.5 miles (4 km) west of Tenaya Lake and just slightly more than 2 miles (3.2 km) east of the May Lake turnoff. Here the grandeur of the granite walls of Tenaya Canyon is revealed. Beyond loom the less-seen northern and eastern faces of Half Dome and Clouds Rest. To the east, the landscape includes Tenaya Lake and the many domes and peaks of the Tuolumne Meadows region. A short nature trail leads down from the point; watch for fat and sassy marmots in the rocks (but please don't feed them).

## Harden Lake

This is a 3-mile (4.8-km) walk to an attractive little lake that offers picnicking, swimming, and fishing. Start in front of the White Wolf Campground and head north on what was the original Tioga Road. The trail soon becomes unpaved and descends gradually to the lake; the walk back up may feel steeper and longer under the summer sun. There's a good view of the Tuolumne River Canyon from the far side of the lake. The round-trip is about 6 miles (9.7 km) and should take about 4 hours.

## Lukens Lake

It's somewhat uphill, but this hike of less than 1 mile (1.6 km) terminates at a lovely spot amid meadow flowers and grasses. Being so close to the road, Lukens Lake is perfect for families with young (but not infant) children. Take your fishing poles and a picnic lunch. The trailhead is found 1.8 miles (2.9 km) to the east of the White Wolf intersection, or 3 miles (4.8 km) west of the spot where Tioga Road crosses Yosemite Creek. Head north up the hill, then drop down to the lake. This easy hike is not quite 2 miles (3.2 km) up and back and requires about an hour to cover (a little longer for families!). You can also reach Lukens Lake from White Wolf. Ask for trail directions at the lodge.

## Yosemite Creek to the Valley

From the point on Tioga Road where it crosses Yosemite Creek (about 5 miles or 8 km east of the White Wolf turnoff), a trail leads southward over level and downhill terrain all the way to Yosemite Valley. Because it's a one-way hike of 13 miles (21 km), you'll have to arrange for a ride to the trailhead, plan on shuttling back to pick up your car on Tioga Road, or use the hikers' bus mentioned on page 132. The trail follows Yosemite Creek down to Yosemite Creek Campground and eventually to the top of Yosemite Falls. Check out the spectacular view from the top (see page 95) before descending the final 3.5 miles (5.6 km) to the Yosemite Valley floor. This is a hike for the physically fit, demanding but satisfying. Allow at least 8 hours.

## North Dome

This strenuous hike to one of the best views of Yosemite Valley (see page 104) takes off to the south of Tioga Road, about 5 miles (8 km) beyond the point where the road crosses Yosemite Creek (this is also 2 miles or 3.2 km west of the May Lake turnoff and just east of Porcupine Flat Campground). The walk is mostly downhill and flat for 4.2 miles (6.8 km) to the dome. Watch for the erratic boulders left by the glaciers here, and check out the impressive view of Half Dome directly across from you. Because

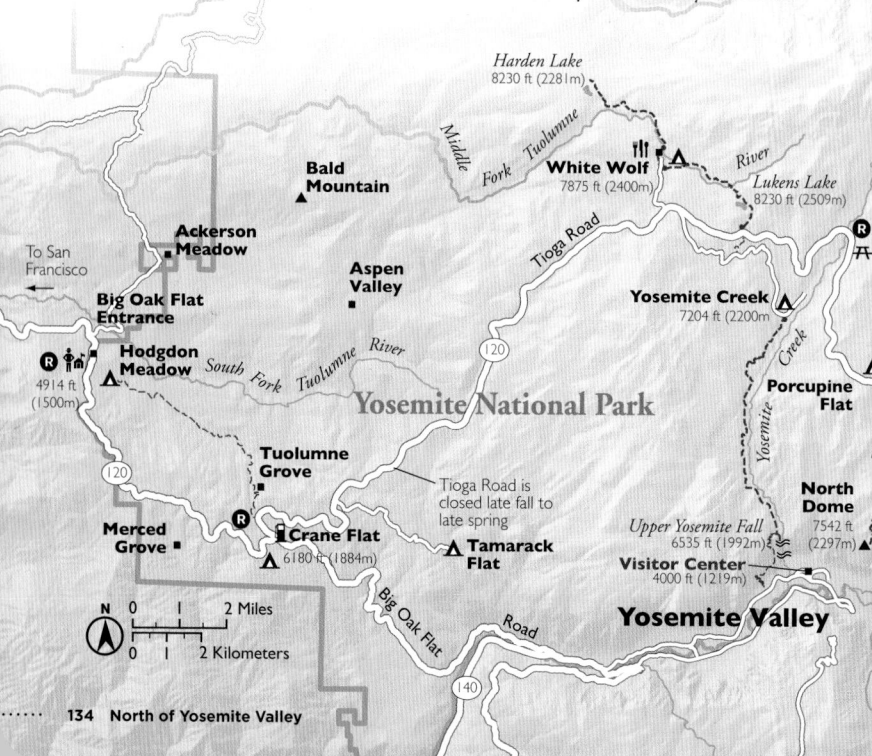

the return trip to Tioga Road is mostly uphill, give yourself 6 to 8 hours for the 8.5-mile (13.7-km) trip out and back.

## May Lake and Mount Hoffmann

Mount Hoffmann is the geographic center of Yosemite National Park. It offers superb views of the park's high country from its 10,850-foot (3,307-m) summit. The route up the mountain leads past idyllic May Lake, the location of one of the High Sierra Camps (see page 136). Start your hike at the May Lake parking area. Turn north off Tioga Road about 5 miles (8 km) west of Tenaya Lake and drive 2 miles (3.2 km) to the parking lot. It's an easy 1.25 miles (2 km) to May Lake, and the 2 miles (3.2 km) beyond to the top of Mount Hoffmann are much more strenuous but worth the effort (you will gain about 1,500 feet or 457 m in elevation). Plan on 2 hours round-trip for May Lake, and add 3 to 4 more for the ascent of Mount Hoffmann.

## Mono Pass

This high-elevation hike is a comparatively easy 4 miles (6.4 km) with an elevation gain of only 1,000 feet (305 m). The route, however, begins at nearly 10,000 feet and almost reaches the 11,000-foot (3,353-m)

level (prepare for some heavy breathing). The trail begins 1.5 miles (2.4 km) west of Tioga Pass and heads south along an old Indian trading route. At Mono Pass are the remains of several mining buildings and cabins from the late 1800s. Views of Mount Gibbs and Mount Dana are extremely fine. This 8-mile (12.9-km) round-trip takes from 4 to 6 hours.

## Gaylor Lakes

Here's another trip for high-elevation fans who love to huff and puff. The trail ascends steeply to the north from just a few feet west of the Tioga Pass Entrance Station, which is 9,945 feet (3,031 m) high. Middle Gaylor Lake is about 1 mile (1.6 km) from the trailhead, but it's no easy climb. Follow the inflowing creek to Upper Gaylor Lake and the remnants of a stone shelter at the Great Sierra Mine 900 feet (274 m) to its north. This is truly an alpine environment, with few trees, strong winds, and often harsh weather. Allow 3 hours for this moderately difficult hike of 4 miles (6.4 km) round-trip.

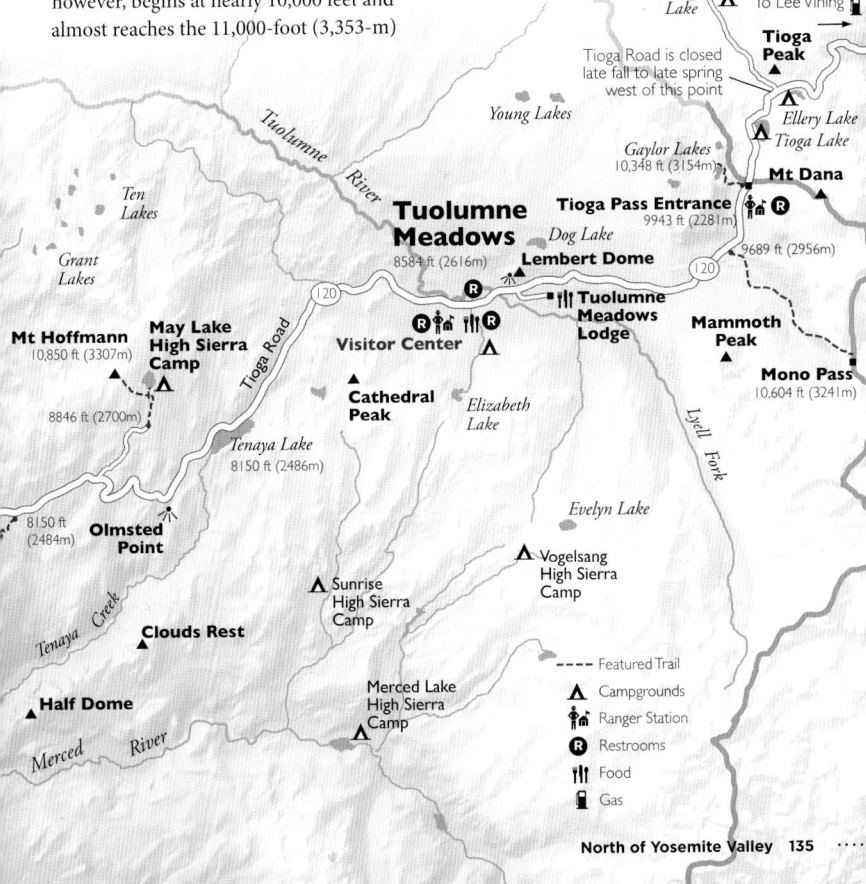

**Five rustic colonies** of tents in the park's loftier regions constitute an institution unique to Yosemite called the High Sierra Camps. Placed in a roughly circular pattern about 1 day's hike apart, the camps allow visitors to enjoy high-elevation backcountry in semi luxury, with wholesome hot meals prepared by the camp staff, and regulation beds with mattresses, pillows, woolen blankets, and comforters that await weary travelers. There are even showers!

The idea for the camps originated with Washington B. Lewis, Yosemite's first NPS superintendent. He wanted hikers to enjoy Yosemite's high country free from the "irksome" load normally needed for a backcountry trip. In 1924 the first camps were installed at a number of locations.

Over the years there have been as many as 8 different camps, including Little Yosemite Valley, Boothe Lake, Lyell Canyon, and Tenaya Lake, but the present configuration has been set for a while. The camps are open for a short season (roughly late June/early July to Labor Day) and are operated by Yosemite Hospitality.

Many people use Tuolumne Meadows Lodge (see page 145) as a starting or ending point for the High Sierra Loop Trip. In a counterclockwise direction from Tuolumne Meadows, the other camps are Glen Aulin, May Lake, Sunrise, Merced Lake, and Vogelsang. The distance from one to the next averages 9 miles (14.5 km). Guests at the High Sierra Camps are accommodated in dormitory-style tents that sleep either 4 or 6. The communal bathhouses offer running water, toilets, and 3 of the camps have showers. Guests must provide their own sleeping bags or sleep-sacks and towels. Hearty breakfasts and dinners are served daily, and bag lunches can be ordered. Sizes of the camps vary, but about 35 people on average can be lodged.

A favorite of many High Sierra Camp users is the 7-day guided loop trip (there's also a 5-day option). A naturalist accompanies a maximum of 14 people, providing ongoing interpretation of the geology and natural history of Yosemite's wilderness. There are campfire programs nightly, and members of the group develop a real spirit of camaraderie and friendship.

Despite the price (around $146 plus tax per one unguided, overnight stay including two meals), the camps are fully booked almost every night of the summer. There is also a meals-only option if you camp in your own tent, as well as saddle trips. Reservations are essential and are handled by lottery. Applications are accepted each year between September 1 and November 1 for the lottery and applicants are notified of the results in the spring. For more information and to submit an application, look for High Sierra Camps at travelyosemite.com.

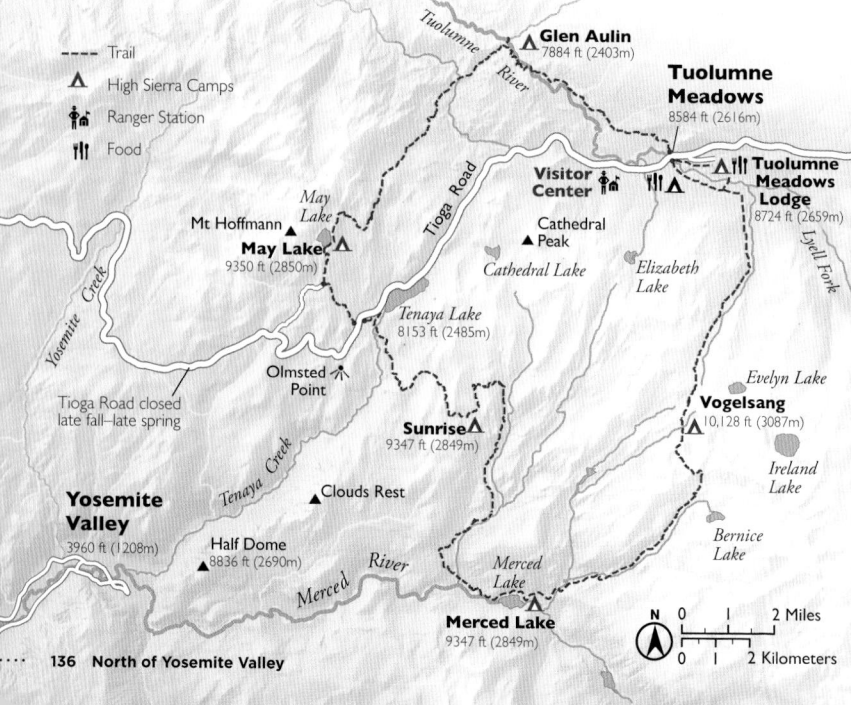

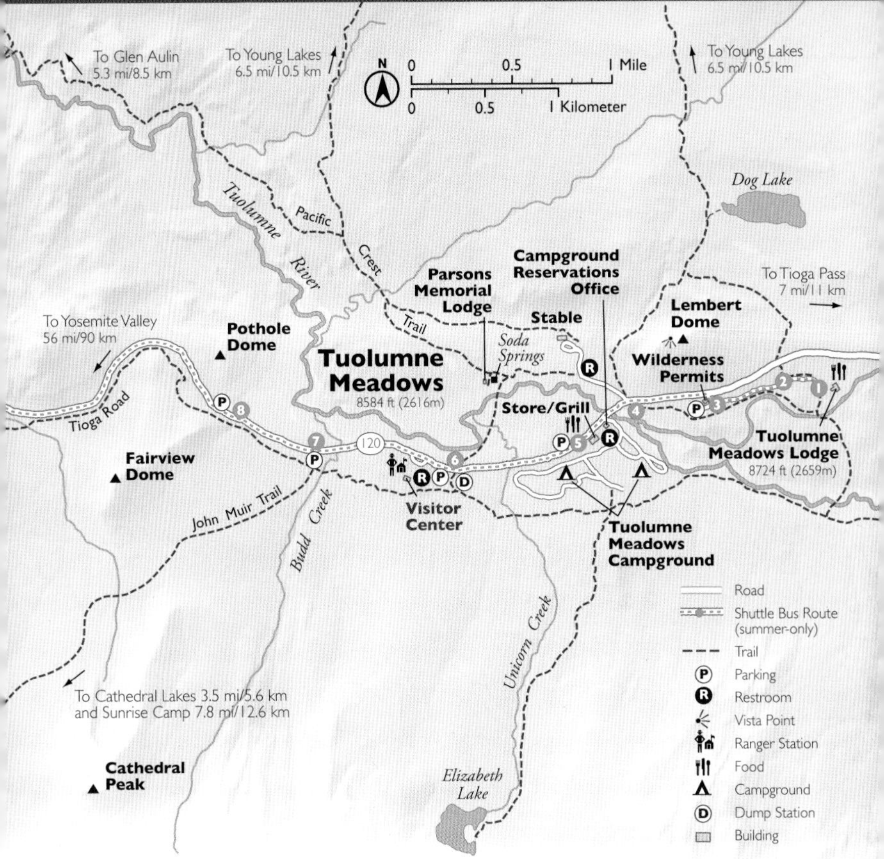
To Glen Aulin
5.3 mi/8.5 km
To Young Lakes
6.5 mi/10.5 km
N
0
0.5
1 Mile
0
0.5
1 Kilometer
To Young Lakes
6.5 mi/10.5 km
Dog Lake
Tuolumne River
Pacific Crest Trail
Campground Reservations Office
Parsons Memorial Lodge
Stable
To Tioga Pass
7 mi/11 km
Lembert Dome
To Yosemite Valley
56 mi/90 km
Pothole Dome
Soda Springs
Wilderness Permits
Tuolumne Meadows
8584 ft (2616m)
Tioga Road
Store/Grill
120
Tuolumne Meadows Lodge
8724 ft (2659m)
Fairview Dome
John Muir Trail
Budd Creek
Visitor Center
Tuolumne Meadows Campground
Unicorn Creek
Road
Shuttle Bus Route (summer-only)
Trail
Parking
Restroom
Vista Point
Ranger Station
Food
Campground
Dump Station
Building
To Cathedral Lakes 3.5 mi/5.6 km
and Sunrise Camp 7.8 mi/12.6 km
Cathedral Peak
Elizabeth Lake

**This stunningly** picturesque region sits 8,600 feet (2,600 m) up in the transparent sky of Yosemite's high country. Contained in a basin about 2.5 miles (4 km) long, the meadow system may be the largest in the Sierra Nevada at the subalpine level. Tuolumne Meadows is only 55 miles (88.5 km) by road from Yosemite Valley, but it's a world apart.

Called by some the "hub" or "heart" of the high country, Tuolumne is a seasonal phenomenon. It is closed by snow to visitation during the bulk of year, but when summer comes, the action is impressive. Hikers flock here, both day trippers and backpackers. Rock climbers who winter in Yosemite Valley adopt Tuolumne as a summer home. And visitors arrive in cars to revel in the awesome beauty of the place, and to enjoy a less-developed part of the park.

Sunrise High Sierra Camp

There's plenty to gawk at, too. The Tuolumne River winds its way sinuously through the meadows, while an array of unusually shaped domes rings the area. There are smooth-bottomed canyons and jagged peaks; delicate lakes and odorous springs. These multiple elements combine to create a landscape both wonderful and inspiring.

During the summer months there's a wilderness center at Tuolumne Meadows operated by the National Park Service, along with a small visitor center. The wilderness center is just off Tioga Road along the way to Tuolumne Lodge, and the visitor center is located near the halfway point of the meadows about .25 miles (.4 km) west of the store. For information or assistance call (209) 372-0263.

### Climb a Dome

Scrambling to the top of one of Tuolumne's granite domes can be fun and exhilarating. It can also be hazardous to your health. Try one of the easier rocks, like Lembert Dome (see page 141) or Pothole Dome (adjacent to the road at the west end of the meadows). Wear proper footgear and don't go up anything you aren't sure you can get down. If you are planning on climbing in Yosemite, be sure to check nps.gov/yose for current climbing restrictions, safety advice, and more. Climbing lessons are available from the Yosemite Mountaineering School & Guide Service. Check out rock climbing at travelyosemite.com or call (209) 372-8344 for details.

Pothole Dome

### Take a Swim

Because they are fed by the melting snow nearby, most of the streams, rivers, and lakes of the Tuolumne region are freezing cold. As the summer progresses they warm a bit, but swimming is not for the weak of heart. There are plenty of good swimming holes along the Tuolumne River as it passes the campground, and on its fork that winds lazily through Lyell Canyon (see hiking section below). Lake swimmers should try Tenaya Lake, 7 miles (11.3 km) to the west, Elizabeth Lake, or Dog Lake (see pages 140 and 141).

### Become a Sheepwatcher

Sierra Nevada bighorn sheep are native to Yosemite, but were eliminated here by disease and hunting before 1900. Efforts to reintroduce these amazing rock climbers to the area began in the late 1970s. In 1986, a small herd was transplanted to the park in the Tioga Pass region, and in 2015 a herd was released in the Cathedral Range area. Over the years, smaller groups and individual sheep have been added to supplement specific herds, and the effort is considered a success, with the wild herds now being able to reproduce and survive on their own. Your best bet to see bighorns is along the Sierra Crest, at Mono Pass or Parker Pass. Check at the visitor center for information and directions.

### Walk a Mile in Your Shoes

The hiking around Tuolumne Meadows is first-rate. The trails are varied, the scenery is exceptional, and the weather is usually cooperative (but plan for afternoon thunder showers, particularly in August). A person staying at Tuolumne could take a different hike every day for a week and still not exhaust the possibilities. Be sure to follow normal hiking precautions (see page 97) and drink extra water to keep yourself hydrated at this high elevation.

Hiking distance signs along the trails in Tuolumne Meadows and Tioga Road may vary, as updates have been made to maps and signs over the years. Do not be too concerned about a slight difference in mileage from one sign to the next, but do carry a good map and be conscious of your conditioning and abilities when hiking in the high country.

A shuttle bus runs between Tuolumne Meadows and Olmsted Point, providing service to several stops along the way for a nominal fee, from approximately June through mid-September. It's a good way to get to your trailhead and leave your car behind. Hours are posted on signs at bus stops throughout the Tuolumne area. The Yosemite Hospitality bus and the YARTS

Elizabeth Lake

bus both visit Tuolumne Meadows from Yosemite Valley at least once a day from July 1 through Labor Day, weather and road conditions permitting. You can be dropped off at the trailhead of your choice and, if the timing works out, be picked up later. Contact Yosemite Hospitality at (888) 540-5794 or travelyosemite.com under shuttles, or YARTS at (877) 989-2787 and yarts.com for more information.

### Get Centered

To learn more about the Tuolumne Meadows region, visit the visitor center located south of Tioga Road a short way west of the store. There you'll find exhibits, knowledgeable rangers, and books and maps for sale. It's also a good place to find out about free ranger walks and programs that will be happening during your visit (or check the *Yosemite Guide*). If you need to call the Tuolumne Meadows Visitor Center, the number is (209) 372-0263.

Children can participate in the junior ranger program by purchasing a copy of the *Junior Ranger Handbook* (ages 7 to 13) or the *Little Cub Handbook* (ages 3 to 6) at the center. By completing the activities outlined in the handbook, they can earn certificates and badges while they learn lots more about the park. The handbooks are available at all park visitor centers.

### Do Something Fishy

Tuolumne Meadows is loaded with family fishing opportunities for high-country trout. Your kids will find great places to practice their angling techniques. The Tuolumne River and its tributaries are excellent spots. You can also try Cathedral Lake, Gaylor Lakes, Spillway Lake, and Elizabeth Lake. Follow park fishing regulations (see page 91) and check at the visitor center for information.

· · · · · · · · · · · · · · · · · · · · · · · · · · · · · · · · · · · · · · · · ·

**Q: How should a hiker behave in a lightning storm?**

**A: There is no safe place outdoors when thunder is audible, but some places are more dangerous. To increase your safety, lose elevation and avoid rocky outcroppings. Do not be in open areas or near the tallest object; better to be in a forest of trees of similar height. Spread out from other hikers in your party. If you feel static in the air, sit on your pack and keep your feet off the ground.**

Hikers on the trail to Soda Springs

## Cathedral Lakes

Taking off from the obvious parking area at the west end of Tuolumne Meadows (south of the road), this trail is fairly strenuous, gaining about 1,000 feet (300 m) in under 4 miles (6.4 km). The route is uphill, then relatively flat for a while, then uphill again before it drops into the Cathedral Lakes basin. Take the right fork in the trail to reach the lower lake, which is the larger of the two. Have a swim, enjoy your lunch, or fish a little. Your view of Cathedral Peak will be outstanding. The round-trip hike is less than 8 miles (13 km) and should take 4 to 6 hours.

## Elizabeth Lake

It's steep and short and well worth the effort. Elizabeth Lake is a lovely spot nestled against the base of Unicorn Peak, one of Tuolumne's most recognizable landmarks. The 2.3-mile (3.7-km) hike begins

Soda Springs

at the back side of the Tuolumne Meadows Campground (across from the bathrooms for the group camp area), and it is just about all uphill. Given the elevation (you climb to about 9,500 feet or 2,900 m), it's a good idea to take your time and adopt a slow but steady pace. The water's cold though swimmable, and fishing is fair. Allow from 3 to 4 hours for the 4.6-mile (7.4-km) round-trip.

## Soda Springs

Here's an easy hike that's flat and perfect for all ages. The trail leads out into the middle of Tuolumne Meadows and to a naturally carbonated mineral spring that bubbles mysteriously to the surface. Park in the parking lot just north of Tioga Road, adjacent to Lembert Dome (just east of the bridge over the Tuolumne River). Follow the gravel road to the north, and where the road turns right, walk around the brown metal gate and continue north. (If you get to the stable, you're off-route.) Besides the Soda Springs, you'll find Parsons Memorial Lodge (erected in 1914 by the Sierra Club) and the McCauley Cabin, a pioneer structure now used as a ranger residence. You'll be close to the river and will get a sense of the size and beauty of the meadows. You can make the 1.5-mile (2.4-km) walk in an hour.

### Glen Aulin

To reach this aspen-studded hollow along the Tuolumne River, walk to Soda Springs (see above for hike information). The trail continues past the springs and roughly follows the river 7 miles (11.3 km) to a small campground and one of the High Sierra Camps (see page 136). The trail is slightly downhill all the way, and that makes the hike back a stiff one. Watch for Tuolumne Falls and White Cascade as you hike. If you are truly a glutton for hiking punishment, Waterwheel Falls, one of the park's most unusual cascades, is 3.3 miles (5.3 km) past Glen Aulin. The trip to Glen Aulin is a very strenuous hike of 14 miles (22.5 km) round-trip; give yourself 8 to 10 hours to accomplish it.

## Lembert Dome

From the top of this oddly shaped dome, the 360-degree panorama of Tuolumne Meadows is fantastic. At the east end of Tuolumne Meadows turn onto the road that leads to Tuolumne Lodge. Past the ranger station but before the lodge is a parking lot on the left side of the road. Park there, walk up the bank to the north, carefully cross the main road, and begin your hike up the hill. After some steep switchbacks, the spur trail to the summit of Lembert Dome heads left. Emerge from the trees and walk the (usually) sunny, windswept granite to the top of the dome. Take your topo map for identification of the many peaks and mountains around you. There is also a nature trail from the parking lot at the base of the dome itself, but this is relatively difficult to find and follow. Up and back is about 3 miles (4.8 km) and should require 3 hours of your time.

## Dog Lake

This easily reached spot is perfect for swimming, but not fishing. Fish at this site have naturally gone extinct due to lack of spawning habitat. Because there are no fish, if you look carefully, you may see one of the rare and endangered Sierra Nevada yellow-legged frogs. (Please only look and don't touch because their skin is sensitive to oils and sunscreen commonly found on our hands.) Follow the directions for the Lembert Dome trailhead. Once you've found the trailhead, the most challenging part of the hike is over! The trail is steep at first, then levels off for a final gradual ascent to the lake. A moderate hike of 3 miles (4.8 km) round-trip; allow 4 hours.

## Lyell Canyon

This hike is the proverbial stroll in the park. The trail follows the Lyell Fork of the Tuolumne River out through the beautiful canyon that shares its name. The trailhead is at the west end of the parking lot for Tuolumne Meadows Lodge, but park your car in the lot for the Dog Lake hike. Head into the forest, cross a bridge, then continue to double bridges over the Lyell Fork (less than .5 miles or .8 km out). You leave the river at this point and follow the trail, which rejoins the river farther out the canyon. It's a flat hike the entire route and as scenic and relaxing as they come. Lyell Canyon is about 8 miles (13 km) long and you can hike as little or as much as you like. Give yourself enough time to make it back before dark.

Dog Lake

**The campgrounds** at the north end of the park can be characterized as more primitive and remote and generally smaller (with Tuolumne Meadows Campground being the main exception). Only a few are handled by Recreation.gov; the balance are operated on a first-come, first-served basis. For campgrounds that can't be reserved in advance, remember that the check-out time is noon; this is the perfect hour to attempt to secure a site (although it doesn't hurt to arrive earlier, especially on weekends).

Pets are not allowed in some campgrounds, or on any of the trails in the high country. Check the listings below to see if you can legally bring your pet, and always indicate that you'll be camping with a pet when you make your reservation. See page 15 for the specifics about successfully arranging a campsite reservation.

There are also campground reservation offices at the Big Oak Flat Entrance (where Highway 120 enters the park from the west) and in Tuolumne Meadows (at the entrance to the campground). At times campsites can be arranged at the last minute by stopping at one of these offices. For information only, call (209) 379-2123 for the Big Oak Flat and (209) 372-4025 for the Tuolumne Meadows offices. The summer camping limit is 14 days outside of Yosemite Valley, and most of the campgrounds are open only in the summer. The limit extends to 30 days the rest of the year, but be aware that you may only camp in Yosemite a total of 30 days in any one calendar year. For general park camping regulations, see page 15.

## Hetch Hetchy Area Campgrounds

### CRANE FLAT CAMPGROUND

This camping area of 166 sites is situated at the 6,200-foot (1,900-m) level, where Big Oak Flat Road and Tioga Road meet. Of all the campgrounds located outside Yosemite Valley, it's the closest—only 17 miles away. The nightly fee is $26, and reservations are required. Normally open from late June through early October, Crane Flat is close to the Merced and Tuolumne Groves and the Tioga Road attractions. Pets okay.

### HODGDON MEADOW CAMPGROUND

Here is the first place to camp when you enter Yosemite from the west on Highway 120 (you'll be 25 miles or 40 km from Yosemite Valley). All types of campers are welcome in this campground consisting of 105 sites. To reach Hodgdon Meadow, turn down the hill just south of the Big Oak Flat Entrance. It's less than .5 miles or .8 km to the campground entrance. Reservations are required April through September ($26 per site); the rest of the year, it's a first-come, first-served facility. Pets okay.

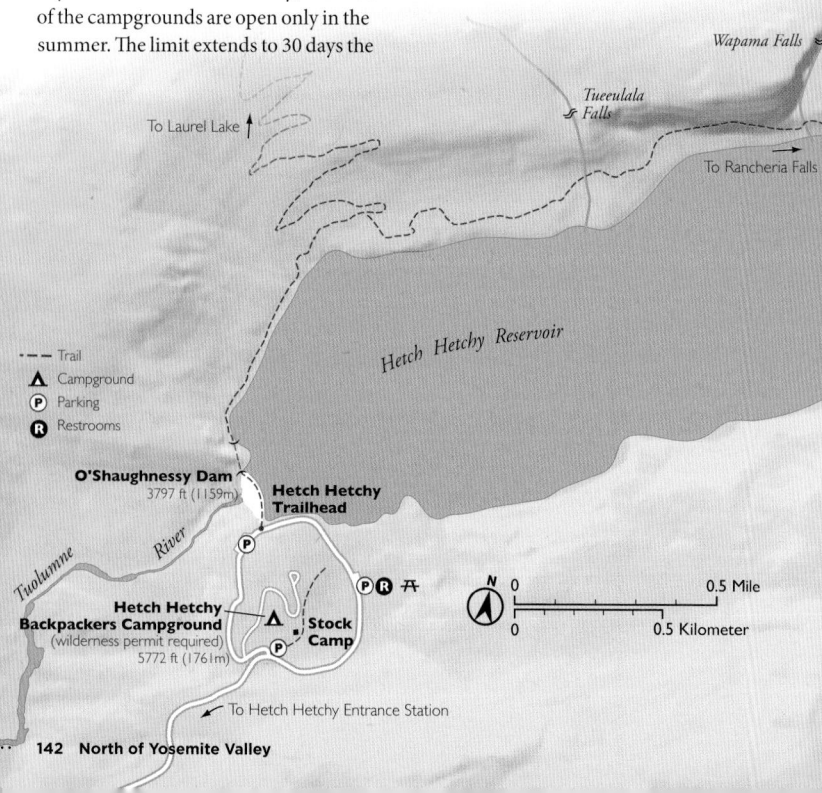

Legend:

- – – Trail
- ▲ Campground
- Ⓟ Parking
- Ⓡ Restrooms

Wapama Falls
Tueeulala Falls
To Laurel Lake
To Rancheria Falls
Hetch Hetchy Reservoir
O'Shaughnessy Dam 3797 ft (1159m)
Hetch Hetchy Trailhead
Tuolumne River
Hetch Hetchy Backpackers Campground (wilderness permit required) 5772 ft (1761m)
Stock Camp
N
0     0.5 Mile
0     0.5 Kilometer
To Hetch Hetchy Entrance Station

### HETCH HETCHY BACKPACKERS CAMPGROUND

This campground is exclusively for back-country users (with wilderness permits) who are beginning their trips from the Hetch Hetchy trailhead. Open all year, stays are limited to 1 night at the beginning and end of wilderness outings. Located at Hetch Hetchy Reservoir, the campground features 19 backpacker sites (6 persons per site), 2 organized group sites (one accommodating 18 persons, the other 25), and 2 stock use sites (6 persons and 6 head of stock per site). Parking is provided near the campground, which has running water and flush toilets. No recreational vehicles, trailers, or pets are allowed. Prior arrangements should be made for the organized group and stock use sites. The fees are $6 per night for backpackers and $50 per site for the group and stock sites. Call (209) 372-0740 for a wilderness permit.

## Tioga Road Campgrounds

### TAMARACK FLAT CAMPGROUND

If you enjoy a more primitive camping experience (creek water that must be boiled and pit toilets), this campground fits the bill. It's located at 6,300 feet (1,900 m) down a 3-mile (4.8-km) dirt road that takes off Tioga Road about 4 miles (6.4 km) east of Crane Flat (not suitable for large recreational vehicles or trailers). There are 52 first-come, first-served campsites, and the fee is $12 per night. Usually open from late June through early October. Pets okay.

### WHITE WOLF CAMPGROUND

A favorite of many high-country campers, White Wolf is set on a beautiful meadow alongside a bubbling creek. Added amenities are the White Wolf Lodge with a small store and restaurant, and public showers for a fee. The 8,000-foot (2,400-m) setting 14 miles (22.5 km) east of Crane Flat makes for cold nights and brilliant days. There are 74 first-come, first-served sites which rent for $18 per night (not suitable for RVs over 27 feet or 8.2 m long). The camping season here is approximately July through September. Pets okay.

### YOSEMITE CREEK CAMPGROUND

Another primitive campground, the Yosemite Creek camping area is located .5 miles (8 km) down a narrow dirt road to the south of Tioga Road (the turnoff is less than .5 miles or .8 km east of the White Wolf turnoff). Don't, repeat don't, even think about trying to take an RV or a trailer into this campground. The 75 sites utilize pit toilets and water from nearby Yosemite Creek (be sure to treat it). First-come, first-served, $12 per night, and open July through early September only. Pets okay.

### PORCUPINE FLAT CAMPGROUND

There are flatter campgrounds in the world. There is no running water and no flush toilets here, but Porcupine Creek wanders by and the lodgepole pines make a fine canopy. Because the roads in the campground are very bad, recreational vehicles are limited to a few campsites at the entry to the campground; there are 52 sites total. The fee is $12 per night for these first come, first served sites. Open usually from July to October 15. Pets okay.

## Tuolumne Meadows Campgrounds

### TUOLUMNE MEADOWS CAMPGROUND

Here is the park's largest single campground, with 304 sites. The road complex throughout the area is confusing, but once you get the hang of it, you'll love this campground. Families return here year after year for the camping, fishing, hiking, and scenery. Reservations are required for half the campsites; the balance are first come, first served. There's a store nearby, a restaurant at Tuolumne Meadows Lodge, horseback riding at the stable, and fishing in the adjacent Tuolumne River. A sanitary dump station is also available. Backpackers and visitors without vehicles may take advantage of 25 walk-in sites for a fee of $6 per night, with a 1-night maximum stay. Regular sites rent for $26 per night, and the camp is kept open from July through September in a typical year. Pets okay.

### TUOLUMNE MEADOWS GROUP & HORSE CAMPGROUND

Special campsites within this campground are available for organized groups or people traveling with horses. Reservations must be made in advance (see page 15). Each site, for tent camping only, can accommodate no fewer than 13 and no more than 30 people. You must have a horse with you to use the horse campsites, no exceptions. No pets are allowed. Contact (877) 444-6777 or Recreation.gov for reservations.

## Gas

There is only one gas station in the north portion of Yosemite, at Crane Flat, which is open all year and accepts credit cards. There is a small store at this location that is open seasonally. If you are traveling Tioga Road, be sure to check your gas gauge, as it's a stretch of more than 50 miles where no services are provided. Check the *Yosemite Guide* for hours of operation. There is one gas station just a few miles west of Yosemite on Highway 120, at Yosemite Lakes RV Park on Hardin Flat Road, which is open 24 hours a day, year round, and takes credit cards. There are several gas stations in the town of Lee Vining, east of Yosemite near the junction of highways 120 and 395.

A repair garage is open all year in Yosemite Valley, and towing service can be arranged 24 hours a day by calling (209) 372-1060.

## Food: Restaurants

The north end of the park is relatively undeveloped. While there are a few options for hearty meals in generally rustic facilities, you should plan on picnicking a lot and preparing your own food when you travel to Yosemite's north country. The following is a list of your choices (open only during the visitor season of July through September) should you choose to "dine out." Check the *Yosemite Guide* for dates and hours of operation.

### EVERGREEN LODGE

Not technically within the park, this old wooden lodge exudes unpolished charm. It is is 7 miles (11.3 km) out Evergreen Road on the way to Hetch Hetchy. They serve dinner 7 nights a week and breakfast on weekends (lunch items are available at the small store on the premises); the food is remarkably good. The Evergreen Lodge is not listed in the *Yosemite Guide*, so call (209) 379-2606 or go to evergreenlodge .com for hours of operation and to make a reservation. Their normal season is from April through October. Moderate to expensive.

### RUSH CREEK LODGE

Rush Creek Lodge is located on Highway 120 just a few miles west of the Big Oak Flat entrance and park boundary, and is open for breakfast, lunch, and dinner, with full bar service. Visit rushcreeklodge.com or call (209) 379-2373. Moderate to expensive.

### WHITE WOLF LODGE

With its covered porch and its low-key, intimate dining room, the whitewashed White Wolf Lodge is an enjoyable spot to eat. Buffet breakfast and family-style dinner are served (grab a table on the porch if they're serving outdoors), and box lunches can be ordered and items can be purchased from the adjacent store. There's a fine old fireplace, adequate food, and beer and wine. Dinner reservations are recommended; make them at the front desk when you arrive. Moderate to expensive.

### TUOLUMNE MEADOWS LODGE

The dining room at the lodge is located in a canvas-sided tent-like structure that captures the feeling of roughing it in the high country. But the food will make you think you're someplace fancy. Breakfast and dinner are served from a menu family style; that is, you get seated with whoever happens to be present for mealtime when you are. It's good fun, and many fast friendships have been initiated in the lodge dining room. Beer and wine are served, and box lunches are available to order the evening before you need them. Dinner reservations are required and can be made by calling (209) 372-8413. Moderate to expensive.

### TUOLUMNE MEADOWS GRILL

Located adjacent to the Tuolumne store and post office, the grill is a great place for a hamburger. Pull up a stool or stand and wolf. Fry-cooked meals are served at breakfast, lunch, and dinner (but the Lodge is preferred for breakfast if you're in no hurry). No reservations accepted (it's not that kind of place), and you can order menu items "to go." It also features delicious, cheap soft-serve ice cream. Inexpensive.

## Food: Groceries

The following outlets are basic convenience stores with limited selections. Check the *Yosemite Guide* for operating hours.

### CRANE FLAT GAS STATION

Located in the main building of the gas station at the intersection of Big Oak Flat and Tioga Roads.

### WHITE WOLF LODGE

A very small camp store adjacent to the dining room at the lodge.

### TUOLUMNE MEADOWS STORE

This facility offers the largest selection and variety north of Yosemite Valley.

## Lodging

As in the Wawona area, there are overnight accommodations in the north part of the park that are not operated by Yosemite Hospitality. For reservations for concessioner facilities, follow the steps outlined on page 14. You must deal directly with the other independent lodging providers to reserve with them. The quoted rates for the following listed lodging facilities are approximate and are subject to change.

### EVERGREEN LODGE

Open March through December. Here are 88 cabins spread over 20 acres along the road to Hetch Hetchy. Each cabin includes a private bath, but there are no kitchens. Other amenities are a restaurant, bar, and small convenience store. For reservations call (800) 935-6343 or (209) 379- 2606 or visit evergreenlodge.com. Moderate to expensive.

### RUSH CREEK LODGE

Rush Creek Lodge is a sister property to the Evergreen Lodge, open year round and located on Highway 120 .5 miles (.8 km) west of the Big Oak Flat entrance and park boundary. It offers 143 rooms, suites, and villas spread over 20 acres with amenities that include a full restaurant and bar, a small store, swimming pool, family activities and games, guide services and more. Go to rushcreeklodge.com, email info@ rushcreeklodge.com, or call (209) 379- 2373 for more information.

### WHITE WOLF LODGE

Open in summer only. These rustic accommodations are situated at delightful White Wolf, bordered by meadow and forest both. There are 4 cabins with a private bath (about $122 to $155 plus tax) featuring propane heating, a desk, chair, dresser, and 2 double beds. Limited electricity is provided for lighting and heat. The 24 canvas tent cabins share a communal bathroom and shower house (about $131 plus tax). The canvas cabins are equipped with beds with linens, candles for lighting, a wood-burning stove, and wood. There is no electricity. Special amenities include a dining room and store. Reservations should be made at travelyosemite.com or by calling (888) 540-5794 or international (602) 278-8888 (see page 14).

### TIOGA PASS RESORT

Usually open seasonally from around the end of May until mid-September, this resort was damaged by the snows of 2017. Fingers crossed that it reopens as planned in 2019. Nestled on the side of a hill at well over the 9,000-foot (2,700-m) level, the resort consists of 10 housekeeping cabins, 4 motel-type rooms, and a central building with a restaurant, store, and coffee bar. It's 2 miles (3.2 km) beyond Tioga Pass Entrance and just outside of the park. Weekly rates are offered. For reservations send a booking request online at tioga-passresort.com or by email to tiogapass-resortllc@gmail.com; there is no phone service. Moderate to expensive.

### TUOLUMNE MEADOWS LODGE

Open in summer only. Here are 69 canvas tent cabins set close by the Tuolumne River in a picture-book setting. The tents are rustic and utilize wood stoves and candles (there's no electricity), but there are mattresses and linens on the beds. Bathrooms and showers are communal and anything but fancy. But that's part of the fun of the Tuolumne Meadows Lodge— it's roughing it easy. The tents rent for about $122 plus tax and will sleep up to 4. Reservations (which are much sought and highly coveted) should be made through travelyosemite.com or by calling (888) 540-5794, or international (602) 278-8888 (see page 14).

Yosemite Falls

# 7 GETTING TO YOSEMITE

**Most visitors to Yosemite** arrive in private automobiles, but there are public transportation alternatives. Following are brief descriptions of those various alternatives, as well as detailed descriptions of the highway routes to Yosemite and amenities in the Yosemite gateway communities. For further information about transportation to Yosemite National Park, check nps.gov/yose under Plan Your Visit.

## By Air

Most people traveling to Yosemite by air fly into San Francisco, Oakland, or San Jose, roughly 4 hours from the park. Sacramento International Airport (SMF) is also a viable destination for air travel to the Yosemite area. With fewer crowds and busy highways, it is also about 4 hours from the park. The largest air terminal close to Yosemite served by a number of major airlines and several smaller ones is the Fresno Yosemite International Airport (FAT); go to flyfresno.com for information on ground transportation. Rental cars are available and there is public transportation from the airport, including YARTS daily. Call (877) 989-2787 or check yarts.com.

Some visitors choose to fly into Reno, Nevada, and approach the park from the east side via Interstate 395 and Tioga Road. From the Reno International Airport (RNO) a rental car is needed; go to renoairport.com for more information. Or consider flying into the much smaller Mammoth Yosemite Airport (MMH), also located on the east side of Yosemite National Park near Mammoth Lakes, where public transportation is available via YARTS in the summer season only in addition to rental car services. But be aware that access to Yosemite National Park via Highway 120 from the east is only available on a seasonal basis; Tioga Road is closed in winter which can begin as early as November and may last into June.

## By Train

Train transportation is available to Yosemite from many locations in California. From some some stations you can take a combination of a train and a connecting bus, while from other locations the full trip is made via various connections of the Amtrak Thruway bus. There is also a packaged vacation option. Plan your trip at amtrak.com or call (800) USA-RAIL.

## By Bus

For those staying in visitor accommodations surrounding the park, there is a car-free option: the Yosemite Area Regional Transportation System (YARTS) provides bus service from many of the communities outside Yosemite. Along the Highway 140 route, service is available year round from Merced, Catheys Valley, Mariposa, Midpines, and El Portal. From Highways 120 and 132, buses can be caught in the summer season at stops in Sonora, Jamestown, Coulterville, Greeley Hill, Groveland, and Buck Meadows. Highway 41 also offers a summer service YARTS bus line between Fresno and Yosemite, with stops along the way including Oakhurst and Fish Camp. Service also is available from Mammoth Lakes over Highway 120 during summer only. For information, call toll free to (877) 989-2787 or visit yarts.com.

### Mileages to Yosemite Valley

**Via Highway 41 from**

| | |
|---|---|
| Los Angeles | 313 miles / 504 km |
| Bakersfield | 201 miles / 323 km |
| Fresno | 94 miles / 151 km |
| Oakhurst | 50 miles / 80 km |
| Fish Camp | 37 miles / 60 km |

**Via Highway 140 from**

| | |
|---|---|
| Merced | 81 miles / 130 km |
| Mariposa | 43 miles / 69 km |
| El Portal | 14 miles / 23 km |

**Via Highway 120 from the West from**

| | |
|---|---|
| San Francisco | 195 miles / 314 km |
| Sacramento | 176 miles / 283 km |
| Stockton | 127 miles / 204 km |
| Manteca | 117 miles / 188 km |
| Oakdale | 96 miles / 154 km |
| Groveland | 49 miles / 79 km |

**Via Highway 120 from the East from**

| | |
|---|---|
| Reno | 218 miles / 351 km |
| Carson City | 188 miles / 303 km |
| Bishop | 146 miles / 235 km |
| Mammoth Lakes | 106 miles / 171 km |
| Lee Vining | 74 miles / 119 km |

## By Automobile

There are 4 major routes to Yosemite National Park. Following is information on points of interest, restaurants, and motels along each route. The list is not meant to be exhaustive. Because motels and restaurants are often short-lived, be sure to call ahead to avoid disappointment. All directions and orientations assume that one is traveling toward Yosemite.

Highway 140 to Yosemite

## Highway 41 from Fresno

### POINTS OF INTEREST

**Fresno Flats Historic Village and Park:** 49777 High School Road, Oakhurst (turn right at Road 426 stoplight, go .5 miles or .8 km to High School Road/Road 427, turn left and follow signs). This park includes a collection of old buildings depicting the lives of early settlers; open daily until dusk; fresnoflatsmuseum.org, (559) 683-6570.

**Oakhurst Visitor Center:** 40343 Highway 41, Oakhurst. A great place for information, books, and maps about Yosemite. yosemite thisyear.com, (559) 683-4636.

**Yosemite Mountain Sugar Pine Railroad:** 56001 Highway 41 (1 mile or 1.6 km south of Fish Camp). Take a 4-mile (or 6.4-km) ride on a historic logging train; many special events are offered, including dinner trips. A fee is charged. ymsprr.com, (559) 683-7273.

**Tesla Supercharger:** 1122 Highway 41, Fish Camp (at the Tenaya Lodge).

### RESTAURANTS

**Erna's Elderberry House Restaurant:** 48688 Victoria Lane, Oakhurst (on the left on the final descent into town). This 5-star epic dining experience is a French-California "farm-to-table" feast for the eyes, palate, and soul and has received numerous honors. Call for dress code and reservations. Chateau du Sureau is onsite luxury lodging. (559) 683-6800

**South Gate Brew Company:** 40233 Enterprise Drive, Oakhurst (turn onto Highway 49, turn left in .3 miles or .5 km). A craft beer eatery with an industrial vibe and a classic pub menu, serving lunch and dinner. (559) 692-2739

**DiCicco's Italian Restaurant:** 40282 Highway 41, Oakhurst. Serving great Italian food for lunch and dinner, this spot is well-liked by locals. (559) 641-5588

**Oka Japanese Restaurant:** 40291 Junction Drive, Oakhurst (turn left onto Highway 49, turn right at first stoplight). Authentic Japanese food and sushi served for lunch and dinner around a Teppanyaki table; full bar. (559) 642-4850

**Crab Cakes:** 49271 Golden Oak Loop, Oakhurst (turn right onto Road 426, then immediate left on Golden Oak). This friendly eatery serves crab cakes, fresh fish, steak, chicken, and pasta for dinner only. There's patio seating and a full bar. (559) 641-7667

**El Cid Mexican Cuisine:** 41939 Highway 41 (2 miles or 3.2 km north of Oakhurst). Another locals' hangout for lunch and dinner, with patio dining and a full bar. (559) 683-6668

### LODGING

**Best Western Plus Yosemite Gateway Inn:** 40530 Highway 41, Oakhurst. A larger option, with 132 units, indoor and outdoor pools and spas, plus a restaurant. Moderately priced. bestwestern.com, (559) 683-2378.

**Yosemite South Gate Hotel and Suites:** 40644 Highway 41, Oakhurst. Eighty-one mini-suite units, plus a pool; lodging includes complimentary continental breakfast. Moderately priced. yosemitesouthgate.com, (559) 683-3555.

**Yosemite Sierra Inn:** 40662 Highway 41, Oakhurst. With 42 units and an outdoor pool; continental breakfast is available. Moderately priced. yosemitesierrainn.com, (559) 642-2525.

**Tenaya Lodge:** 1122 Highway 41, Fish Camp (on the right as you enter town). Beautiful resort with many activities and a variety of excellent restaurants and bars, indoor and outdoor pools, and a full spa and fitness center. Electric car charging on premises. Expensive. tenayalodge.com, (559) 683-6555.

## Highway 140 from Merced

### POINTS OF INTEREST

**California State Mining and Mineral Museum:** 5005 Fairgrounds Road, Mariposa (at the Mariposa County Fairgrounds, 1.8 miles or 2.9 km south of town). A well-exhibited collection of minerals plus a mine tunnel and gold displays. An entrance fee is charged. Open Thursday through Sunday. parks.ca.gov, (209) 742-7625.

**Mariposa County Courthouse:** 5088 Bullion Street, Mariposa (turn right on 8th Street near the middle of town, then left on Bullion Street). Built in 1854, this California Historical Landmark (No. 670) is the oldest courthouse in continuous use in the western United States. Self-tour only, Monday through Friday, 8 a.m. to 4 p.m. (209) 966-2456.

**Mariposa Museum and History Center:** 5116 Jesse Street, Mariposa (watch for a sign along Highway 140 on the left). Historic displays of Mariposa's Gold Rush days. Open year round, 7 days a week. mariposa-museum.com, (209) 966-2924.

**Mariposa County Visitors Center:** 5158 Highway 140, Mariposa (at the intersection of Highway 140 and 49). Great place for information, maps, and books. Open year round, 7 days a week. mariposachamber. org, (209) 966-7081.

**Yosemite Rail Exhibit:** El Portal (turn left from Highway 140 onto El Portal Road, go one block). View relics of early railroad activity including a locomotive and turntable. El Portal was the terminus of the Yosemite Valley Railroad.

### RESTAURANTS

**Castillo's Mexican Restaurant:** 4995 Fifth Street, Mariposa (1 block off Highway 140). Excellent Mexican food for lunch and dinner; served on the patio in summers. (209) 742-4413

**Savoury's:** 5034 Highway 140, Mariposa (on the right side in the historic downtown). Very popular with tourists and locals; tasty food for dinner only with a full bar. (209) 966-7677

**Charles Street Dinner House:** Highway 140, Mariposa (at 7th Street, downtown). Good traditional food for lunch and dinner, plus beer and wine. (209) 966-2366

**1850 Restaurant and Brewing Company:** 5114 Highway 140 (on the right), Mariposa. Open for lunch and dinner, this spot serves a seasonal menu food and their own craft beer, and is deservedly liked by locals. (209) 966-2229

**High Country Health Foods and Cafe:** 5186 Highway 49, Mariposa. Open for breakfast and lunch with healthy, delicious sandwiches and salads. There's a market, too. (209) 966-5111

### LODGING

**Best Western Yosemite Way Station:** 4999 Highway 140, Mariposa (at the intersection of Highway 140 and 49). Outdoor pool and free breakfast. Moderately priced. bestwestern.com, (209) 966-7545.

**Comfort Inn Yosemite Valley Gateway:** 4994 Bullion St., Mariposa. Outdoor pool and a free breakfast. Moderately priced. choicehotels.com, (209) 966-4344.

**Mariposa Lodge:** 5052 Highway 140, Mariposa (on the right midway through town). Lovely gardens, outdoor pool and spa. Moderately priced. mariposalodge. com, (209) 966-3607.

**Yosemite Bug Rustic Mountain Resort:** 6979 Highway 140, Midpines (on the left, 10 miles or 16 km east of Mariposa). A member of Hostelling International, "The Bug" is very popular with backpackers and draws an international clientele. Accommodations include dorms, tent cabins, and private cabins. There's a spa and a restaurant on site that serves breakfast, lunch, and dinner. Beer and wine are available. Inexpensive to moderately priced. yosemitebug.com, (209) 966-6666.

**Yosemite Cedar Lodge:** 9966 Highway 140, El Portal. This lodge about 8 miles (13 km) from the Arch Rock Entrance Station hosts a YARTS bus stop, and features indoor and outdoor pools, a restaurant and bar, and a pathway along the Merced River. Moderately priced. stayyosemitecedarlodge.com, (209) 379-2612.

**Yosemite View Lodge:** 11136 Highway 140, El Portal. Located just 2.4 miles (3.8 km) from the park along the Merced River, this large motel complex sports a gift shop, indoor and outdoor pools, and two restaurants. All rooms have kitchenettes. Moderate to expensive. stayyosemiteview-lodge.com, 209-379-2681.

## Highway 120 from Manteca

POINTS OF INTEREST

**Historic Jamestown:** Highway 108 (a few miles from the Highway 120 intersection). Main Street is lined with shops and restaurants housed in historic, Gold Rush–era buildings.

**Railtown 1897 State Historic Park:** 18115 5th Ave, Jamestown (just beyond town). This state park features historic trains, a roundhouse, and seasonal locomotive rides. A fee is charged. Open year round, 7 days a week except Thanksgiving, Christmas and New Years Day; trains operate weekends April through September. Check hours at railtown1897.org, (209) 984-3953.

**Moccasin Creek Fish Hatchery:** Moccasin (on Highway 49 near the Highway 120 intersection). Take a self-guided tour of this visitor-friendly trout hatchery operated by the California Department of Fish and Wildlife. Open year round, 7 days a week, 7:30 a.m. to 3:30 p.m. (Red Hills Interpretive Nature Trail is nearby, too.) (209) 989-2312.

**Tesla Supercharger:** 11875 Ponderosa Lane, Groveland (in the county parking lot, walking distance to the Hotel Charlotte).

**RESTAURANTS**

**Priest Station Café:** 16756 Old Priest Grade, Big Oak Flat (at the intersection of Highway 120, west of Groveland). This spot has a nice deck with view; open for breakfast, lunch, and dinner, plus beer and wine. (209) 962-1888

**Fork & Love Restaurant (in the Hotel Charlotte):** 18736 Main Street, Groveland (on the left side of Highway 120 in the center of town). A seasonal dinner menu inspired by world cuisine with a full bar. (209) 962-1912

**Buck Meadows Restaurant:** 7647 Highway 120, Buck Meadows (about 13.5 miles or 22 km from the Big Oak Flat Entrance Station). Offers classic American cuisine, plus beer and wine. (209) 962-5281

**Rush Creek Lodge:** 34001 Highway 120 (just a few miles west of the Big Oak Flat entrance and park boundary). Open for breakfast, lunch, and dinner, with full bar service. Moderate to expensive. Visit rushcreeklodge.com or call (209) 379-2373.

**LODGING**

**Hotel Charlotte:** 18736 Main Sttreet, Groveland. Comfortable historic hotel with complimentary breakfast. Vacation rentals also available. Moderately priced. hotelcharlotte.com, (209) 962-6455.

**Groveland Hotel:** 18767 Main Street, Groveland. Beautifully restored, very pet-friendly historic hotel with 17 guestrooms and an extensive wine list. Room 15 reputedly comes with its own ghost. Moderately priced. groveland.com, (800) 273-3314.

**Yosemite Westgate Lodge:** 7633 Highway 120, Buck Meadows (the address is listed as Groveland). Recently remodeled 48-room hotel with a pool, children's playground, and restaurant. Inexpensive to moderate. yosemitewestgate.com, (209) 962-5281.

**Rush Creek Lodge:** 34001 Highway 120 (just a few miles west of the Big Oak Flat entrance and park boundary). This 143-room lodge offers many daily activities. Moderate to expensive. Visit rushcreeklodge.com or call (209) 379-2373.

## Highway 120 from Lee Vining

**POINTS OF INTEREST**

**Mono Lake Committee Information Center and Bookstore:** Highway 395, Lee Vining. Operated by the Mono Lake Committee, the group primarily responsible for saving and restoring Mono Lake, this outlet offers free educational exhibits and films, plus

Highway 120 toward Tioga Pass

an excellent gift and book store. Open year round, 7 days a week, 8 a.m. to 9 p.m. monolake.org, (760) 647-6386.

**Mono Lake Visitor Center:** 1 Visitor Center Drive, Lee Vining (north of town off Highway 395). Impressive multiagency facility with exhibits, bookstore, movie, and a great deck overlooking the lake. Open year round, 7 days a week, 8 a.m. to 5 p.m. fs.usda.gov, (760) 647-3044.

**Mono Lake County Park:** Highway 395 (5 miles north of Lee Vining). This is a terrific spot for picnicking and bird watching.

### RESTAURANTS

**Epic Café:** 349 Lee Vining Ave., Lee Vining. A community-minded café with a patio serving fresh, delicious food for breakfast, lunch, and dinner, plus beer and wine. (760) 965-6282

**Whoa Nellie Deli:** Highway 120 (Lee Vining (near the 395 intersection). A local institution located inside the Mobil Gas Mart. Excellent food, including burgers and fish tacos. Open seasonally. (760) 647-1088

**Tioga Pass Resort:** Highway 120 (9 miles or 14.5 km west of Lee Vining). As of this writing, it was unclear if this resort would reopen as planned in 2019. With that in mind, this spot is famous for homemade pies. Rustic lodging is also available. Open summers only; no phone service. Stop by if it's open.

### LODGING

**El Mono Motel and Latte Da Coffee Café:** Highway 395, Lee Vining (at 3rd Street). Small, family-run motel with bustling coffee shop; closed winters. Inexpensive. elmonomotel.com, (760) 647-6310.

**Lake View Lodge:** 51285 Highway 395, Lee Vining. A family-owned lodge with gardens and a view of Mono Lake. Epic Café is nearby. Inexpensive. lakeviewlodgeyosemite.com, (800) 990-6614.

**Murphey's Motel:** Highway 395, Lee Vining. Dog-friendly motel open year round; AAA discounts offered. Inexpensive. murpheysyosemite.com, (800) 334-6316.

Mono Lake sunrise

**There are lots** of online resources available about Yosemite. Whether found on sites maintained by the government or on the personal pages of passionate Yosemite lovers, information, photographs, maps, and stories are abundant. Here are some of the best available at this time.

## Yosemite National Park

### NPS.GOV/YOSE

This is the official park website, maintained by the National Park Service. Here you will find lots of visitor information, nuts and bolts data, the latest weather conditions, government news releases, sections about park planning and management issues, volunteer opportunities, safety info, and a park map. Don't miss the Plan Your Visit section. Also available online are a series of interesting videos on topics such as fire ecology, birding, and bears.

## yosemitenationalpark

### YOUTUBE.COM CHANNEL

You'll find videos galore, including the incredible Yosemite Nature Notes series (a video podcast focused on natural and human history), Visiting Yosemite (videos presented by National Park Service rangers on trip planning and safety), and videos in American Sign Language from Yosemite Deaf Services.

## Yosemite Conservancy

### YOSEMITECONSERVANCY.ORG

This site offers opportunities for Yosemite lovers to deepen their connection with the park, as donors, as volunteers, and as participants in Yosemite Conservancy's art, adventure, and theater programs. The site also features real-time webcam views of world-famous scenery; a regularly updated blog; descriptions of grants that donors fund in Yosemite; and an online store with books, gifts, apparel, and more. Easy-donate links allow site visitors to support projects that preserve and protect Yosemite for the future. Donors receive a discount on bookstore products and certain park-based activities.

## Yosemite Guide Online

### NPS.GOV/YOSE/PLANYOURVISIT/GUIDE

This page allows prospective visitors to download the *Yosemite Guide* in a PDF version. The *Yosemite Guide* contains a calendar of guided programs and park activities, as well as hours of operation for visitor centers and museums.

## Yosemite Hospitality

### TRAVELYOSEMITE.COM

Operated by the park's chief concessioner, this site is most important for the information it provides about lodging options in Yosemite, including online reservations. There's also information about activities, special events, and jobs in the park.

## Recreation.gov

### RECREATION.GOV

This site provides an easy and convenient way to make camping reservations by credit card for Yosemite and other national park campgrounds. It certainly beats trying to use their phone-in system. Options are available for individual, family, and group sites at all campgrounds that require reservations (see page 15).

## NatureBridge

### NATUREBRIDGE.ORG

This organization offers environmental education in the park, and their site offers videos and slide shows from their programs and participants, information about the educational curriculum, organizational data, and teacher resources. For school groups interested in a high-quality learning experience in Yosemite, this is the place to check.

# PHOTO CREDITS

1: October in Yosemite Valley, Yosemite Conservancy/Keith Walklet

2: El Capitan in close-up, haveseen/Shutterstock.com

3: Lone hiker with Half Dome, Aaron Rockefeller/Shutterstock.com

5: Mule deer, Henk Bouma/Shutterstock.com

6: Hikers with Vernal Fall, Maridav/Shutterstock.com

7: Tuolumne Meadows beauty, Yosemite Conservancy/Keith Walklet

### ■  1. Welcome to Yosemite

8–9: Summer sunrise at Tunnel View, Bill45/Shutterstock.com

14: Half Dome Village, Kit Leong/Shutterstock.com

15: Happy campers, Blend Images/Shutterstock.com

17: Half Dome and Giant Staircase, Patricia Hamila/Shutterstock.com

18: Backpacking, Galyna Andrushko/Shutterstock.com

19: Black bear, Josef Pittner/Shutterstock.com

20: View from Washburn Point, Joaquin Ossorio Castillo/Shutterstock.com

21: Ranger on horseback, National Park Service/Cindy Jacoby

22: Valley View in winter, Pung/Shutterstock.com

24: The Village Store, courtesy of Yosemite Hospitality

25: Relaxing by a lake, Bill45/Shutterstock.com

25: Squirrel, Wonder Life/Shutterstock.com

27: Bridalveil Fall, Gary C. Tognoni/Shutterstock.com

28: Glacier Point, Pung/Shutterstock.com

29: Climber hand jamming, Greg Epperson/Shutterstock.com

30: Climber in silhouette, Greg Epperson/Shutterstock.com

31: Scaling a rock face, mikeledray/Shutterstock.com

31: Climber in helmet, Greg Epperson/Shutterstock.com

32: Tuolumne Meadows Visitor Center sign, Matthew Corley/Shutterstock.com

### ■  2. Yosemite History

34–35 Holmes Brothers, San Jose, and Old Stanley Steamer, c. 1901. Courtesy National Park Service, NPS History Collection, HPC-001808

36: RL 14089 Image of "Paiutes from Mono Lake in Yosemite for acorns," by Thrasher, c. 1902–1903, courtesy of the Yosemite National Park Archives, Museum, and Library

38: RL 002663 Image of Lithograph of Thomas Ayres' drawing of *Yose-mite Falls*, 1855, courtesy of the Yosemite National Park Archives, Museum, and Library

39: Galen Clark in Yosemite, George Fiske, c. 1900. Courtesy National Park Service, NPS History Collection, HPC-001826

39: RL13774 Image of "Group portrait in front of Yosemite Falls," by Gustav Fagersteen, 1880, courtesy of the Yosemite National Park Archives, Museum, and Library

40: YM 20916 Image of "Troop F, 6th US Cavalry on Fallen Monarch, Mariposa Big Tree Grove," by Tibbets, 1899, courtesy of the Yosemite National Park Archives, Museum, and Library

41: RL 005701 Image of "Negro Troopers of 1899, 24th Infantry," by Celia Crocker Thompson, 1899, courtesy of the Yosemite National Park Archives, Museum, and Library

42: RL 004475 Image of "John Muir and Theodore Roosevelt at Glacier Point," by Underwood and Underwood, May 1903, courtesy of the Yosemite National Park Archives, Museum, and Library

43: Ackerson Meadow, National Park Service

44: Ranger with banjo, National Park Service

45: Swinging Bridge picnic area, OLOS/Shutterstock.com

46: Yosemite chapel, Andrew Zarivny/Shutterstock.com

48: Grizzly Giant, Stephen Moehle/Shutterstock.com

50: RL 002521 Image of "Galen Clark," by Houseworth, 1945, courtesy of the Yosemite National Park Archives, Museum, and Library

51: RL 14396 Image of "James Mason Hutchings," courtesy of the Yosemite

National Park Archives, Museum, and Library

51: RL 004398 Image of "John Muir," by Francis Fultz, 1907, courtesy of the Yosemite National Park Archives, Museum, and Library

52: RL 002501 Image of "David Curry," by Newton Studio, Palo Alto, CA, c. 1900, courtesy of the Yosemite National Park Archives, Museum, and Library

52: RL 002499 Image of "Mrs. David Curry," by Ben Tarnutzer, 1940, courtesy of the Yosemite National Park Archives, Museum, and Library

52: RL 16641 Image of "Ansel Adams," by J. Malcolm Greany, 1950, courtesy of the Yosemite National Park Archives, Museum, and Library

54: Half Dome from Olmsted Point, bjul/Shutterstock.com

55: Tenaya Lake, Luca Moi/Shutterstock.com

## ▪ 3. Yosemite's Natural World

56–57: Coyote, Gleb Tarro/Shutterstock.com

58: Erratic boulder, Dan Schreiber/Shutterstock.com

59: Tunnel View, f11photo/Shutterstock.com

60: Half Dome, Nina B/Shutterstock.com

61: Yosemite Falls, Dennis Michael Photography/Shutterstock.com

63: Controlled burn, Paul Richard Jones/Shutterstock.com

64: Burned pine trees, Sergey Yechikov/Shutterstock.com

65: Spring flooding, Sasha Buzko/Shutterstock.com

66: Black oak, Colnago 95310/Shutterstock.com

67: All images from Shutterstock.com: TOP ROW: Alpine lily, Holly Zynda / western azalea, Sundry Photography / sneezeweed, Iva Vagnerova / SECOND ROW: fleabane daisy, Luka Hercigonja / Henderson's shooting star, Sundry Photography / Lewis's monkeyflower, Bob Coffen / THIRD ROW: Leichtlin's mariposa lily, Sundry Photography / western monkshood, Jill Richardson / pussypaws, Sundry Photography / FOURTH ROW: alpine gold, Sundry Photography / snow plant, Asif Islam / Sierra stickseed, Sundry Photography

68: Giant sequoia, Galyna Andrushko/Shutterstock.com

69: Black bear, unavailable/Shutterstock.com

70: Mule deer, ksb/Shutterstock.com

71: Pika, Tom Reichner/Shutterstock.com

72: Mountain lion, sirtravelalot/Shutterstock.com

73: Coyote, Aspen Photo/Shutterstock.com

73: Western gray squirrel, mccw thissen/Shutterstock.com

74: Marmot, Fremme/Shutterstock.com

74: Bighorn sheep ewe, California Department of Fish and Wildlife

75: American dipper, Steve Byland/Shutterstock.com

75: Acorn woodpecker, OfeMartinez/Shutterstock.com

75: Clark's nutcracker, vagabond54/Shutterstock.com

76: Black-headed grosbeak, birdiegal/Shutterstock.com

76: Peregrine falcon, neelsky/Shutterstock.com

76: Great horned owl, artcphotos/Shutterstock.com

77: Sierra Nevada yellow-legged frog, Jason Mintzer/Shutterstock.com

77: Sierra fence lizard, fotogestoeber/Shutterstock.com

78: Rainbow trout, MediaFuzeBox/Shutterstock.com

79: Northern Pacific rattlesnack, fivespots/Shutterstock.com

80: Poison oak, ShutterstockProfessional/Shutterstock.com

80: Black widow, Jay Ondreicka/Shutterstock.com

81: Deer mouse, Close Encounters Photo/Shutterstock.com

81: California ground squirrel, Marci Paravia/Shutterstock.com

82: Peregrine falcon, Robert L. Kothenbeutel/Shutterstock.com

82: Bighorn sheep, Josh Schulgen/California Department of Fish and Wildlife

83: Sierra Nevada yellow-legged frog, Tom Grundy/Shutterstock.com

83: Bald eagle, Kane513/Shutterstock.com

83: Willow flycatcher, Steve Byland/Shutterstock.com

### ■ 4. Yosemite Valley

84–85: Meadow in Yosemite Valley, haveseen/Shutterstock.com

88: Valley Visitor Center, Yosemite Conservancy

90: Lee Stetson, Yosemite Conservancy/Keith Walklet

90: Vernal Fall, topseller/Shutterstock.com

92: Shelton Johnson, Yosemite Conservancy/Keith Walklet

93: Outdoor Adventure, Yosemite Conservancy/Keith Walklet

94: Mirror Lake, Pung/Shutterstock.com

96: Climbing Half Dome with the cables, David Prosser/Shutterstock.com

96: The 10 Essentials, National Park Service/Alan Hageman

98: River, sergioboccardo/Shutterstock.com

100: Setting up the tent, Yosemite Conservancy/Keith Walklet

102: Half Dome Village, Yosemite Hospitality

103: The Majestic Yosemite Hotel, Yosemite Hospitality

### ■ 5. South of Yosemite Valley

106–7: Mariposa Grove, Jane Rix/Shutterstock.com

110: The Bachelor and Three Graces, turtix/Shutterstock.com

112: RL 002749 Image of "Troop K, 4th Cavalry," 1896, courtesy of the Yosemite National Park Archives, Museum, and Library

113: The Wawona Tunnel Tree, Henry G. Peabody, 1929. Courtesy National Park Service, NPS History Collection, HPC-000099

114: Chilnualna Fall, Mordy Neuman/Shutterstock.com

114: Wawona stage coach, National Park Service

115: Big Trees Stable, Yosemite Hospitality

118: Grizzly Giant, Yosemite Conservancy

120: View from Sentinel Dome, Richard Bizick/Shutterstock.com

121: Camping, Alex Brylov/Shutterstock.com

122: Big Trees Golf Course, Yosemite Hospitality

123: Big Trees Lodge, Yosemite Hospitality

### ■ 6. North of Yosemite Valley

124–25: Tuolumne Meadows, Pung/Shutterstock.com

128: Tenaya Lake, turtix/Shutterstock.com

128: White Cascade, Robert Bohrer/Shutterstock.com

129: Hetch Hetchy Reservoir, Nickolay Stanev/Shutterstock.com

130: Wapama Falls bridge, Radoslaw Lecyk/Shutterstock.com

132: Cathedral Lake and Peak, Adonis Villanueva/Shutterstock.com

133: Olmsted Point view, JessK89/Shutterstock.com

137: Sunrise High Sierra Camp, Yosemite Hospitality

138: Pothole Dome, Maridav/Shutterstock.com

139: Elizabeth Lake, All a Shutter/Shutterstock.com

140: Hikers, pixy/Shutterstock.com

140: Soda Springs, ArnaudS2/Shutterstock.com

141: Dog Lake, Hans Debruyne/Shutterstock.com

### ■ 7. Getting to Yosemite

146–47: Yosemite Falls, A.Homung/Shutterstock.com

149: Road to Yosemite, Machmarsky/Shutterstock.com

151: Highway 120, Christopher Boswell/Shutterstock.com

152: Mono Lake, Rick Whitacre/Shutterstock.com

160: Dogwood, Yosemite Conservancy/Keith Walklet

**Pages with maps are in bold.**

accessibility, 93
Ackerson Meadow, 43
Adams, Ansel, 52
The Ahwahnee. *See* The Majestic Yosemite
    Hotel
air travel, 148
American Indians, 26, 35–38, 50, 61
amphibians, 77
animals. *See* wildlife
Ansel Adams Gallery, 52, 90
art classes, 91–92
ATMs, 24
Ayres, Thomas, 38, 42

babysitting, 24
Backpacker Walk-In, 16, 100
backpacking. *See* hiking and backpacking
Badger Pass. *See* Yosemite Ski & Snowboard
    Area
bars, 24
baskets, 37
bears, 19, 45, 69–70, 99
beer, 24–25
bicycles, 26, 91
Big Oak Flat, 32, 53
Big Trees Lodge (formerly Wawona Hotel),
    20, 110, 112, 114–15, 122, 123
birds, 75–76, 82, 83
black widows, 80
Bracebridge Dinner, 23, 90
Bridalveil Creek Campground, 16, 121
Bridalveil Fall, 27, 45, 61, 62
Bridalveil Meadow, 45
Buffalo Soldiers, 41, 92
buses, 27, **88–89**, 91, 148

California State Mining and Mineral
    Museum, 150
Camp 4, 16, 23, 29, 100
camping
    chart, 16
    north of Yosemite Valley, 142–43
    regulations, 18
    reservations, 15
    south of Yosemite Valley, 121
    US Forest Service areas, 15
    winter, 23
    Yosemite Valley, 99–100
cars, 41, 148, 149–52. *See also* gas
Cathedral Lakes, 132, 140
cell phones, 33, 118
cemetery, 47, 93
children, 26, 92
Chilnualna Fall, 53, 114, 116
chipmunks, 73
Clark, Galen, 39, 42, 45, 47, 50, 53, 54, 93,
    111, 112
climate change, 20
climbing, 29–31, 138
coffee, 24, 101
Conness, John, 53

coyotes, 73
Crane Flat, 16, 53, 130, 142
Curry, David and Jennie, 52, 53
Curry Village. *See* Half Dome Village

Dana, James Dwight, 53
deer, mule, 5, 70–71
Dewey Point, 105, 120
Dog Lake, 138, 141
drones, 33
dump stations, 99

Eagle Peak, 104
El Capitan, 29, 30, 31, 45, 53, 60
Elizabeth Lake, 138, 139, 140
El Portal, 53
endangered species, 82–83
entrance fees, 12
environmental issues, 20, 48

Firefall, 43, 44, 52
fires, 18, 26, 63–64, 99, 130
fish, 78, 91, 131, 133, 139
floods, 64–65
food
    groceries, 25, 102, 122, 145
    restaurants, 101–2, 122, 144
    storage, 19, 69, 70, 99
Four-Mile Trail, 95, 120
Fresno Flats Historic Village and Park, 149
frogs, 77, 78, 83

gas, 101, 122, 144
Gaylor Lakes, 135
geology, 58–60
giardia, 79
Glacier Point, 28, 32, 42, 95, 104, 110,
    119, 122
Glacier Point Road, **119,** 120
glaciers, 59, 60, 61
Glen Aulin, 53, 136, 140–41
golf, 110, 114–15, 122
Grizzly Giant, 28, 48, 68, 117, 118
groceries, 25, 102, 122, 145

Half Dome, 17, 53, 54, 60, 96, 105, 133
Half Dome Village (formerly Curry Village),
    14, 32, 53, 101, 102–3
hantavirus, 80
Happy Isles, 26, 27, 53, 91–92
Harden Lake, 134
Hetch Hetchy, 41, 54, **126,** 128, 129–30,
    **131, 142**
Hetch Hetchy Backpackers Campground,
    16, 143
High Sierra Camps, 128, **136**
hiking and backpacking. *See also individual
    trails*
    with children, 26
    essentials for, 96, 97
    Glacier Point Road, 119–20
    Half Dome, 96
    Hetch Hetchy, 130–31

hiking and backpacking, *continued*
  High Sierra Camps, 128, **136**
  in lightning storms, 139
  losing the trail, 97
  Mariposa Grove, 117–18
  regulations, 18
  rescues, 98
  route planning, 18
  Tioga Road, 132–33, **134–35**
  tips, 18–19
  Tuolumne Meadows, 138, 140–41
  Wawona, 115, **116**
  wilderness permits, 17
  Yosemite Valley, 92, 94–95
Hill, Thomas, 115
Hodgdon Meadow, 16, 34, 142
Hoffmann, Mount, 128, 135
horseback riding, 110, 115, 121
Horsetail Fall, 62
Housekeeping Camp, 102, 103
Hutchings, James, 38, 39, 42, 47, 50–51, 54, 93

ice skating, 23, 26
Illilouette Fall, 54, 62
Internet
  access, 33
  resources, 153
Inyo National Forest, 15

Jamestown, 151
John Muir Trail, 94, 95, 120
Johnson, Robert Underwood, 39, 51
Junior ranger program, 26, 27, 92, 139

laundry, 24, 100
Lembert, John Baptiste, 54
Lembert Dome, 141
Lewis, Washington B. "Dusty," 42, 44, 136
lightning, 139
lizards, 77
lodging. *See also* camping
  north of Yosemite Valley, 145
  reservations, 14
  south of Yosemite Valley, 123
  Yosemite Valley, 102–3
Lower Pines, 16, 100
Lukens Lake, 134
Lyell, Charles, 54
Lyell, Mount, 12, 42, 54
Lyell Canyon, 128, 138, 141

The Majestic Yosemite Hotel (formerly The Ahwahnee), 20, 23, 24, 46, 90, 102, 103
Mariposa, 150
Mariposa Battalion, 36, 38, 42, 45, 50, 53, 54, 55
Mariposa Grove, 28, 32, 42, 54, 68, 110, 116, **117,** 118
marmots, 74
May Lake, 135, 136
Meadow Loop, 116
Merced Grove, 128, 130

Merced Lake, 136
Merced River, 45, 54, 59, 64–65, 115
mice, 80, 81
Mirror Lake, 27, 94
Mist Trail, 27, 90, 94, 95, 120
Moccasin Creek Fish Hatchery, 151
Mono Lake, 54, 151–52
Mono Pass, 135
mosquitoes, 79
mountain lions, 72–73
Muir, John, 39, 40, 42, 45, 47, 51, 53, 60, 90, 92, 129

National Park Service, 21, 44
NatureBridge, 153
Nevada Fall, 54, 61, 62, 95
newts, 77
911 service, 118
North Dome, 95, 104, 134–35
North Pines, 16, 100

Oakhurst Visitor Center, 149
Olmsted, Frederick Law, Sr. and Jr., 38, 44, 48, 54
Olmsted Point, 54, 128, 133, 138
Ostrander Ski Hut, 23, 42, 110

Panorama Trail, 120
Parker, Julia, 37
peaks, highest, 12
peregrine falcons, 43, 76, 82
pets, 18, 24, 99, 142
phones
  cell, 33, 118
  contact numbers, 12
picnics, 93
pikas, 71
Pioneer Yosemite History Center, 110, 114
plague, 81
plant life, 12, 66–68, 83
poison oak, 80
Porcupine Flat, 16, 143
post offices, 24
Pothole Dome, 138

Railtown 1897 State Historic Park, 151
rainfall, 13
rangers, 21, 26, 115
rattlesnakes, 77, 79
reptiles, 77
rescues, 98
restaurants, 101–2, 122, 144
Ribbon Fall, 62
Rim Fire, 43, 64, 131
rockfalls, 65
Roosevelt, Theodore, 42, 45
Royal Arch Cascade, 62

salamanders, 77
scorpions, 79
Sentinel Dome, 104, 120
Sentinel Falls, 62
Sentinel Rock, 45

sequoias, giant, 68, 117, 118, 130
sheep, bighorn, 74, 82, 83, 138
showers, 24, 100
shuttle buses, 27, **88–89,** 91
Sierra Club, 40, 92, 129, 140
Sierra Nevada, 18, 54, 58–59
Silver Strand Falls, 62
skiing and snowboarding, 22–23, 26, 110, 119
snakes, 77, 79
Snow Creek Trail, 95
snowshoeing, 23, 26
Soda Springs, 140
spiders, 80
squirrels, 73, 81
Staircase Falls, 62
Stanislaus National Forest, 15, 64
star gazing, 119
Stoneman Meadow, 46, 55
Sunrise High Sierra Camp, 136, 137
swimming, 92, 98, 115, 132, 138
Swing Bridge, 45

Taft Point, 105, 120
Tamarack Flat, 16, 143
Tenaya, Chief, 36, 50, 55
Tenaya Lake, 25, 55, 128, 132, 138
ticks, 79
Tioga Road, 28, 32, 43, 55, 125, **126–27,** 132–33, **134–35,** 143
toads, 77
trains, 148, 149, 150
transportation, 147–52
Tunnel View, 8–9, 27, 90, 105
Tuolumne Grove, 130
Tuolumne Meadows, 7, 16, 28, 125, **127, 137,** 138–41, 143, 144, 145
Tuolumne Meadows Lodge, 136, 144, 145

Upper Pines, 16, 23, 100

Vernal Fall, 6, 27, 61, 62, 90, 94, 95
views, **104–5**
Village Store, 24, 25, 46
Vogelsang, 55, 136

Walker, Joseph R., 38, 42
Wapama Falls, 130, 131
Washburn brothers, 112, 113
Washburn Point, 20
water
  accidents related to, 78, 98
  purification, 19, 79
waterfalls, 61–62. See also individual waterfalls
Wawona, 32, 55, **111,** 112–15, **116,** 122, 123
Wawona Campground, 16, 34, 121
Wawona Hotel. See Big Trees Lodge
Wawona Point, 110
Wawona Tunnel Tree, 28, 43, 113, 116, 117, 118
weather, 13
White Cascade, 128

White Wolf, 16, 55, 128, 143, 145
Whitney, Josiah D, 53, 60
Wilderness Center, 93
wilderness permits, 17
wildlife. See also individual species
  birds, 75–76
  climate change and, 20
  dangerous, 19, 69–70, 72–73, 79–81
  diversity of, 12, 57
  endangered species, 82–83
  fishes, 78
  mammals, 69–74
  observing, 71
  reptiles and amphibians, 77
winter, 13, 22–23

Yosemite Area Regional Transportation System (YARTS), 148
Yosemite Chapel, 46
Yosemite Conservancy, 93, 122, 153
Yosemite Creek, 16, 134, 143
Yosemite Falls, 27, 38, 47, 61, 62, 90, 94–95
Yosemite Hospitality, 12, 14, 153
Yosemite Lodge. See Yosemite Valley Lodge
Yosemite Mountain Sugar Pine Railroad, 149
Yosemite Museum, 26, 42, 44
Yosemite National Park. See also individual attractions
  annual visitors to, 12, 43, 44
  in fiction, 49
  future of, 48
  history of, 35–47
  map of, **10–11**
  naming of, 36, 55
  one day in, 27–28
  sister parks of, 43
  statistics for, 12
  website of, 153
Yosemite Point, 105
Yosemite Ski & Snowboard Area (formerly Badger Pass), 13, 22–23, 26, 42, 110, 119
Yosemite Theater, 90, 92
Yosemite Valley
  activities in, 91–96
  best bets in, 90
  camping, 99–100
  circle tour of, 91
  creation of, 59–60
  food, 101–2
  gas, 101
  historical sites in, 45, **46–47**
  lodging, 102–3
  map of, **86–87**
  mileages to, 148
  size of, 85
  views from above, **104–5**
Yosemite Valley Lodge (formerly Yosemite Lodge), 20, 24, 47, 65, 101, 102
Yosemite Valley Visitor Center, 27, 43, 88–89, 90
Yosemite Village, 32, **88–89,** 101
Yosemite West, 123

Author **Steve Medley** spent 35 of his 57 years in Yosemite National Park, starting out as a ranger before moving to the Yosemite Association, which he led for more than 2 decades. He was one of Yosemite's greatest supporters, building the Yosemite Association into a tremendous force on behalf of the park and leaving a legacy of educational publications for park visitors to enjoy. His energy, drive, and great good humor made him as beloved around Yosemite as Yosemite was to him. He is greatly missed.

Dogwood in autumn